The Rise of Coptic

THE ROSTOVTZEFF LECTURES

INSTITUTE FOR THE STUDY OF THE ANCIENT WORLD

NEW YORK UNIVERSITY

The Rostovtzeff lectures are named for Michael I. Rostovzteff, a Russian ancient historian who came to the United States after the Russian Revolution and taught at the University of Wisconsin and then for many years at Yale University as Sterling Professor of Ancient History. Rostovtzeff's prodigious energies and expansive interests led him to write on an almost unimaginable range of subjects. The Institute for the Study of the Ancient World Rostovtzeff lecture series presents scholarship embodying its aspirations to foster work that crosses disciplinary, geographical, and chronological lines.

The Rise of Coptic: Egyptian versus Greek in Late Antiquity,
JEAN-LUC FOURNET
The Political Machine: Assembling Sovereignty in the Bronze Age Caucasus,
ADAM T. SMITH
The Origins of Monsters: Image and Cognition in the First Age of Mechanical Reproduction,
DAVID WENGROW

The Rise of Coptic

EGYPTIAN VERSUS GREEK IN LATE ANTIQUITY

Jean-Luc Fournet

PRINCETON UNIVERSITY PRESS
Princeton & Oxford

This work is published in association with the Institute for the Study of the Ancient World at New York University.

Published by Princeton University Press
41 William Street, Princeton, New Jersey 08540
6 Oxford Street, Woodstock, Oxfordshire OX20 1TR

press.princeton.edu

First paperback printing, 2021
Paperback ISBN 9780691230238

The Library of Congress has cataloged the cloth edition of this book as follows:

Names: Fournet, Jean-Luc, author.
Title: The rise of Coptic : Egyptian versus Greek in late antiquity / Jean-Luc Fournet.
Other titles: Rostovtzeff lectures.
Description: Princeton ; Oxford : Princeton University Press, 2019. |
Series: The Rostovtzeff lectures
Identifiers: LCCN 2019018022 | ISBN 9780691198347 (hardcover)
Subjects: LCSH: Coptic language—History. | Greek language, Hellenistic (300 B.C.-600 A.D.)—History.
Classification: LCC PJ2025 .F68 2019 | DDC 493/.209—dc23 LC record available at https://lccn.loc.gov/2019018022

British Library Cataloging-in-Publication Data is available

Editorial: Rob Tempio and Matt Rohal
Production Editorial: Sara Lerner
Text and Cover Design: Pamela Schnitter
Production: Erin Suydam
Publicity: Amy Stewart and Alyssa Sanford
Copyeditor: Hank Southgate

Cover Credit: The Weill codex, 6th century AD. Photo courtesy of the Musée du Louvre, distr. RMN–Grand Palais/Christian Larrieu

This book has been composed in Adobe Text Pro and Caslon Pro

CONTENTS

LIST OF IMAGES

Graphs

Figures

PREFACE

The chapters of this book correspond to the four lectures that I gave at the Institute for the Study of the Ancient World (New York University) in March and April 2017 as part of the Rostovtzeff Lectures series and of my teaching at the Collège de France. I am grateful to ISAW and its current director, Alexander Jones, for having invited me to deliver them, and to its former director, Roger Bagnall, who was so kind as to honor me by scheduling me as his last invited speaker in the Rostovtzeff Lectures. I would like these four lectures to be considered a modest testimony to my immense admiration for Roger's work and an homage to his relentless activity in both papyrology and ancient history, which has not only driven them forward but also irreversibly changed their composition in terms of organization, methodology, and ways of operating.

To this end, I wanted to choose a subject dear to Roger, namely that of the relations between Egyptian and Greek, which were the constant focus of his attention over the past twenty or so years, as chapter 4 of his *Everyday Writing in the Graeco-Roman World* (Berkeley-Los Angeles-London 2011) notably attests. Interest in this subject also encounters a direction in current research, because multilingualism has in recent years acquired an unprecedented importance in the field of linguistic studies (with the development of a branch of sociolinguistics devoted to languages in contact): the cloistered study of ancient societies long practiced by researchers specializing in only one area has given way in recent times to a more open approach that is alert to cultural interactions. Moreover, contemporary Western societies have increasingly had to face the problem of multilingualisms and of the coexistence of multicultural practices for which they are often ill prepared, because the monocultural national models in which they have developed have not prepared them to understand and manage these types of combinations. The theme of these lectures is thus at the intersection of historical investigation, methodological necessity, and societal preoccupation.

I should like to express my gratitude to the entire ISAW team, which welcomed me during my month's stay with unforgettable care and kindness.

I am also indebted to the audiences at the lectures for their suggestions and comments, from which the present book has profited greatly, and to the two anonymous peer reviewers. In the preparation of the lectures I also benefited from the help of Dominique Benazeth, Betsy Bolman, Anne Boud'hors, Florence Calament, Marie-Pierre Chaufray, Willy Clarysse, Muriel Debié, Alain Delattre, Alain Desreumaux, Stephen Emmel, Jean-Marc Mandosio, Roberta Mazza, Leila Nehmé, and Jean-Baptiste Yon. My warmest thanks to all. I am particularly indebted to Antonio Ricciardetto and Loreleï Vanderheyden for their work compiling the data that allowed me to generate graph 1 and for reading the manuscript of this book, and to Valérie Schram for compiling the index of ancient sources. I am also grateful to Princeton University Press for agreeing to publish this book and for their excellent cooperation in the publication process. I should like, finally, to express my gratitude to Roger Bagnall, who, in addition to everything else, read through the entire manuscript, thus helping me to make it less imperfect, and to my wife, Caroline Magdelaine, without whose help and encouragment none of this would have seen the light of day. The translation is for the most part due to Elizabeth Libbrecht, with the help of Céline Surprenant (Collège de France).

The Rise of Coptic

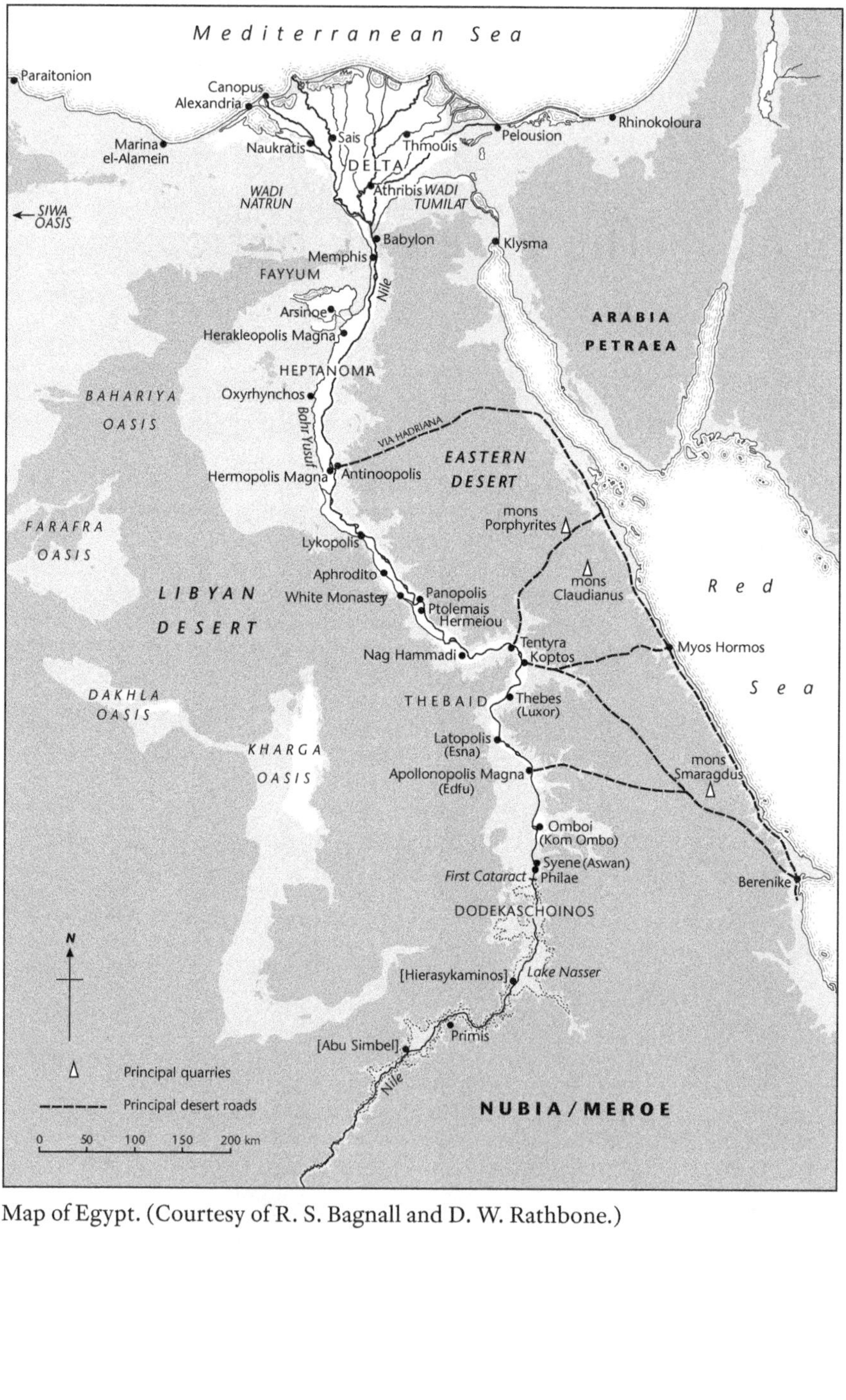

Map of Egypt. (Courtesy of R. S. Bagnall and D. W. Rathbone.)

CHAPTER I

An Egyptian Exception?

It is a particular aspect of the relations between Egyptian and Greek that I would like to examine here: the way in which the Egyptian language, in the new form that it took on during Late Antiquity in Christian milieus, namely that of Coptic,[1] developed and attempted to undermine the monopoly

[1] Coptic is the last stage of the Egyptian language, written with Greek letters. The term *Coptic* must give rise to a preliminary warning of a terminological as well as methodological nature. It is commonly used to designate several realities: it refers to various phenomena connected to the Egyptians who speak and write that language, otherwise known as the Copts. This last word goes back to the Arabic *Qibṭī*, which was derived from the Greek word Αἰγύπτιος "Egyptian" (itself, it seems, in turn derived from an Egyptian designation of Memphis, *Ḥwt-kꜣ-Ptḥ*, lit. "The house of the *ka* [i.e., spiritual double] of Ptah," which, by metonymy, would have been used by the Greeks to designate Egypt at a time when their knowledge was limited mainly to Lower Egypt). The Arabs, long after the conquest of Egypt in 642, used indeed this term to characterize the Christian community constituting the population of the conquered country, as opposed to the Muslim conquerors. It then moved on to European languages through the neo-Latin *coptus*. This usage is the only one that is historically valid—even if it fits a context much later than the period that will be treated here, and one during which Egypt was, at least initially, not totally Christian and the Egyptians did not identify themselves as such by their religion. But the word *Coptic* was also used to describe the writing of the Christians of Egypt, the Copts, as well as the state of the language that it renders. This is a modern use, which has given rise to the creation of the term *Coptology* (study of the Coptic writing system and language and, by extension, of the civilization of those who used this writing). It should be noted that the use of this word not only for the writing but also for the state of the language that corresponds to its emergence has led some to use the term *Coptic* also for texts that are not written in Coptic *stricto sensu* (see, for example, very recently Quack 2017, 27). In any case, we must be wary about (and even banish) secondary uses, especially in terms of chronology or material culture: we must absolutely avoid speaking of a "Coptic period," as so often happens; in the same way, one can question the relevance of defining as Coptic an object of everyday life, such as a ceramic or a fabric—as has become customary in museum or collection catalogs. Here, I will use this term only for the language and writing that transcribes it as well as for those who use it. As Coptic is Egyptian, I will

that the Greek language had held for centuries as the official language. What I will analyze, then, is a very specific domain of written culture.

The written culture of Egypt and the interlinguistic relationships that it involves can be studied through two types of sources: (1) sources pertaining to writing that I will call "enduring," in other words, the books and publications created to last and to be disseminated beyond the circle of the people commissioning their writing; and (2) sources pertaining to "everyday" writing, which we modern scholars have typically come to designate with the term "documents"—a conveniently broad term, yet one that is nonetheless very vague in that it covers, as generally used, a wide variety of artifacts. Without entering into an excessively nuanced typology, these can consist of (a) writings that an individual writes for him- or herself (reminders, lists, accounts); (b) writings exchanged between two individuals (private or business letters); (c) documents that testify to an exchange between two individuals, but within a legal framework (contracts, etc.); (d) documents addressed by an individual to the administration (petitions or various requests) or, conversely, (e) by the administration to an individual (tax receipts, administrative letters, various orders)—both of which therefore pertain to the regulated context of public law; and lastly, (f) internal administrative documents. As opposed to the first category, sources pertaining to "everyday" writing are normally set in the urgency of the present and are not intended for intergenerational dissemination (except for some kinds of legal documents).

I will focus in this book on documentary sources and, more specifically, on those produced within a context regulated by the law and the state (categories c–f according to the above typology), which in Egypt had long been subject to the monopoly of Greek, namely legal texts that the ancients called *dikaiōmata*, as well as texts pertaining to the judicial and administrative domain. Our task will be to establish the chronology and mechanisms whereby Egyptian came to enter the domain of *regulated* writing, thus acquiring an official dimension and becoming an actor in public written culture, to the detriment of the monopoly that Greek had acquired for itself. Through this problematic, which clearly relates to the broader subject of the emergence of Coptic, its development, and its coexistence with Greek, we will develop a genuine sociological account of bilingualism in Egypt during Late Antiquity. This is relevant given that the official use of a language reveals and determines to a large extent both

---

also use "Egyptian" as a synonym. It is, moreover, the only word known to the Greek language (Αἰγύπτιος "Egyptian") and to the Coptic one (ⲙⲛⲧⲣⲙⲕⲏⲙⲉ lit. "which is peculiar to the inhabitants of Egypt").

how this language is collectively perceived and how it relates to other languages.

In 1993, Roger Bagnall wrote, "The relationship of Greek and Coptic documentary usage would repay further study."[2] Recent years have seen their share of discoveries that renew our understanding of the subject—and I myself have had the opportunity to find and recently publish a few key pieces—that modify the chronology that had been established.[3] There is still much to be done on this subject. In this book, I will attempt a synthesis on this important issue, basing my investigation on the re-examination of isolated papyri or of dossiers of papyri (and, in chapter 4, on the presentation of new pieces) that I believe can help us renew our perspective.

The Egyptian Situation (250–550)

During the first three centuries of its history, Coptic was limited exclusively to nonregulated written exchanges. In this and the following chapter, we will ask whether this state of affairs is historically noteworthy or significant and, if so, what makes it so. However, I first need to present the linguistic context in Egypt at the time.

As is well known, a consequence of the Graeco-Macedonian conquest of Egypt and the establishment of the Ptolemaic Dynasty was the institution of Greek as the official language. This situation remained unchanged when Egypt came under Roman domination (30 BC). In the name of a very Roman type of pragmatism, the new power did not attempt to break with the previous linguistic tradition; rather, by availing itself of existing structures, it accepted that the administration continued using Greek while introducing Latin into it under certain circumstances (some documents originating in the army or regarding it, as well as those related to Roman citizenship). Compared to Greek, Egyptian—the language of the large majority of the population—was employed in multiple written forms depending on the context, of which only one was in common usage: Demotic (as opposed to Hieratic, which was reserved for the writing of literary and religious texts, and hieroglyphics, which were restricted to epigraphy [Fig. 1]). Even though the last example of Demotic is a graffito left on a wall at the Temple of Philae (452) [Fig. 2], its "natural" use disappeared much earlier. This writing ceased to be used in letters and tax receipts during the middle of the first century and, except in Egyptian temple environments,

[2] Bagnall 1993, 241n51.

[3] Fournet 2010b; Förster, Fournet, and Richter 2012; Delattre and Fournet 2018.

Fig. 1. The last hieroglyphic inscription (394) on the wall of Hadrian's Gate at Philae. It accompanies a representation of the Nubian god Mandoulis. We can note the presence, at the bottom, of a contemporary inscription in Demotic. (Photograph courtesy of J. H. F. Dijkstra.)

no longer served for legal transactions as well after the first century. I will not dwell on the cause of this disappearance, which was the economic decline of temples: Roger Bagnall shed light on this almost thirty years ago.[4] What is of interest to me here are its sociolinguistic consequences. Apart from the temple milieus, the population no longer had a form of writing its primary language at its disposal, and from the first century found itself in a situation of collective "agraphia," condemned to having to make

[4] Bagnall 1988. See also Lewis 1993 and more recently Stadler 2008.

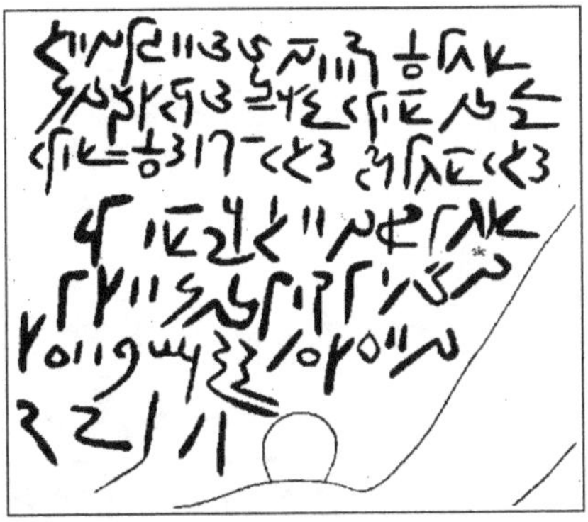

Fig. 2. The last testimony of Demotic (452) in a graffito carved in the Temple of Philae. (From F. Ll. Griffith, *Catalogue of the Demotic Graffiti of the Dodecaschoenus*, Oxford 1935–37, pl. LIV.)

use of Greek for its written communication. The only way to escape this linguistic schizophrenia was to reinvent a new form of writing. The former system was intrinsically bound to temples (which imparted its teaching through "Houses of Life"); and while temples continued to writhe in their death throes, Christianization, which was gaining significant ground during the third century, triggered this reinvention. In a context characterized by the hegemony of Greek and a departure from writing systems derived from ancient hieroglyphics, the new Egyptian writing could only be Greek. Following experiments (called "Old Coptic"[5]) that had already been performed by Egyptian priests who were increasingly unable to master the ancient Pharaonic writing, Greek graphemes were borrowed [Fig. 3]. To these were added others, for rendering phonemes specific to Egyptian that Greek letters could not express. The process was certainly neither organized nor linear, but among the multiple trials that were attempted independently, one came to be one step ahead of the others. It spread through stages and mechanisms unknown to us, and spawned Coptic in the traditional sense.[6]

What I am interested in here is the profile of Coptic writings from the first centuries. While these writings pertain both to the literary and

[5] Quaegebeur 1982, 1991a; Aufrère 1999; Bosson 1999, 72–77; Quack 2017. These experiments were themselves preceded by others ("Pre-Old Coptic"): cf. Quaegebeur 1991b; Aufrère 1999, 48–51 ("pré-vieux-copte I"); Quack 2017, 30–37 ("'Graeco-Egyptian' writing system"). Kasser 2004, 78, distinguishes two types of Old Coptic: "vieux-copte ancien" (I–II AD) and "vieux-copte tardif" (III–IV AD).

[6] From the recent bibliography I retain Bagnall 2005; Choat 2012; Zakrzewska 2015; and Quack 2017.

Fig. 3. School exercise from the Temple of Narmouthis (*O.Narm.Dem.* II 37, second/third century): the hieroglyphic or Hieratic signs are accompanied by their transliteration into Old Coptic. In the latter, we can see some letters derived from Demotic. (Facsimile courtesy of Paolo Gallo.)

documentary domains, it was with literary texts that Coptic made its appearance in the third century,[7] and not just with any form of literary texts, given that the five examples that have been attributed to this century take

[7] I do not take here into account the texts written in what is called Old Coptic, even if I am well aware that the line dividing Old Coptic and Coptic is a modern construction that is essentially based on the difference between milieus and not entirely on specific philological and linguistic traits. As Tonio S. Richter notes, "It would be hard to draw a sharp line between those Old-Coptic efforts, which were situated in the pagan contexts of Roman Egypt, and the earliest evidence of what is usually classified as Coptic and is associated with Christian contexts in a broad sense" (Richter 2008a, 413).

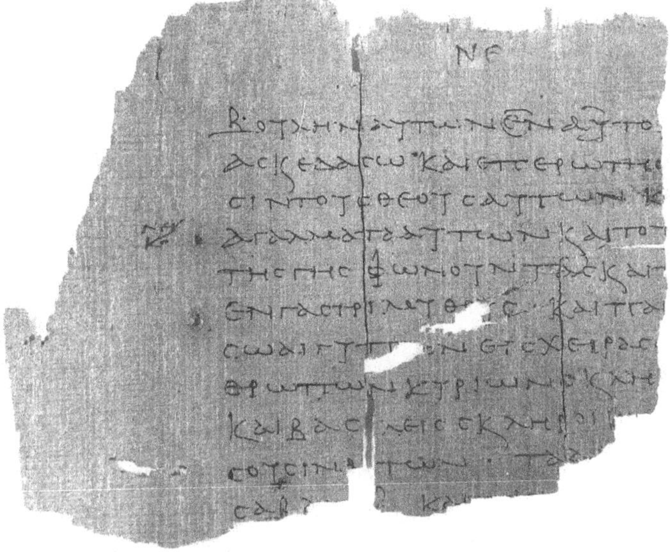

Fig. 4. This Greek edition of *Isaiah* (here *PSI* XII 1273) contains marginal annotations in Coptic that are the earliest testimony of this new writing (third century). (Photograph courtesy of the Biblioteca Medicea Laurenziana, Florence.)

the form of annotations to Greek biblical texts or bilingual versions of the Bible:[8]

(1) Marginal annotations in a Greek edition of *Isaiah*, the majority of which belongs to the Chester Beatty Library, and which can be dated by its writing to the third century (more likely the first half, according to Frederic G. Kenyon) [Fig. 4].[9] According to the edition,

[8] On these texts (and others dated to the third century but more probably to the the fourth century), see the lectures I gave in 2017 at the Collège de France (http://www.college-de-france.fr/site/jean-luc-fournet/course-2016-2017.htm). I exclude here the Kieseleff Papyrus (ed. Brashear and Satzinger 1990 = TM 64362), a Christian acrostic hymn in Greek and Coptic; *P.Bodmer* VI (ed. Kasser 1960 = TM 107761) containing *Proverbs* 1–21; and P.ChesterBeatty AC 1390 (ed. Brashear, Funk, Robinson, and Smith 1990 = TM 61614): all of them must be dated more probably to the fourth century than to the third. There is doubt regarding the date of P.Mich. inv. 5421 (ed. Browne 1979, no. 2 = TM 107779) containing *Job* 30:21–30: its editor favored the fourth–fifth century, but, according to the stratigraphic data, it should be from the end of the third or fourth century (van Minnen 1994, 72). See also TM 107771, 107888, 107910, 107962, and 108146, all dated to the third–fourth century.

[9] P.ChesterBeatty VII (= *P.Beatty* VI, ed. Kenyon 1937) + *PSI* XII 1273 + *P.Merton* I 2 = TM 61951. According to Paola Degni (Cavallo, Crisci, Messeri, and Pintaudi 1998, 111–12), this manuscript could be from the second century.

these Coptic annotations could be from the "middle of the third century or a little later," but we cannot rule out the end of the century. Its origins remain uncertain, even though the Coptic dialect used for these annotations, which is a form of ancient Fayyumic, seems to point to the Fayyum.[10]

(2) A Graeco-Coptic glossary to the minor prophets *Hosea* and *Amos* (kept in London), written on the reverse side of a Greek land register and which was paleographically dated from the "late third century" by its editors, "if not fourth" according to Arthur S. Hunt.[11] A recent study has shown that the land register probably dates from the "third quarter of the second century" and that it originates from Oxyrhynchus, which tallies with the dialect used for the Coptic part of the glossary (Mesokemic).[12]

(3) The Coptic version of *Psalm* 46:3–10 copied among exercises in Greek (declension of pronouns, a paraphrase of Homer, fraction tables, declension of a *chreia*, conjugation of a verb) in a school notebook composed of seven tablets, kept at the Bodleian Library.[13] According to the editor of the Coptic portion, this educational codex dates from the second half of the third century.[14] Purchased in Luxor, its exact origin is unknown, but the Akhmimic dialect characteristic of the Coptic used to copy the *Psalm* seems to confirm that it has been written in Upper Egypt, perhaps in the Theban area.

(4) A bilingual papyrus codex of sixty-four folios containing the *Acta Pauli* (Greek), the *Canticum* (Coptic), the *Book of Lamentations* (Coptic), and *Ecclesiastes* (Greek and Coptic), copied by at least two hands, maybe as writing exercises in both languages.[15] The editors,

---

[10] According to TM 61951, the following origins have been proposed: Aphroditopolis/Aṭfih (Schmidt), Upper Egypt/Panopolis (Sanders), Arsinoe (Kilpatrick).

[11] P.Brit.Mus. EA 10825 (ed. Bell and Thompson 1925, reprinted in *P.Rain.Unterricht. Kopt* 257a) = TM 61982. Hunt's opinion about the date is given by Bell and Thompson 1925, 241.

[12] Benaissa 2016.

[13] T.Bodl. Greek Inscr. 3019 (= TM 61276): Coptic text edited by Crum 1934; Greek text edited by Parsons 1970 (Mertens-Pack[3] 2732; Cribiore 1996, no. 388).

[14] Parsons 1970 and Cribiore 1996, 273, date it to the end of the third century.

[15] Hamburger Papyrus bilinguis 1 (ed. Diebner and Kasser 1989) = TM 61979. I am inclined to think that our two copyists were bilinguals with a better command of Greek, trying to learn Coptic writing or perfecting themselves in Coptic at the same time as they compiled collections of texts for personal use. Even if this codex is not strictly speaking a school text, it had an educational purpose. See Diebner and Kasser

following Eric G. Turner, proposed a date between 275 and 350, but according to a recent re-examination of the script of this codex, the end of the third century should be preferred.[16] The Fayyumic dialect used for the Coptic parts points to a Fayyumic provenance.

(5) A set of annotations to a Greek edition of the minor prophets in a papyrus codex from the Freer Gallery,[17] dated by its writing from the end of the third century. Although this dating was accepted by most scholars, some prefer the fourth century—in my view, correctly.[18] Although it could have been acquired in the Fayyum, nothing can actually confirm its provenance.[19]

As opposed to the typical ratio between literary and documentary texts (usually one to six or seven), we have only one document for this century:[20] a private letter preserved on an ostracon from Kellis (Dakhla Oasis), which is written in a form of archaic Coptic, dating from the later third century [Fig. 5].[21]

During the following century, Coptic documentation became far more visible: the number of literary texts (almost all biblical) proliferated, although they came to be very clearly surpassed by the number of documentary ones. Documentary Coptic truly developed during this century. Rather than going over examples of this, which would be time-consuming

1989, 21 ("Schreibübung [. . .], bei der Buchstabenformen und Orthographie des Schülers z. T. von Lehrerhand, z. T. vom Schüler selbst (auf Anweisung des Lehrers?) verbessert wurden"); and Crisci 2004, 114–15 ("Anche senza voler escludere istanze di perfezionamento di competenze grafiche individuali (in certo senso inevitabili quando si ha a che fare con scritture manoscritte), non penso che fosse questa la principale ragion d'essere di una operazione che aspirava invece a costituire una raccolta di testi religiosi, greco-copti, per letture edificanti, individuali o collettive").

16 Diebner and Kasser 1989, 51; Crisci 2004, 114.

17 Freer MS V (ed. Sanders and Schmidt 1927) = TM 61966.

18 Turner 1977, 181 (OT 187). A comparison with *P.Bodmer* XXV (now attributed to the fourth century) favors this later dating. For the various opinions on the date of this codex, see Choat 2006b, 91–97.

19 See Choat 2006b, 88–91.

20 I am excluding *P.Mich.Copt.* 1 (TM 86539), of unknown provenance, dated by its editors from the third or early fourth century. This letter cannot be this old, because it follows the new-style format of letters, and the writing would be compatible with the fifth to sixth centuries, which the use of an initial cross and final crosses confirms.

21 O.KellisCopt. Inv. D/1/234 (ed. Gardner 1999, reed. *P.Kellis* VII 129 = TM 88395). On this text, see Kasser 2004; Bagnall 2005; and Quack 2017, 72–73.

Fig. 5. The most ancient document in Coptic: a private letter from Kellis (*P.Kellis* VII 129, later third century). (© Dakhleh Oasis Project and C. A. Hope.)

and pointless,[22] I would like to characterize briefly their nature with regard to Greek documents found in the same context. To do so, I will focus primarily on homogeneous groups of texts, in particular on archives that have the merit of contextualizing the concomitant use of Coptic and Greek.

The oldest such archive is that of the Melitian monastery of Hathor (Cynopolite/Heracleopolite), consisting of two subarchives, those of the elder Apa Paieous (330–40) and of his (whether direct or not) successor

[22] We find a list of Coptic documents from the mid-third to the early fifth century in Choat 2006a, 178–85, to be completed in particular by the editions of texts from Kellis (*P.Kellis* VII, published in 2014).

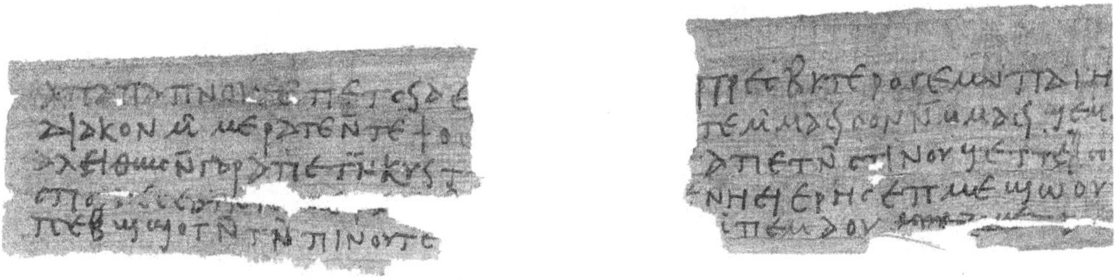

Fig. 6. A Coptic letter sent by Apa Papnoute to Nepheros, the elder of the Hathor monastery (*P.Neph.* 15, ca. 360–70). (© Institut für Papyrologie, Universität Heidelberg.)

Nepheros (360–70).[23] The former contains ten letters, six of which are in Greek and four in Coptic,[24] and a Greek legal text ("contract for the appointment of a deputy");[25] the second contains twenty-six letters, twenty-four of which are in Greek and two in Coptic [Fig. 6], and sixteen other documents (contracts, tax receipts, etc.), all in Greek. Note that the editor believes that the author of one of the Greek letters addressed to Paieous concerning relations between the Melitian congregation and the Bishop of Alexandria (*P.Lond.* VI 1914) is Egyptian, judging by the mistakes he makes. It can therefore be argued that the choice of Greek is related to the nature and importance of this letter, which acts as an official report.

The documents found in the bindings of the codices from Nag Hammadi date from the same era, and also appear to pertain to a monastic circle (especially in those of Codices VII and VIII).[26] Apart from numerous accounts, they contain sixteen Greek letters revolving around the monk Sansnos, and about the same number of Coptic letters, which are most often fragmentary.[27]

---

23 A third group of texts, that of Papnouthios (*P.Lond.* VI 1923–29), is less clearly related to these. It consists entirely of Greek letters. On the monastery of Hathor or Phathor, cf. Hauben 2002.

24 *P.Lond.* VI 1914–19 (Greek); 1920–22 (= *SBKopt.* III 1311–13) and *SBKopt.* III 1310 (Coptic).

25 *P.Lond.* IV 1913.

26 I am referring here just to the texts included within the covers and do not want to get into the debate surrounding the "monastic connexion" of the codices themselves (see, for instance, Wipszycka 2000 and the bibliography that she mentions).

27 Greek letters: *P.Nag Hamm.* 66–81; Coptic letters: *P.Nag Hamm.Copt.* 3 (letter or homily), 4–8 (letters), 9–14 (undetermined fragments, probably letters), 15–19 (letters). Wipszycka 2000, 190–91, gives a list of documents that she considers to be of monastic origin.

Texts from the same period or slightly later originate from the oases of Kharga and Dakhla in the Western Desert of Egypt. They are significantly larger in number owing to the excavations carried out in this region over the past several decades. For Kharga, it is the site of Douch (Kysis) that has been the most prolific, although only eleven texts, out of the 639 published ostraca (350–400), have been identified as Coptic,[28] all of which are private letters.[29] However, this is a large number if we compare it to the number of private or business letters in Greek, which makes up barely more than twenty texts. The same goes for Aïn Waqfa (a village): of the seventy-nine published documents (350–400), there is only one Coptic letter[30]—the only letter in this group of texts that includes delivery orders, receipts, agreements, or accounts. Finally, of the six documents found at Chams el-Din (Mounesis), one is a record of bookkeeping in Greek in which a line of Coptic managed to slip in.[31]

The Kellis excavations in the Dakhla Oasis have delivered a considerable number of both Coptic and Greek texts, originating from circles professing Manichaeism. While it is difficult to compare the near 450 Greek documents (ca. 290–390)[32] and the 207 Coptic documents (datable from ca. 355 to 380+)[33] in terms of typology, given that their publication is not yet entirely completed, we can get a more precise image of the Coptic documents through a summary given in *P.Kellis* VII (2014). Out of the 207 Coptic documents identified, 199 are letters and 8 are lists or accounts; on the other hand, Greek documents are composed of legal documents and petitions, in addition to private and administrative letters. Therefore, while Coptic documents are almost all letters, the bilingualism of the actors in this dossier is

---

[28] These ostraca (*O.Douch* I 40, 44, 49; II 183; IV 369; V 508, 524, 547, 606, 636) are as yet unpublished, except for *O.Douch* I 40 (ed. Bagnall, Choat, and Gardner 2004) and 49 (ed. Choat and Gardner 2003 = *SBKopt.* III 1292)—on these two texts, see also Schenke 2007. G. Roquet wrote a note about them in Sauneron et al. 1978, 32–33.

[29] I will return later to the case of *O.Douch* I 49.

[30] *O.Waqfa* 77, yet unpublished.

[31] *O.Chams el-Din* 3 = *SB* XX 14823, 4.

[32] I obtain this number by adding the 81 documents in *P.Kellis* I, the 16 in *P.Gascou*, the 62 currently being published in the two sets of *APF* by K. A. Worp (19 documents in the first set, 41 in the second, which moreover includes 2 transcriptions of letters by R. S. Bagnall), and the 289 in *O.Kellis*. K. A. Worp has also informed me of the forthcoming publication of a letter in a volume of *Mélanges*. In fact, to be more precise, it would be necessary to compare by sector: Greek and Coptic papyri come from Area A, House 1–3, which provided only very few of the 289 published ostraca (House 2: 2; House 3: 3; House 4: 10; and House 5: 3). Cf. *O.Kellis*, 14.

[33] *P.Kellis* V 6. The edition of the Coptic texts is now finished.

striking, as they are capable of switching from one language to the other without it always being easy to justify the use of the language. For example, a father writes to his son in Coptic, whereas the latter writes to him in Greek;[34] meanwhile, both of them receive letters in Greek.[35] Another writes to his "brother" sometimes in Greek, sometimes in Coptic.[36] The same person may switch from Coptic to Greek within the same letter for no specific reason.[37] The bilingual nature of this community is summarized well by the recommendation that Makarios makes to his "son" Matheos in a Coptic letter: "Study your Psalms, whether Greek or Coptic."[38]

The last group of texts dating from the fourth century will take us to the Nile Valley, albeit to its outskirts, more particularly to the archive of the anchorite Apa John (Lycopolis, ca. 375–400), which for the moment is composed of thirty-four papyri, all of which are letters, fourteen of them in Greek, and twenty in Coptic. These letters were addressed by monks, clerics, soldiers, state officials, and individuals to Apa John, who has to be identified as the famous John of Lycopolis known by literary sources, so that he would pray for them or intercede in their favor in dealings with the authorities.[39] As the senders did not always state their position, it is difficult to explain the choice of language. While the majority of the Cop-

---

[34] *P.Kellis* V 12 (Coptic); *P.Kellis* I 12 (Greek). See also *P.Kellis* VII 66 and 67 (Coptic letter of Pamour to his "brother" Pekysis) and *P.Kellis* I 72 (Greek letter of Pekysis to Pamour).

[35] *P.Kellis* I 10 and 11.

[36] *P.Kellis* I 71 (Greek) and *P.Kellis* VII 64, 72, and perhaps 65 and 70 (Coptic). The term *brother* often used in ancient letters does not necessarily imply family relationship.

[37] *P.Kellis* V 43. See also *P.Kellis* V 35, a Coptic letter starting with a magical charm in Greek, written by the same hand (that of Valens). On this letter, see Mirecki, Gardner, and Alcock 1997.

[38] *P.Kellis* V 19, 13–14.

[39] Concerning these archives, cf. van Minnen 1994, 80–84; Zuckerman 1995, 188–94 (both independently identified—in my view, correctly—the Apa John of this archive with the John of Lycopolis known by literary sources); Choat 2007a (who has announced its planned re-edition). The Greek texts are *P.Amh.* II 145 (= *W.Chr.* 53) with the subscription of John in Coptic; *P.Herm.* 7–10 and 17; *W.Chr.* 130 (= *P.Lond.* III 981, 241); *SB* XIV 11882 (connected to this archive by Choat 2007a, 180, about which Gonis 2008, 69n2, has some reservations); XVIII 13612; five documents (two of them possibly belonging to this archive) edited by Gonis 2008. The Coptic ones are *P.Lond.Copt.* I 1123; *P.Ryl.Copt.* 268–76 and possibly 292, 301, 310–14, 396; *SBKopt.* IV 1695 (ed. Choat and Gardner 2006); perhaps also *P.CrumST* 172. A Coptic unpublished piece cited by Choat 2007a, 180, must be added (P.Mich. inv. 6626).

tic letters originate from monks,[40] others are addressed to John in Greek (such is the case of Psoïs, *P.Herm.* 7, to which I will return in chapter 2[41]), despite being written by Egyptians.

Isolated texts must be added to these groups, from a list of which I spare the reader because they contribute nothing more: they are letters, and less commonly record-keepings. The same goes for the two following centuries and a half: while Coptic documents during that period (and especially during the fifth century) are less abundant and do not benefit from the contextualization of archives as homogeneous as those that I have just discussed, their nature is identical to what we have seen concerning the fourth century. It was only in the second half of the sixth century that the profile of the documentation changed, as we will see in chapter 3. What conclusions can we draw, then, from this rapid overview of the first centuries in which Coptic was used?

I will not dwell on the geography of this documentation, which has already been analyzed by Roger Bagnall:[42] it is most often found in oases and the desert-like outskirts of the valley, where monasteries and other (semi-)anchoretic settlements came to be established. The villages of the Fayyum have not yielded any document in Coptic, at least not until the Arab Conquest (with very rare exceptions), despite providing so many documents in Greek. I am tempted to think that this is probably not by chance, considering that it is also the region where Demotic was used for the longest period of time, as much in the religious and the magical domain, as in contractual documents, a testament to the persistence of an indigenous language school for notaries that attempted to resist Greek. The link between Demotic and paganism may explain why Christians, in a highly Hellenized region, continued to use Greek, at least in the beginning and in their everyday writing. I will have the opportunity to come back to this point in chapter 3. Last of all, cities were almost entirely absent from our survey. Although the publication of previously unpublished Coptic texts from Oxyrhynchus may somewhat modify this assessment, their number for the period that concerns us definitely

[40] Almost all the letters whose author indicates his status are written by monks (*P. Ryl.Copt.* 268, 269; *SBKopt.* IV 1695). For the others, the names and titles are lost in lacunae, but the use of the expression "brother" ("my brother," "our brother," etc.) strongly suggests that we are dealing with monks or maybe clerics (*P.Ryl.Copt.* 271, 273, 276, 292, 313, 314).

[41] Cf. chapter 2, pp. 50–53.

[42] Bagnall 2011, 81–85.

appears to be very low.[43] As we can see, urban milieus are almost completely absent, to the benefit of monastic ones (or "sectarian" groups such as the Manichaeans).

However, are the conclusions of this sociological approach, which only the documents allow us to establish, also valid for literary texts? This is a tricky question that is made significantly more complex by the absence of provenance and stratigraphic data allowing us to place Coptic books in their geographical and sociocultural context. What is now certain is that the use of Coptic for nondocumentary purposes tends to precede that for documentary ones. Moreover, we note that it does not take on the form of works in the traditional sense but rather that of annotations to Greek texts, Graeco-Coptic glossaries, or school exercises in Greek sets or bilingual writing exercises. We are therefore faced with a subliterary usage intended for learning oriented toward Greek or based on Greek.[44] Moreover, some of these texts appear to originate from cities (Oxyrhynchus) or Fayyum, as opposed to our finding about the provenance of documents. The few pieces that are available and the absence of irrefutable provenance must encourage us not to come to overly definitive conclusions. It is nevertheless tempting to think that the first generations to use Coptic (in the latter half of the third century) lived in urban milieus—the very same ones that led to the formation of municipal elites[45]—or in villages that were significantly Hellenized. It furthermore appears that the use of this new writing aimed to create a version of the Scriptures in vernacular based on Greek editions, rather than to produce an original literature. It was not until several decades later that this writing, once it had been perfected and had proven itself, seems to have spread to the least Hellenized milieus (monastic ones in particular), which apparently used it for documentary purposes, to communicate among themselves. Given that monastic communities were also centers for the copying of Christian works, they were able to establish the link between the two usages.[46] I will not focus on this

[43] Cf. Clackson 2007 and the discussion of Bagnall 2011, 84–85.

[44] In the glossary to *Hosea* and *Amos* (P.Brit.Mus. EA 10825 = *P.Rain.UnterrichtKopt.* 257a), the lemmas are Greek and the annotations are Coptic. The point was thus to understand the Greek version.

[45] Cf. Bagnall 2009b, 71–72; Bagnall 2009a, 67–69; Camplani 2015, 138. On the Coptic elites, see also Wipszycka 1992b, 118; and Camplani 2003.

[46] I do not share E. Zakrzewska's opinion that the invention of Coptic took place in a monastic milieu (Zakrzewska 2016, 216): "Now, as mentioned-above, the earliest Coptic writings come from monastic, Manichaean or Gnostic communities. As is well known, these pioneers of the monastic movement were, in the eyes of their

now, as I will come back to this problem in chapter 2. For the moment, I am merely sowing a few seeds.

The precedence of literary Coptic is also possibly at the origin of one of the most noteworthy paleographic features of Coptic writing in general: its tendency for a noncursive form and a capital letters look, which is peculiar to the copying of literary papyri. With the noteworthy—but for the moment inexplicable—exception of texts from Kellis,[47] Coptic writing from the first centuries stands in sharp contrast to the cursive of Greek documentary texts, especially that of notary deeds, to such an extent that during the sixth century the notary and amateur poet Dioscorus of Aphrodite used the same style of writing for Coptic documents and his Greek poems, as opposed to the style used in his Greek documents [Fig. 7]. This link between Coptic and book writing, which Leslie S. B. MacCoull originally proposed, was called into question by Roger S. Bagnall, who considered that it was based on an oversimplification of "book hands" as opposed to "cursive business hands."[48] The fact that the typology of writing forms in use is much more complex than this understanding does not contradict the theoretical, and ideal, opposition developed by the ancients, between book and documentary writing—and by that I mean legal and administrative writing, and not that of private letters, which are often placed halfway between the two. Admittedly, we can ask whether the graphic style of Coptic is motivated by a usage that was originally exclusively literary, or by the fact that Coptic started to be employed, in the domain of documents, exclusively for private epistolography (as we are going to see in greater detail), at a time when the trend was to "literatize" the writing of private letters. In any case, it is undeniable that from the beginning

contemporaries, indeed 'underconforming to the point of deviance.' They consciously distanced themselves from their original social milieu and networks in order to create an alternative lifestyle that can only be characterized as innovative in the extreme. Part of this alternative lifestyle could be a different linguistic behavior, in this case the use of Coptic in writing." But I agree with her conclusion: "To put it somewhat sharply: literary Coptic was originally constructed not to convert Egyptian farmers but to discuss new ideas with like-minded, well-educated 'counterculturists.'" Camplani 2015, 146–47, seems to me closer to the truth, although he links the first phase too tightly with clerical milieus ("in sintesi, possiamo affermare che la pratica del copto conosce una prima fase in ambienti clericali e episcopali, per poi essere fatta propria dal monachesimo e da questo ricevere un impulso alla sua diffusione oltre il contesto monastico"), whereas it is due, in my opinion, rather to secular Christian milieus (a hypothesis that he considers too: 141).

[47] Noted, for example, by Gardner and Choat 2004, 499–501.

[48] MacCoull 1997, 350; Bagnall 2011, 79–80.

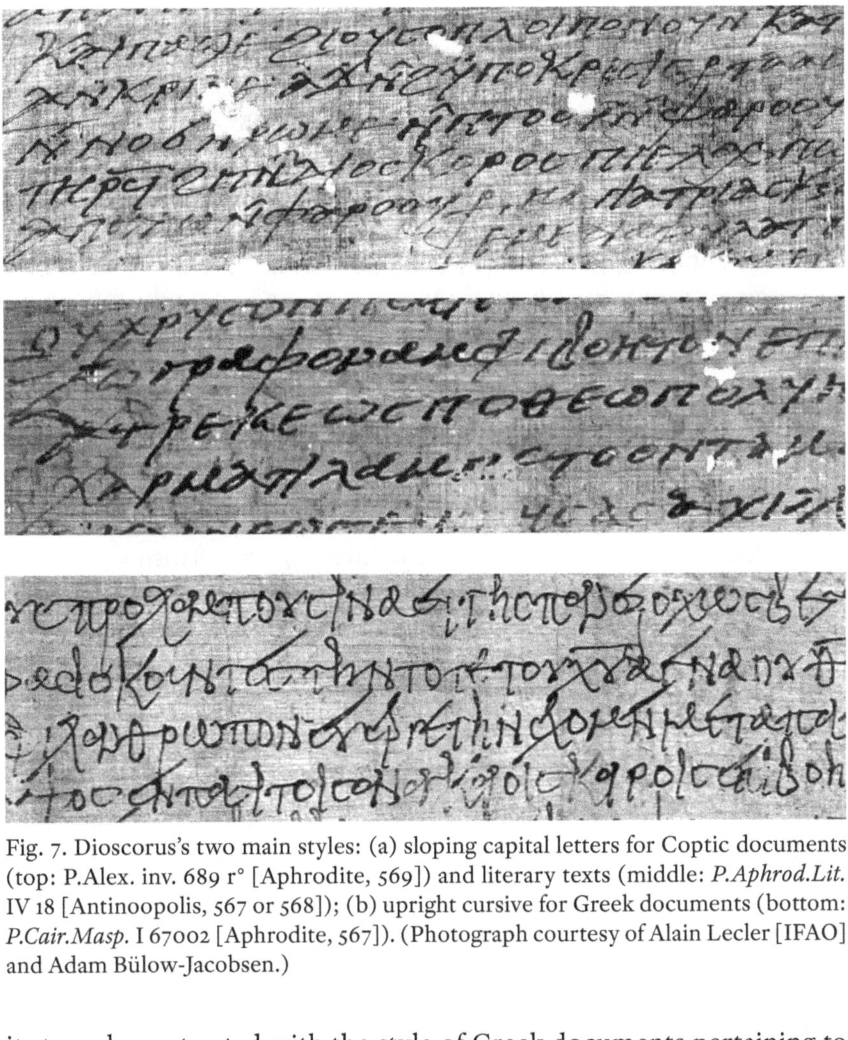

Fig. 7. Dioscorus's two main styles: (a) sloping capital letters for Coptic documents (top: P.Alex. inv. 689 r° [Aphrodite, 569]) and literary texts (middle: *P.Aphrod.Lit.* IV 18 [Antinoopolis, 567 or 568]); (b) upright cursive for Greek documents (bottom: *P.Cair.Masp.* I 67002 [Aphrodite, 567]). (Photograph courtesy of Alain Lecler [IFAO] and Adam Bülow-Jacobsen.)

it strongly contrasted with the style of Greek documents pertaining to notarial or administrative practices. Moreover, this contrast was maintained for such a long time and so systematically that I am tempted to see it as the result of a conscious and deliberate social distribution of the two forms of writing: that is, a socially organized digraphia.[49] I see evidence of

[49] This contrast is all the more necessary since the two languages share the same graphic system (the Greek alphabet), and the shift from one to the other within the same text may not always be very clear and may cause misunderstanding. One could neutralize this risk only by using a different graphic style for each of the languages, which makes it possible to grasp at a glance the language that is used. Cf. Fournet 2018a, 80–81.

this in the fact that Coptic writing ended up adopting a cursive style when it ceased to be employed solely for literary and epistolary purposes—in other words, when it came to be used for legal texts.[50] I therefore think that it is legitimate to relate paleography to the field of use. In my opinion, the capital letters aspect of Coptic would seem to be the graphically translated acknowledgment of its unsuitability for legal or administrative uses. Once again, we see that paleography reflects the history of a society and its cultural choices.

For now, what primarily interests me—and here I am returning to my initial problem—is the nature of the fourth-century documentary texts. Except for a few bookkeeping records, as I have just mentioned, these consist solely of letters, and specifically of private or business letters—texts, in other words, that lie outside the public or legal sphere. The exceptions are very rare: one is possibly *O.Douch* I 49, a letter addressed by a *princeps* (that is, a military officer) regarding wheat distribution:

> Pistoïs, *princeps*, writes to the beloved brother Sansnos: in the Lord—greetings. See, nine artabas of wheat: I have sent them over so that you (pl.) might apportion them amongst you. Give part (i.e., as payment) to Dio (the) camel-herder, corresponding as if you might sell it; and write how much then you have been paid. Be well in the Lord.[51]

As this case most likely refers to military provisions, we could consider this document an administrative letter *stricto sensu*, which should follow an official procedure. But it may also be an unofficial missive sent to a coreligionist who knew Pistoïs well. In any case, the diplomatics of this letter contrasts sharply with Greek administrative letters from the same period, in which the Christian greeting is absent.[52] In fact, the only indisputable exception is a recently published text (2014), which has received little attention since then, *P.Kellis* VII 123, overlooked perhaps because it

[50] Among ancient examples, see *CPR* IV 23 (610); *SBKopt.* III 1369 (ed. Alcock and Sijpesteijn 2000; 646/647); and *P.Vat.Copt.Doresse* 1 (ed. Förster and Mitthof 2004; mid-seventh century). However, even once "cursivized," it would continue to develop features distinctive from those of Greek, which made it possible to distinguish the two within a single given text (cf. Fournet 2009c, 443, fig. 18.12; Cromwell 2010).

[51] Trans. Choat and Gardner 2003, 145.

[52] *O.Douch* II 183 is also a Coptic letter written by an officer (an *optio*). However, we know nothing of its contents. *O.Douch* I 44 is written to a πρ( ) which may be, according to the editors, either a *praepositus* or a priest (*presbyteros*).

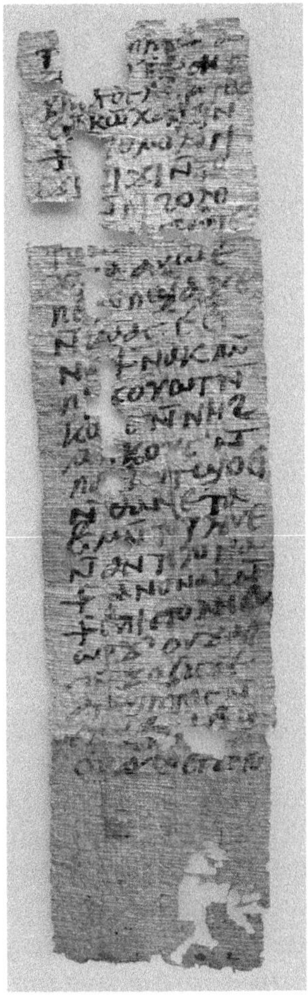

Fig. 8. A Coptic loan receipt in the form of a letter (*P.Kellis* VII 123 [Kellis, ca. 355–80]). (© Dakhleh Oasis Project and C. A. Hope.)

was published in the midst of private letters. Although written in an epistolary form, "this is essentially a loan receipt and an agreement to repay in kind (sometimes called a 'sale in advance')" [Fig. 8][53]:

> Τ[ῶι ἀγα]πητ̣ῷ̣ι ἀ|δε̣[λφῶ]ι̣ Ἰω̣σὴφ | Βη̣σ̣ᾶ̣τος Λ[ου]ιω̣ρ̣ος | ἐν κ(υρί)ω̣ χαίρειν.
> | ϯ[ⲣ̅]ϩⲟⲙⲟⲗⲟⲅⲓ | ϫⲉ̣ ϩ̣ⲓϫⲓ ⲛ̅ⲧⲟ|[ⲧⲕ̅] ⲛ̅ⲡⲓϩⲟⲗⲟ|ⲅⲟⲧ̣ⲓ̣ⲛ̣ⲟ̣ⲥ ⲉⲧⲉ|ⲭⲣ̣ⲓ̣ⲁ ⲁⲩⲱ ⲉ| ⲡⲉϥ̣ⲙ̅ⲡϣⲁ ϫⲉ | ⲛ̅ⲕⲁⲁⲥ ⲉⲉⲓ|ⲛⲁϯ ⲛⲁⲕ ⲙ̅|ⲡⲓϫⲟⲩⲱⲧ ⲛ̅|ⲕⲟ[ⲩ]ⲥ ⲛ̅ⲛⲏϩ | ⲙ̅ⲡ̣ⲕⲟⲩ̣ⲥ ⲛ̅|ⲡⲁⲉ̣ⲓⲱ̣ⲧ ϣⲟⲉⲓ |

[53] *P.Kellis* VII, p. 272.

ⲛ̅ⲑⲁⲛⲉⲧⲁ | ⲉⲙⲛ̅ⲧⲟⲩ ⲗⲁⲩⲉ | ⲛ̅ⲁⲛⲧⲓⲗⲟⲅⲓⲁ | ϯ`ⲧⲁⲛⲟ ⲛⲁⲕ ⲛ̅|ϯ`ⲉⲡⲓⲥⲧⲟⲗⲏ ⲉⲩ|ⲱⲣϫ` ⲟⲩϫⲁⲉ̣ⲓ̣ | ϩⲛ̅ ⲡ̣ϫⲟⲉ̣ⲓ̣ⲥ̣ .ⲉ|ⲁⲅⲁ̣ⲡⲏⲧⲟⲥ ⲛ̅| ⲥ̣ⲟ̣ⲛ̣ ⲉⲧ̣ⲧ̣ⲁ̣ . ` . ´ⲏ|ⲟⲩ ⲁⲩⲱ ⲉⲧⲥ̣ⲟⲉ̣ⲓ̣.

To my beloved brother Joseph son of Besas. (From) Louioros; in the Lord,—greetings. I acknowledge that I have received from [you] this *holokottinos* for my need and its worth, so that I will pay you these twenty choes of oil per the *chous* (-measure) of my father Shoei of the monastery; for they are not disputed. I am drawing up this letter for you as a deed of security. Be well in the Lord my (?) beloved brother, who is honored (?) and . . . [54]

This document follows the formulary of the Greek receipts. But, at the same time, it is explicitly presented as a letter (l. 21, *epistolē*), which is a way of recognizing that it does not have the same status as a Greek legal document even if it claims the same effects. We have here an attempt at drawing up a legal document in Coptic, which nevertheless is formally hybrid and which does not seem to have been imitated. It is an isolated case.

Apart from this one exception, Coptic is exclusively limited to private letters—in any case to texts involving communication.[55] This does not mean that in bilingual environments such as Kellis, private letters were always written in Coptic. In fact, we observe the interchangeability of languages for the epistolary function: both Greek and Coptic were used between the same individuals, and sometimes in the same letter. In other environments, such as Kharga, we find, on the contrary, a preference for Coptic (Douch), or even its exclusive use (Aïn Waqfa) in nonregulated epistolary communication (excluding delivery or payment orders, which also take on an epistolary form and are always in Greek). Are we dealing with less Hellenized milieus, or did the authors deliberately choose to use Coptic for private communication?

In any case, no matter how hard we search for them, we have found no judicial or legal document in Coptic from this period. Greek was used whenever someone wanted to write a petition[56] or make a transaction.

---

[54] Translation from *P.Kellis* VII.

[55] I am omitting the somewhat marginal case of bookkeeping records.

[56] The petition was a complaint addressed to the authorities to institute a legal proceeding. See chapter 3.

Failing to master that language, the person would go to a bilingual notary who would draw up the deed in question in Greek and translate it orally from Greek into Coptic for his client. If the person was not capable of understanding the text of the contract in Greek, he was often—but not always—incapable of writing in Greek his subscription (the equivalent of our modern signature), which constituted agreement. In this case, he called upon a third party, the *hypographeus*, who would subscribe at his request. This situation is noted at the end of a settlement of claims from 545: "and when all terms had been read and translated to them and had satisfied them, they subscribed by agency of Pamouthios at their request because they are illiterate" (it is not necessary to specify that "illiterate" here clearly means illiterate *in Greek*!).[57] The translation of acts for the attention of the parties was so frequent that usually the notary did not even take the time to specify it, except in the case of a few talkative or pedantic notaries.[58]

Therefore, there was no question of writing the text of a contract in Coptic or of providing a subscription in a language other than Greek.[59] It would have been possible to attach a summary in Coptic, in line with notarial practices during the Ptolemaic period or the beginning of the Roman period, in which it was possible to provide a summary in Greek or in Demotic,[60] depending on the language in which the contract was written. I am nevertheless unaware of an example of such a practice.

Admittedly, at times, scholars mention Coptic "summaries" found on the reverse side of Greek legal acts; some are even described as "chancellery notes," which would give them an official nature.[61] However, the study of these texts, which have never been gathered together or ana-

[57] *P.Oxy.* LXIII 4397, 186–88: καὶ ἀναγνωσθέντων̣ πάντων καὶ ἑρμηνευθέντων αὐτοῖς καὶ ἀρεσθέντων ὑπέγραψα̣ν̣ διὰ Παμουθίου αἰτηθέντος παρ᾽ αὐτῶν ἀγραμμάτων ὄντων.

[58] Other than *P.Oxy.* LXIII 4397, cf. also *P.Münch.* I 13, 71 (sale; Syene, 594); *P.Mon. Phoib.Test.* 1, 13–15 and 70 (=*P.Lond.* I 77, 12–14 and 69 [231]) (will; Hermonthis, end of the 610s)—concerning this text, see chapter 4. It must be noted that these texts are very long: respectively 245, 85, and 89 lines.

[59] The counterexamples are doubtful: for example, MacCoull 1995, 345 (=*BL* X 282) believes that there is a Coptic subscription in *P.Vat.Aphrod.* 4, 15 (Aphrodite, VIth c.): ⲧ̣ⲥ̣ⲩ̣ⲣ̣ⲁ ⲥⲁⲃⲓⲛⲟⲥ "Tsyra daughter of Sabinos," where it must actually be read as Α̣ὐ̣ρηλία Τσῦρ̣ος.

[60] See Depauw 2009.

[61] *BGU* XVII 2683 intr. (p. 21): "wahrscheinlich eine Notiz der Kanzlei."

lyzed specifically through an interlinguistic perspective, shows a different phenomenon altogether (cf. appendix 1).[62] I was able to identify a dozen Greek contracts with Coptic "summaries," all of which date from the years 520–50 and originate from Hermopolis or an Antinoopolite enclave in Hermopolite territory.[63] They belong to at least three archives: that of Taurinos,[64] that of the monastery of Apa Sabinos (called the "Northern Rock of Antinoopolis"), and that of the monastery of Apa Apollō at Bawīt. Most of the time, these one- or two-line annotations replicate the title of the document—which is written in Greek as required, on the verso—and are always written in another hand. They were therefore added subsequently and are not part of the document as such. They are annotations made by someone more comfortable with Coptic than with Greek, and therefore allowing one more easily to identify a document once it was rolled up: perhaps one of the monastery archivists who spoke less Greek than his predecessors?

We can go even further with the texts of the Taurinos archive. Here we are struck by the clumsiness of the hand or hands responsible for the notations that are found on their reverse side—a characteristic that in my opinion appears to confirm that all four of them do indeed belong to the same archives. In addition to the inexperienced character of the writing, which resembles that of a semiliterate person, we observe, among other errors, graphic confusions that can only be explained through the misunderstanding of a preexisting original.[65] In brief, the writer appears not to understand fully what he is writing. I am also inclined to think that these annotations pertain to a sort of exercise for learning Coptic, and that they must be completely dissociated both from the writing of the act and its subsequent use. We would seem to find still stronger evidence for this idea in *BGU* XVII 2683 [Fig. 9]: the three lines of accounts, which are moreover written in a direction different from that of the Greek endorsement, are written by a hand so untrained that they are difficult to read, and, more

[62] Bagnall 2011, 82, cites only one of these texts without analyzing the relationship between the front and the back sides.

[63] On the location of the monastery of Apa Sabinos (*P.Prag.* I 46), cf. Fournet 2009b, 120; and Gascou 2011.

[64] To which *BGU* XVII 2683 from the Aurelia Kyra dossier and *BGU* XII 2187 must be added.

[65] For example, in *BGU* IV 1094, ⲡⲏⲥⲫⲣⲁⲕⲓ̈ⲥⲙⲁ for ⲡⲉⲕⲥⲫⲣⲁⲅⲓⲥⲙⲁ with a misreading of ⲉⲕ<ⲥ> in ⲏⲥ.

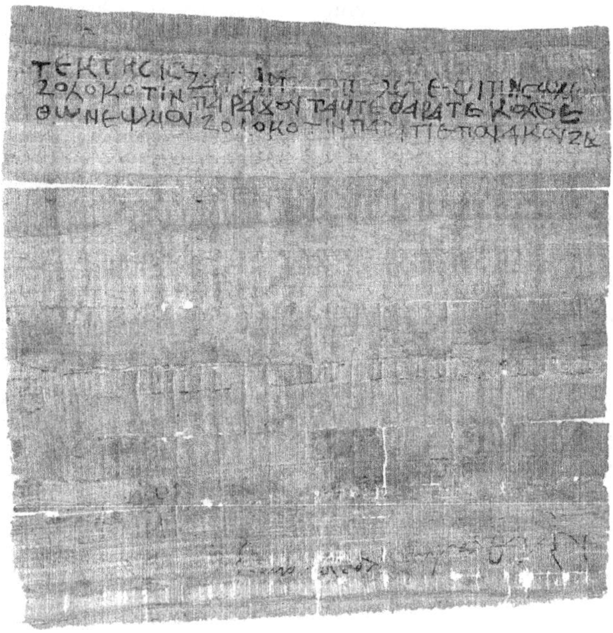

Fig. 9. A Coptic account on the verso of a Greek lease (*BGU* XVII 2683 [Hermopolis, 523?]). Note the clumsiness of the writing. (© Staatliche Museen zu Berlin—Ägyptisches Museum und Papyrussammlung, Scan: Berliner Papyrusdatenbank, P 11746.)

importantly, their content has nothing to do with the contract on the other side.[66] This is clearly nothing but an exercise!

We can therefore affirm that not only were legal texts always written in Greek, but that the titles summarizing their content on the reverse side of the sheet were also always written in Greek. Coptic was not involved at any time during the editorial process of the document.

This invisibility of Coptic in documents pertaining to the non-epistolary sphere also has its parallel in the public space. As Jacques van der Vliet writes, "The public space of Christian Egypt was, up until a time period difficult to specify with certainty, exclusively Greek. It is unlikely that in the

[66] This may also be the case of *P.Athen.Xyl.* 17: the Coptic text states that the declarant is the woman ⲧⲉϭⲣⲟⲙⲡⲉ whereas following the subscription (the beginning of the document has been lost), it is Phoibammōn, son of Khoïs.

fourth and fifth centuries"—I would also include the sixth century—"the Coptic language was ever used for monumental inscriptions."[67] It seems to me that this coincidence in the lack of both public inscriptions and legal or administrative papyrus documents deserves to be highlighted. Even church dedicatory inscriptions—I am not talking about monasteries, which do not really pertain to the public space—are in Greek, the official language of the Church.[68]

To return to Coptic legal texts, their nonexistence during the first centuries of the history of Coptic has piqued the curiosity of the scholarly world. Some have interpreted this as an accident of our documentation. For example, Leslie S. B. MacCoull does not hesitate to state that "the paucity of the pre-conquest Coptic documents"—she means *legal documents*—"is more probably an artefact of our state of preservation down to the present day, than the result of circumstances in the late ancient world."[69] Moreover, she writes,

> When sites in Egypt were explored for papyri, or when accidental discoveries were made, the material later in time occurring in the upper strata suffered the most loss. Owing to the exclusively classical background of workers in the field until recently, Greek papyri were not only what were prized but what were read and published, while Coptic papyri were put away in storage, relegated to the occasional glances of visiting Orientalists or religion specialists. Their loss has been severe, and its extent can only be imagined. Their survival is even more precarious in the political climate of today.[70]

---

[67] Van der Vliet 2006, 304. The first monumental Coptic inscription is, to my knowledge, a dedication commemorating the transformation of a Pagan temple into a church (*FHN* III 330 [Dendur, ca. 536–69, see Ochała 2011]), but its provenance is peripheral, given that it is the Nubian king Eirpanome's doing. Otherwise, the first Coptic inscriptions, the date of which is always difficult to establish, belong to the private sphere and are funerary—they often contain parts written in Greek (initial divine invocation, etc.). On these bilingual inscriptions, cf. Fournet 2018a, 62–64, 72–73, and 80. For the earliest dated funerary inscription (553), see van der Vliet 2017, 412–15.

[68] See chapter 2.

[69] MacCoull 1997, 351. Cf. also MacCoull 1995, 351–52.

[70] MacCoull 1995, 352.

While the two reasons that she proposes are very real,[71] they do not in any way explain the fact that only legal documents are missing: neither the chance of destruction nor the lack of interest that long hindered Coptic papyrology is capable of accounting for this complete absence.[72]

Would an explanation of a legal nature be more legitimate? We could argue that, from the Antonine Constitution of Caracalla (212)—which granted Roman citizenship to all free men in the Empire—the legal context to which relations between individuals were set was Roman law, and this law, while tolerating Greek, left no space for a language as distant from Roman legal concepts as was Egyptian. I will have the opportunity to return to this problem, but, for now, it will suffice to object by arguing that history provides multiple counterexamples to the causal link that we are tempted to draw between law and the language of legal expression.[73] Unless, of course, the Roman authorities formally prohibited the use of vernacular in the production of legal acts? However, we have no traces of such a prohibition on papyri—except perhaps a fleeting allusion in a will from the 610s in which the non-Greek-speaking testator declares "having dictated [his] will in the language of the Egyptians but having ordered it to be written in Greek according to that which is prescribed by the imperial laws properly and piously established."[74] This is, however, the somewhat specific case of a will that, because it pertains to the *jus civile*, is always subject to restrictions in terms of languages (Greek was officially tolerated in Egypt for wills of Roman citizens only at a very late date, under Severus Alexander between 224 and 235).[75] Conversely, we have no traces of a law authorizing the use of Coptic, which might explain, as we will see,[76] the proliferation of Coptic legal acts before the end of Byzantine domination in Egypt (642). The silence of papyri is not enough, however, and it is necessary to expand our investigation to all legislative sources.

---

[71] For the second one, cf. Clackson 2004, 29–30.

[72] Cf. Bagnall 2011, 78–86.

[73] Cf., for example, Cotton 2009, 159; or Richter 2010b, 48n49.

[74] *P.Mon.Phoib.Test.* 1, 13–15 = *P.Lond.* I 77, 12–14 (p. 231): τὸ ἔσχατον̣ [βο]υ̣λημάτιον ἐπαγόρευσα (l. ὑπαγόρευσα) μὲν τῇ τῶν Αἰγυπτίων φωνῇ Ἑλληνικοῖς δὲ καὶ ῥήμασιν ἐπέταξα γραφῆναι κατά τε θειωδῶς ὑπὸ τῶν καλῶς καὶ εὐσεβῶς κειμένων νόμων διηγορευμένα (which here I am citing in the edition of Garel 2015). I will return to this will in chapter 4.

[75] It was not until a Novel of Theodosius II from 439 that Greek was officially authorized for the wills throughout the empire (*Novellae*, XVI, 8).

[76] Cf. chapter 4.

The Legal System on the Scale of the Empire: Legal Sources and Near Eastern Papyri

Although jurists have focused on the language of the writing of legal acts, it was above all to determine whether, from a Latin-centric point of view, Greek had a certain degree of legitimacy.[77] There are nevertheless two texts that focus more specifically on the use of vernacular for legal purposes.[78] The first is a text by the jurist Ulpian (beginning of the third century) transmitted via the *Digest* and regarding the *stipulatio*, the exchange between parties that validates a transaction:

> *Eadem an alia lingua respondeatur, nihil interest. Proinde si quis Latine interrogaverit, respondeatur ei Graece, dummodo congruenter respondeatur, obligatio constituta est: idem per contrarium. Sed utrum hoc usque ad Graecum sermonem tantum protrahimus an vero et ad alium, Poenum forte vel Assyrium vel cuius alterius linguae, dubitari potest. Et scriptura Sabini, sed et verum patitur, ut omnis sermo contineat verborum obligationem, ita tamen, ut uterque alterius linguam intellegat sive per se sive per verum interpretem.* (*D.* 45, 1, 1, 6 = *Ulpianus libro quadragesimo octavo ad Sabinum*)
>
> It makes no difference whether the reply [to a *stipulatio*] is made in the same language or in another. For instance, if a man asks in Latin but receives a reply in Greek, as long as the reply is consistent, the obligation is settled. And the same goes for the opposite case. Whether we extend this rule to the Greek language only or to another, such as Punic or Assyrian [= Syriac] or some other tongue, is a matter of doubt. That is what Sabinus wrote, but the truth also admits that all tongues can produce a verbal obligation, provided that both parties understand each other's language, either of their own accord or by the means of a truthful interpreter.[79]

The main point to retain from this text is that any kind of language can give rise to an obligation.

---

[77] Cf. Dagron 1969, 39–40 (= Dagron 2012, I, 219).

[78] On this problem, cf. MacMullen 1966; and, above all, Wacke 1993.

[79] I am modifying the translation of Watson 1998, IV, 163–64, in particular for *Et scriptura Sabini, sed et verum patitur* (I thank Jean-Marc Mandosio for helping me to understand the structure of this sentence). See also Wacke 1993, 26–27.

The second text concerns *fideicommissa* (the expression of a trust, which was not made in the solemn forms of bequests or institutions of heirs through a Roman will):

> *Fideicommissa quocumque sermone relinqui possunt, non solum Latina vel Graeca, sed etiam Punica vel Gallicana vel alterius cuiuscumque gentis.* (*D.* 32, 11 pr. = *Ulpianus libro secundo fideicommissorum*)
>
> *Fideicommissa* may be left in any language, not only Latin or Greek but Punic, Gallic, or that of any other nation.[80]

The problem of the language of legal transactions arises for jurists mainly in relation to the *jus civile*, which implies *verba solemnia* that can only be uttered in Latin, unlike the deeds that come under the *jus gentium*, where it is possible, indeed necessary in the case of peregrines or even of Roman citizens who are not literate in Latin, to employ Greek and other languages. The obligation to integrate non-Greek-speaking citizens, which had become even more imperative after 212, accounts for the fact that the juridical use of other languages was extended, including of course Greek (which had acquired a special status beside Latin) but also the empire's other vernacular languages. What matters, henceforth, is that the parties can understand each other, whichever language they speak—with the exception of some specific legal acts, such as wills, as we saw above. Justinian, taking up again Ulpian's arguments about *stipulatio*, clearly reaffirms this principle:

> *Utrum autem Latina an Graeca vel qua alia lingua stipulatio concipiatur, nihil interest, scilicet si uterque stipulantium intellectum huius linguae habeat: nec necesse est eadem lingua utrumque uti, sed sufficit congruenter ad interrogatum respondere: quin etiam duo Graeci Latina lingua obligationem contrahere possunt. Sed haec sollemnia verba olim quidem in usu fuerunt: postea autem Leoniana constitutio lata est, quae, sollemnitate verborum sublata, sensum et consonantem intellectum ab utraque parte solum desiderat, licet quibuscumque verbis expressus est.* (*Inst.* 3, 15, 1)
>
> Whether the stipulation is in Latin, or Greek, or any other language, is immaterial, provided the two parties understand

[80] Watson 1998, III, 73.

> one another, so that it is not necessary even that they should both speak in the same tongue, so long as the answer corresponds to the question, and thus two Greeks, for instance, may contract an obligation in Latin. But it was only in former times that the solemn forms referred to were in use: for subsequently, by the enactment of Leo's constitution, their employment was rendered unnecessary, and nothing was afterwards required except that the parties should understand each other, and agree to the same thing, the words in which such agreement was expressed being immaterial.[81]

Such are the rare discussions of the problem in legislative sources. However, what about in practice? We have seen that the papyri do not support jurists' conclusions. Was this the case outside of Egypt? Although it remained exclusively Egyptian for a long time, documentary papyrology has diversified over the past decades, by opening up to other geographical horizons, especially thanks to discoveries in the Near East.[82] Today we have a number of legal acts in various languages derived from Aramaic (Nabataean, Palmyrenian, and above all Syriac).[83] I will skip over acts in Nabataean from the first and second centuries, published particularly in *P.Yadin* (or *P.Babatha*),[84] to focus on those from the third century (which are therefore almost contemporaneous to the era during which Coptic appeared in Egypt) that originated in the Middle Euphrates. They pertain to two collections of texts, that of the papyri from Dura-Europos (*P.Dura*), discovered during the excavations of Yale University and of the Académie des Inscriptions et Belles-Lettres (1928–37), and the Euphrates Papyri (*P.Euphr.*), a group of twenty-one documents that were purchased and most probably came from the former Apadana (slightly to the north of Dura, as Rostovtzeff had already demonstrated) and were published by Denis Feissel, Jean Gascou, and Javier Teixidor from 1989 to 2000.[85] These documents (petitions and contracts), all written under Roman domination, testify to the use of a

---

[81] Trans. Moyle 1913.

[82] Cotton, Cockle, and Millar 1995; Gascou 2009a.

[83] For a brief overview of the dialectical diversity of Syria and Mesopotamia, cf. Taylor 2002, in particular 302. For the relation between Greek and Syriac, cf. Brock 1994; and Millar 2011. For an analysis of the impact of Greek on Syriac, see Butts 2016.

[84] See Cotton 2009 for a presentation of the dossier and its legal aspects.

[85] See Feissel and Gascou 1989, 1995, 1997, and 2000; and Teixidor 1990 and 1993. On the legal aspect of these texts, see now Johannsen 2017.

language other than Greek, in this case, one of the three Aramaic dialects that I cited above. In these papyri, vernacular language comes into play in three different forms:

(a) It can be the main language of the act:

- *P.Dura* 151 (Dura,[86] 200?),[87] possibly a contract for a sale or lease or, according to J. T. Milik, a will, written in Judeo-Aramaic;
- *P.Dura* 152 (Dura, third century?),[88] probably a lease contract, written in Palmyrenian;
- *P.Euphr.* 18 (Marcopolis, 240),[89] an acknowledgment of debt written in Syriac [Fig. 10];
- *P.Euphr.* 19 (Marcopolis, 242),[90] a land lease contract written in Syriac;
- *P.Dura* 28 (Edessa, 243),[91] a contract for the sale of a slave written in Syriac (observing a formulary marked distinctly by Greek[92]).

(b) It may be limited to the subscriptions of the parties and/or certain witnesses:

- *P.Dura* 27 (Dura, ca. 225–40),[93] a sale contract in Greek with subscriptions in Greek and one in Aramaic (the only case in Dura, according to the edition);
- *P.Euphr.* 12 (Beth Phouraia, 244),[94] a deposit contract (*parakatathēkē*) for mobile assets (clothing and jewelry) that belonged to a deceased person, written in Greek with subscriptions in Greek and one in Syriac;

[86] Here and for the following documents, I mention the place of writing and not that of the conservation or discovery of the text.

[87] Milik 1968; TM 171909; Cotton, Cockle, and Millar 1995, no. 152.

[88] *PAT* 1656; TM 171910; Cotton, Cockle, and Millar 1995, no. 153. For the language (given as Aramaic in the *P.Dura*) and the date, cf. *PAT* 237.

[89] = *P.Euphr.Syr.* A (ed. Teixidor 1990, 147–54; reed. Aggoula 1992, 391–97); TM 383599; Cotton, Cockle, and Millar 1995, no. 159.

[90] = *P.Euphr.Syr.* B (ed. Teixidor 1990, 154–59; reed. Aggoula 1992, 397–99; and Teixidor 1993 [1991/1992], 198–202); TM 383600; Cotton, Cockle, and Millar 1995, no. 157.

[91] TM 17225; Cotton, Cockle, and Millar 1995, no. 160. Cf. Goldstein 1966.

[92] "Written in their own native language for members of a Semitic population touched by Hellenism, who are Roman citizens" (Goldstein 1966, 1).

[93] TM 17224; Cotton, Cockle, and Millar 1995, no. 47.

[94] = *SB* XXVI 16655 (ed. Feissel and Gascou 2000, 163–74); TM 44670; Cotton, Cockle, and Millar 1995, no. 29.

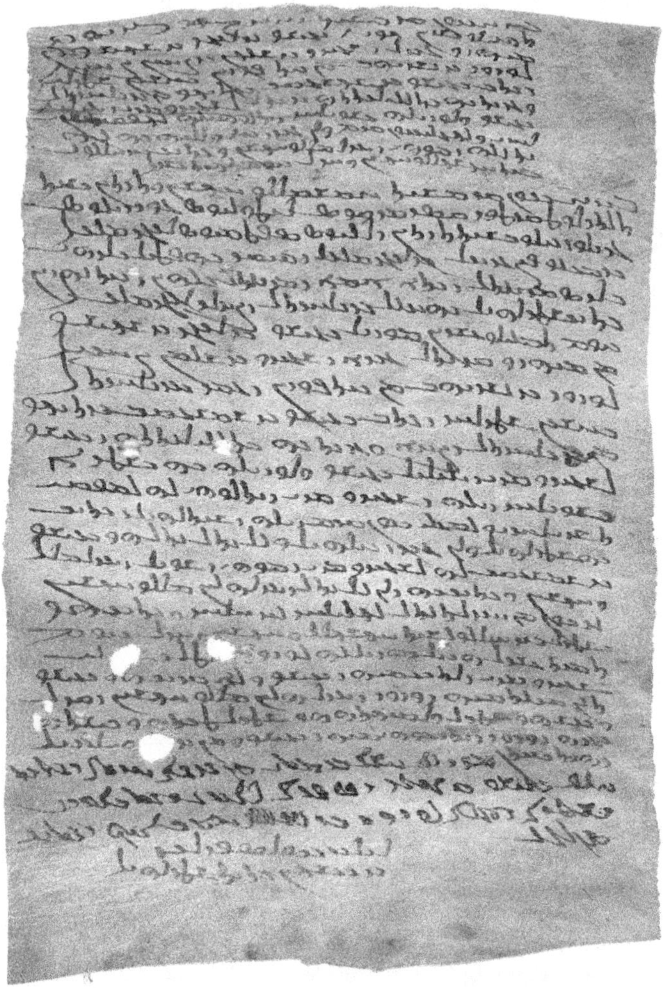

Fig. 10. An acknowledgment of debt entirely written in Syriac (*P.Euphr.* 18 [Marcopolis, 240]). (Photograph courtesy of Adam Bülow-Jacobsen.)

- *P.Euphr.* 6–7 (Marcopolis, 249),[95] a contract for the sale of a slave (and its duplicate) in Greek with four subscriptions in Syriac (and on the reverse side, five subscriptions, four of which are in Syriac) [Fig. 11];

[95] = *SB* XXIV 16167–68 (ed. Feissel and Gascou 1997, 6–26; TM 23926–27; Cotton, Cockle, and Millar 1995, no. 158.

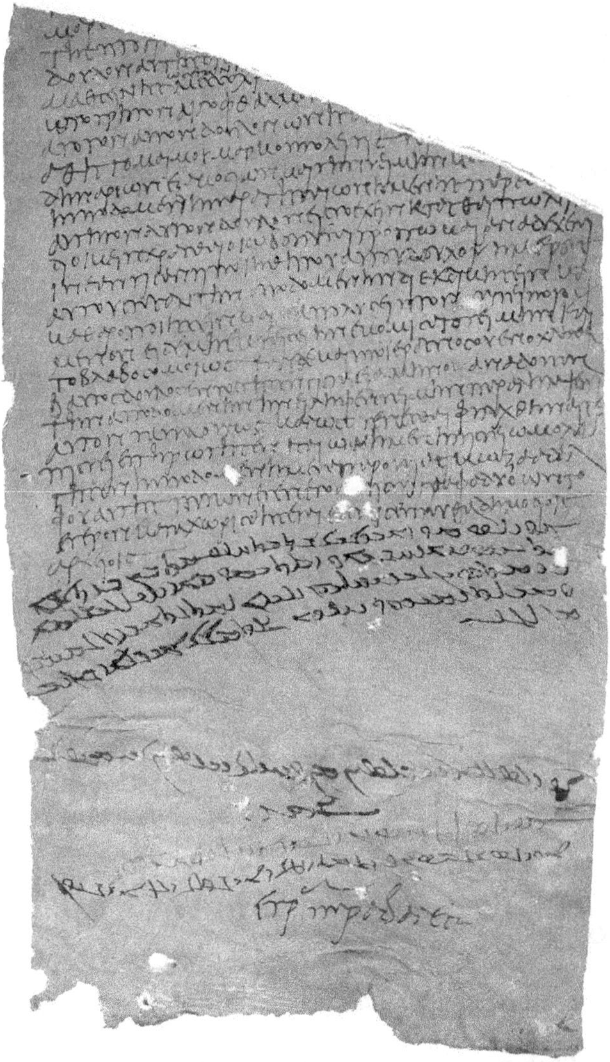

Fig. 11. A sale of a slave written in Greek with four subscriptions in Syriac (*P.Euphr.* 7 [Marcopolis, 249]). (Photograph courtesy of Adam Bülow-Jacobsen.)

- *P.Euphr.* 10 (Carrhae, 250),[96] a sale contract for a mare written in Greek with subscriptions in Syriac, at the bottom and on the reverse side, from the declarant and witnesses (except for one witness subscription in Greek);

96 = *SB* XXIV 16171 (ed. Feissel and Gascou 1997, 45–53); TM 23930; Cotton, Cockle, and Millar 1995, no. 161.

- *P.Euphr.* 3–4 (Beth Phouraia, 252–56 or 245–48),[97] petition (and its duplicate) to the *praepositus praetenturae* written in Greek with the subscription of the petitioner in Syriac;
- *P.Euphr.* 9 (Beth Phouraia, 252),[98] a contract for the sale of a slave in Greek with a subscription by the witness in Syriac.

(c) Here, I will add an unclear use, that of *P.Euphr.* 1 (Antioch, 245),[99] a petition to the governor of Coele-Syria written in Greek with the recipient's subscription in Latin: on the backside, following the Greek endorsement, it shows the traces of "three Syriac (?) signs surrounded by two lines." As the document is a "duplicate of the original prepared immediately by the officer or by an authorized scribe and remitted to the petitioners to support their subsequent actions,"[100] is this a mark of registration? Nonetheless, that would be strange.

The situation reflected by papyri from the Middle Euphrates is therefore opposed to what happened in Egypt: contracts were written in local languages, and people did not hesitate to subscribe in these languages rather than calling upon a *hypographeus*—called *cheirochrētēs* in certain texts from Judea.[101] People were even allowed to do so to append their signature to a petition, that is, when addressing the administrative authority. The contrast is striking[102]—so striking that one is overcome with doubt regarding its validity. Is it truly relevant to compare the Egyptian situation to that of the Middle Euphrates? Are Syriac documents from the Middle Euphrates (such as those from Judea in Aramaic, Hebrew, and Nabataean, more than a century beforehand, published in *P.Yadin*) evi-

---

97 = *SB* XXII 15498–99 (ed. Feissel and Gascou 1995, 94–107; see the corrections in Feissel and Gascou 1997, 54–55); TM 23923–24; Cotton, Cockle, and Millar 1995, no. 26. The first date is that of the edition, the second one is preferred by T. Gnoli (*BL* XII 233).

98 = *SB* XXIV 16170 (ed. Feissel and Gascou 1997, 39–45); TM 23929; Cotton, Cockle, and Millar 1995, no. 28.

99 = *SB* XXII 15496 (ed. Feissel and Gascou 1995, 67–84); TM 23921.

100 "Un duplicatum de l'original préparé immédiatement par le greffe ou par quelque scribe agréé et remis aux pétitionnaires pour étayer leurs démarches ultérieures" (Feissel and Gascou 1995, 76).

101 Cf. Cotton 1995. On subscriptions, see also Schiffman 2003 and Wise 2015, 44–61, who do a sociolinguistic analysis of them.

102 Jones 1964, 991–92, had already signalled the difference in the linguistic situation in Oshroene and Mesopotamia, on the one hand, and Egypt, on the other, at a time when the *P.Euphr.* were still unknown.

dence of the normal use of vernacular in the legal context, or rather the persistence of uses in effect prior to Roman domination? The Euphrates papyri entirely written in Syriac date from 240 to 243, only thirty years after Oshroene became Roman in 212/213 (with the deposition of King Abgar), whereas the last testimonies of the use of Syriac (244–52) are limited to subscriptions in acts written in Greek from then on. The fact that we no longer find anything during the mid-third century seems to confirm the hypothesis that uses dating back to before annexation to the Roman Empire survived. This is the opinion that Fergus Millar recently defended in a 2011 study on "Greek and Syriac in Edessa and Osrhoene, 213–363,"[103] following Naphtali Lewis's position on the subject of older papyri from Judea.[104]

Applied to the Egyptian situation, such reasoning could be supported *a contrario* by the complete absence of legal Coptic. As it appeared following Roman domination, Coptic would not have had the possibility to develop autonomously prior to being subject to the "muzzling" hegemony of Greek, maintained by the new conquerors as the only official language. I will have the opportunity to discuss this again in the following chapters.

If we return to the Middle Euphrates, this survival hypothesis may however raise legitimate and quite disconcerting objections. One of the first scholars to have objected to it was David G. K. Taylor in 2002, although he merely pushed aside the argument about the silence of documentation in the name of a potential continuity:

> Syriac would appear, then, to have been an acceptable language in which to conduct formal business, and it is possible that this practice continued for far longer than our present documentary evidence would suggest, for contrary to expectation and the assertion of some recent surveys, these parchments are not written in the formal Syriac bookhand known

[103] Millar 2011, 566: "What we encounter here is closely comparable to the image of the transition from the Nabataean monarchy to the Roman province of Arabia (see above), where there are quite elaborate Nabataean documents from the end of the regal period, but where Greek rapidly takes over as the established language of public documentary practice. In the case of Edessa it is striking that in the document of 243, deriving from the restored colonia, Syriac is still used for the main text. But in those of 249 and 250 it has been replaced by Greek, with Syriac confined to personal attestations and witness-statements."

[104] Lewis 2001. The title of this study echoes an article on the disappearance of Demotic that the same author had published eight years earlier (Lewis 1993).

> as estrangela, the script of all other surviving manuscripts until the eighth/ninth centuries, but in a cursive documentary or secretarial hand called serta that reappears at that date and becomes the dominant literary hand among the Syrian Orthodox. That in the meantime it had a continued existence outside the main manuscript tradition, presumably in business or administrative texts which have not survived, is clearly attested by a manuscript of AD 509 (BM Add 14542) in which it is employed in the colophon.[105]

Roger S. Bagnall returned to the subject in 2011, developing two objections to the survival hypothesis:

> Edessa and the Middle Euphrates, one may object, had been under Roman rule for a relatively short time in the 240s and 250s, and the extinction of the vernacular contract may have lain in the immediate future, once the Roman grip tightened, as it had in the Dead Sea region. But there are two weighty counter-arguments. First, this objection is untrue of Dura, which had been Roman since 166, and the person who took the Edessa slave sale to Dura must have thought it would be usable there. And, it should be emphasized, the position is much the same as in Judaea and Arabia: with Dura's fall to the Sassanids (it was destroyed in 256), Greek and Latin documents vanished from Syria just as much as Syriac ones did. These are matters of the survival of the documentary record and in the case of Dura of a particular city, not demonstrably of ancient practice. Second, it would be paradoxical to suppose that Syriac contracts of a distinctly Roman legal and formulaic cast came into existence after the coming of direct Roman rule and were thus a result of that rule, while at the same time arguing that their disappearance was a product of the same event.[106]

Hannah M. Cotton adopted the same position in 2009 for papyri from Judea, refuting Lewis's argument according to which Roman domination asphyxiated the legal use of Aramaic: "The Aramaic legal contract in Syria Palaestina remained alive and vibrant—at least in some form—for centuries to come, as must be inferred from the running commentaries in

[105] Taylor 2002, 325.

[106] Bagnall 2011, 104.

Hebrew on its formulae in the Mishnah and the Toseftah. It will resurface, for example, in the late contracts of the Cairo Genizah."[107]

Other objections can be made: the first is the support that epigraphy gives to the hypothesis of the vitality of vernacular beyond the solely private sphere. While we have seen that public epigraphy expressed in Coptic was nonexistent in Egypt, the same is not true of Nabataean, Palmyrenian, and Syriac epigraphy in the Near East. We are acquainted with the famous case of the tax tariff of Palmyra, an excise tariff from 137 that the authorities had engraved in Greek and Palmyrenian, almost 120 years after Palmyra was integrated into the Roman Empire.[108] Up until 279/280, the numerous instances of inscriptions, above all dedicatory, in Palmyrenian, whether associated or not with Greek or Latin, testified to the perfect integration of the Aramaic language into the public space.[109] As for Syriac epigraphy, it experienced a large degree of vitality, which allowed it to persist for many centuries following the disappearance of legal acts, even progressively becoming more present in the public space, starting in the fourth century, in the form of inscriptions on buildings.[110] Many of these involved churches, but also nonreligious urban spaces, such as two Syriac inscriptions from Bābisqā dating from 547, which commemorate the construction of a stoa and the layout of gardens [Fig. 12].[111] In Egypt, it would have been inconceivable for such inscriptions to be engraved in Coptic!

Moreover, the *Syro-Roman Law Book*, which "collected and explained (for law school teaching in an Eastern province) *constitutiones* (statutes) enacted by Roman emperors of the fifth century,"[112] could also in its own way be a testimony to a Syriac language legal tradition insofar as people in the sixth century felt the necessity to translate into Syriac this work, which was originally written in Greek.

Lastly, while there are no longer traces of legal documents in Syriac after the mid-third century, this does not mean that there is no longer evidence of the use of Syriac in documents of an official nature. The Ecumenical Councils that gathered the Eastern Christian bishops under Imperial supervision on many occasions handled countless documents (official letters, reports, petitions) that are preserved for us by the *Acta Conciliorum Œcumenicorum*. The absence of the originals is no reason to doubt their

107 Cotton 2009, 158.

108 Shifman 2014. See also Matthews 1984.

109 Cf. Taylor 2002, 317.

110 Cf. Brock 2009; and Millar 2009, 51–52.

111 *AAES* IV 14–15, with corrections in *PAES* IV B, 64–65.

112 Thür 2013, 6495. This work was edited by Selb and Kaufhold 2002.

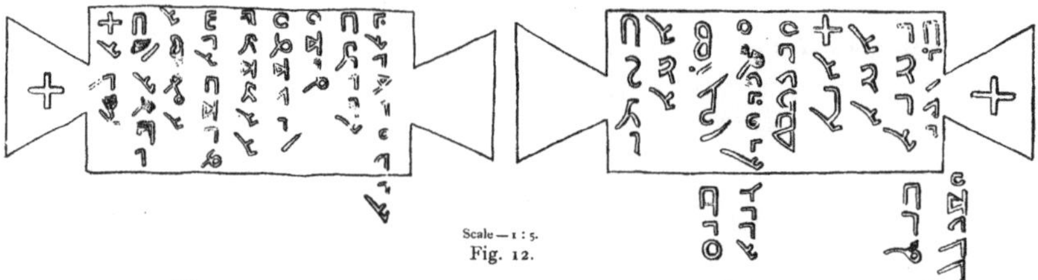

14

ܐܠܗܐ	1	*God*
ܒ[ܪܟ]ܢ، ܐܬ[ܒܢܝ].	2	*[bless us! There was built]*
ܐܣܛܘܐ	3	*this stoa*
ܗܢܐ ܒܫܢܬ	4	*in the year*
ܚܡܫܡܐܐ	5	*five hundred*
ܘܬܫܥܝܢ	6	*and ninety*
ܘܫܬ	7	*and six,*
ܒܚܘܫܒܢܐ	8	*according to the era*
ܕܐܢܛܝܘܟܝܐ	9	*of Antioch.*

15

ܒܝܘܡܝ	1	*In my days*
ܐܚܐ	2	*the brothers*
ܣܪܓܘܢ	3	*Sargon*
ܘܬܐܘܕܘܪܐ	4	*and Theodore*
ܘܒܟܘܣ	5	*and Bakkhos*
ܙܒܢܘ	6	*purchased*
ܓܢܬܐ	7	*the gardens.*
✠ܐܢܐ	8	✠ *I,*
ܐܚܐ	9	*the brother*
ܝܘܚܢܢ	10	*Yōḥannā,*
ܒܪ ܙܟܝ	11	*son of Zakkai,*
ܒܢܝܬ	12	*built*
ܘܫܠܡܬ	13	*and finished.*

Fig. 12. Two Syriac inscriptions from Bābisqā (*AAES* IV 14–15 [547]). (From *AAES* IV, New York 1904, 34.)

authenticity. Yet Syriac is used on multiple occasions, in the subscriptions of petitions or proclamations addressed to the emperor during the councils that took place throughout the fifth and sixth centuries. The Syriac subscriptions have three patterns:

(a) They can be bilingual with a Greek and a Syriac version (the latter one is not given in the proceedings but just mentioned) as in the petition addressed to the bishops Photios and Eustathius by the clergy of Edessa (Council of Chalcedon, 451) subscribed by the parties both in Greek as well as in Greek and Syriac:[113] for example, Εὐλόγιος πρεσβύτερος πεποίημαι τὴν διδασκαλίαν ταύτην ἅμα ἑταίροις. καὶ

[113] *ACO* II/1/3 (Council of Chalcedon, 451), 35, 1–37, 37. The prescript of this petition is Διδασκαλία καὶ παράκλησις τοῖς θεοφιλεστάτοις καὶ ὁσιωτάτοις ἐπισκόποις Φωτίωι καὶ Εὐσταθίωι παρὰ παντὸς τοῦ κλήρου τῆς Ἐδεσσηνῶν μητροπόλεως. On the meaning to be attributed to *didaskalia*, cf. Fournet 2010a, 64–67. For the Syriac subscriptions, see 35, 26–27 (example given here); 29–30; 34–35; 36, 3–4; 5–6; 18–19; 25–26; 26–27; 33–34; 35–36; 37, 9–10; 16–17; 23–24; 28–29; 30–31; 32–33; 34–35; 36–37.

ὑπογραφὴ Συριακή "I, Eulogios, a priest, made this petition with my colleagues. *And his subscription in Syriac*."

(b) They can be just in Syriac (translated into Greek in the proceedings) as in two petitions from 536:[114] for example, Ἰωάννης πρεσβύτερος καὶ ἀρχιμανδρίτης μονῆς Θωμᾶ Συριστὶ ὑπέγραψα "I, John, priest and archimandrite of the monastery of Thomas, have subscribed in Syriac."

(c) They can be just mentioned without any translation. Such is the case of the proclamation made by the Council and sent to the Emperor after having been subscribed by its members in Latin, Greek, and Syriac:[115] in the latter case, subscriptions are indicated by the phrase "subscriptions in Syriac letters" (Ὑπογραφαὶ διὰ Συριακῶν γραμμάτων);[116] however, as opposed to the examples cited above, the translation is not given.

As for the documents from the Middle Euphrates, the signatories to these petitions and declarations felt perfectly authorized to use their own

[114] The first one is *ACO* III, 136, 29–147, 4 (Councils of Constantinople and Jerusalem, 536), a petition addressed to Pope Agapetus I by Marianos, exarch of the monasteries of Constantinople, and by the archimandrites and monks of Jerusalem and Anatolia (136, 29–141, 37). Its prescript is Τῶι δεσπότηι ἡμῶν τῶι ἁγιωτάτωι καὶ μακαριωτάτωι ἀρχιεπισκόπωι τῆς πρεσβυτέρας Ῥώμης καὶ οἰκουμενικῶι πατριάρχηι Ἀγαπητῶι παρὰ Μαριανοῦ πρεσβυτέρου καὶ ἐξάρχου τῶν μοναστηρίων τῆς βασιλίδος καὶ λοιπῶν ἀρχιμανδριτῶν τῆς αὐτῆς καὶ παρὰ τῶν ἐνδημούντων ἐν αὐτῆι Ἱεροσολυμιτῶν καὶ Ἀνατολικῶν ἀρχιμανδριτῶν καὶ μοναχῶν. It is followed by subscriptions in Greek, Latin, and in Syriac for five of them: 144, 32–33 (Ἰάκωβος πρεσβύτερος καὶ ἀρχιμανδρίτης μονῆς Ἀββίβου Σύρος Συριστὶ ὑπέγραψα); 146, 22–23 (Σευηριανὸς πρεσβύτερος καὶ ἀρχιμανδρίτης μονῆς Ζωόρα τῶν θερμῶν Συριστὶ ὑπέγραψα); 146, 24–25 (Κασσίσας πρεσβύτερος καὶ ἀρχιμανδρίτης τῆς εὐαγοῦς μονῆς τῶν Λουκᾶ Συριστὶ ὑπέγραψα); 146, 36 (example provided here); 146, 37 (Θωμᾶς πρεσβύτερος καὶ ἀρχιμανδρίτης μονῆς Ἀαρὼν Συριστὶ ὑπέγραψα). The second petition is *ACO* III, 147, 5–150, 3 (Councils of Constantinople and Jerusalem, 536), addressed by the bishops of Constantinople and of the diocese of Anatolia to Pope Agapetus I (147, 5–150, 3) with the following prescript: Δεσπότηι ἡμῶν τὰ πάντα ἁγιωτάτωι καὶ μακαριωτάτωι πατρὶ πατέρων ἀρχιεπισκόπωι τῆς Ῥωμαίων καὶ πατριάρχηι Ἀγαπητῶι παρὰ τῶν ἐνδημούντων κατὰ ταύτην τὴν βασιλίδα πόλιν ἐπισκόπων τῆς τε Ἀνατολικῆς διοικήσεως καὶ τῶν ὑπὸ τοὺς ἁγίους Χριστοῦ τοῦ θεοῦ ἡμῶν τόπους καὶ ἀποκρισιαρίων καὶ λοιπῶν κληρικῶν. Two of its subscriptions are in Syriac: 150, 8 (Ἰωάννης ἐλέει θεοῦ ἐπίσκοπος Γαβάλων ὑπέγραψα Συριστί); and 150, 12 (Δαυίθος ἐλέει θεοῦ ἐπίσκοπος τοῦ Κιρκινσίου ὑπέγραψα Συριστί).

[115] *ACO* III, 182, 6–189, 17 (Councils of Constantinople and Jerusalem, 536).

[116] *ACO* III, 184, 3 and 185, 32.

language, signing Greek documents not only in a different language but also in a different type of writing.[117] The fact that these texts were written in an ecclesiastical context by no means undermines their significance for my argument. They have all of the characteristics of official documents: the councils were organized under the authority of the Emperor; meetings took place in the presence of officials from the Imperial chancellery; acts were drawn up according to procedures and using wording identical to those of documents from the civil sphere.[118] Moreover, their supraregional nature grants them an even greater degree of "officialdom." Nonetheless, the authors of these documents did not hesitate to use local writing, and often went so far as to call for the use of Syriac in debates:

> Samuel said: "We ask that what is said be translated into Syriac for the sake of the most sacred Bishop Uranius, since he knows exactly what was written about us to the most God-beloved and holy Archbishop Flavian by the most God-beloved and holy Archbishop Domnus, for he was present at Constantinople."
>
> The most God-beloved bishops said: "Let one of those able to interpret for the most God-beloved Bishop Uranius come forward."
>
> The notaries said: "Maras is here, who can interpret for the most God-beloved Bishop Uranius."[119]

---

[117] Moreover, we note that in *P.Yadin* I 11, 29–30; 16, 33–35, subscriptions are given only in the form of a Greek translation (ἑρμηνεία ὑπογραφῆς), as in the majority of acts from the *ACO*, whereas in *P.Yadin* I 27, 15–18, the translation follows the text in Aramaic.

[118] See Fournet 2010a, in which I show that the diplomatic characteristics of the petitions received and sent during these councils are identical to those of the petitions sent by the persons answerable to the judicial proceedings.

[119] *ACO* II/1/3, 20, 24–29 (Council of Chalcedon, 451), trans. Price and Gaddis 2005, II, 278–79. Σαμουῆλος εἶπεν· Παρακαλοῦμεν τὰ λεγόμενα Συριστὶ λεχθῆναι διὰ τὸν ὁσιώτατον ἐπίσκοπον Οὐράνιον, ἐπειδὴ ἀκριβῶς οἶδε τίνα ἐστὶ τὰ γραφέντα τῶι θεοφιλεστάτωι καὶ ἁγιωτάτωι ἀρχιεπισκόπωι Φλαβιανῶι παρὰ τοῦ θεοφιλεστάτου καὶ ἁγιωτάτου ἀρχιεπισκόπου Δόμνου περὶ ἡμῶν· παρῆν γὰρ ἐν Κωνσταντινουπόλει. Οἱ θεοφιλέστατοι ἐπίσκοποι εἶπον· Παρίτω τῶν δυναμένων ἑρμηνεύειν εἷς τῶι θεοφιλεστάτωι ἐπισκόπωι Οὐρανίωι (the last sentence in the translation is provided from the Latin version). See also further on in *ACO* II/1/3, 23, 13–25: Σαμουῆλος πρεσβύτερος εἶπεν· Παρακαλοῦμεν καὶ τοῦτο ὑπάρξαι ἡμῖν παρὰ τῆς ὑμετέρας δικαιοσύνης ὥστε αὐτὰ ταῦτα Συριστὶ ῥηθῆναι τῶι θεοφιλεστάτωι καὶ ἁγιωτάτωι ἐπισκόπωι Οὐρανίωι, ἐπειδὴ παρῆν ἐν Κωνσταντινουπόλει, ἡνίκα τὰ γράμματα περὶ τούτου γραφέντα παρὰ τοῦ ἀρχιεπισκόπου Δόμνου πρὸς τὸν ἀρχιεπίσκοπον Φλαβιανὸν

And yet is it necessary for me to specify that at no time in the *Acta Conciliorum Œcumenicorum* was Coptic involved, and that none of the Egyptian bishops ever subscribed in Coptic? Some of them, however, did not understand Greek. An example is Kalosiris, Bishop of Arsinoe, who was accompanied to Chalcedon by his deacon, who translated the debates for him.[120]

We therefore have to acknowledge that, contrary to what was taking place elsewhere with other local languages in the provinces of the Eastern Roman Empire, the Egyptian language was not granted official recognition or used in official contexts during the first three centuries of its history. On the contrary, it remained in the shadows of private relations. Therefore, an Egyptian exception does exist.

ἀνεγνώσθη. Καὶ πάλιν παρῆν ἐν Ἀντιοχείαι, ὅτε περὶ τούτου ἐμέλλομεν κινεῖν λόγον· καὶ περὶ τούτου οἷα αὐτῶι διελέχθη καὶ τί αὐτῶι εἶπεν, παρακαλοῦμεν αὐτὸν εἰπεῖν. Οἱ θεοφιλέστατοι ἐπίσκοποι Φώτιος καὶ Εὐστάθιος εἶπον· Ἅπαντα ἅπερ ἐζήτησας, ὁ παρεστὼς τῶι θεοσεβεστάτωι ἐπισκόπωι Οὐρανίωι διὰ τῆς οἰκείας ἑρμηνεύσει γλώττης. Καὶ ἡρμηνεύθη "The presbyter Samuel said: 'We request another favour from your righteousness—that this be read out in Syriac for the benefit of the most God-beloved and holy Bishop Uranius, since he was present in Constantinople at the reading of the letter on the matter from Archbishop Domnus to Archbishop Flavian. He was again present at Antioch, when we were about to make a proposal on the matter. We ask him to say what he uttered to him on the matter and what he said to him.' The most God-beloved bishops Photius and Eustathius said: 'Everything you have requested will be translated for the most religious bishop Uranius into his own tongue by his assistant.'—It was translated" (trans. Price and Gaddis 2005, II, 282, slightly modified).

120 *ACO* II/1/1, 185, 21 and 194, 11: Καλοσίριος ἐπίσκοπος Ἀρσινοίτου ἑρμηνεύοντος αὐτὸν Ἰουλίου διακόνου αὐτοῦ. The Greek documents received or sent by the same Kalosiris (for the latter, see *P.Prag.* I 100–101) do not imply that he was able to read or write them or that he knew enough Greek to be able to follow the debates of the Council. Moreover, the identity claim that the use of Coptic could convey before the Synod of Bishops is, in my opinion, an unlikely explanation (see Camplani 2015, 147, who seems to have changed his mind).

CHAPTER 2

Why Was Greek Preferred to Coptic?

We have just seen that Coptic was absent from the public scene and formal exchanges between individuals. Its use was restricted to private relations of an informal nature.[1] Our task is now to seek the cause of this silence, which was all the more "deafening" for its systematicity and duration of several centuries.

One explanation for the absence of legal acts—that is, conventions regulated by law and therefore subject to state arbitration in case of conflicts—could be the fact that there was no court operating in Egyptian and therefore capable of settling the disputes related to these acts. This, however, merely reformulates the essential question: why were there no courts that accepted the use of Egyptian, as there had been during the Ptolemaic period with the *laocritai*, the Egyptian judges who moderated conflicts between Egyptians or more generally involving agreements written in Egyptian? Moreover, the relationship of causality between court and language is not restrictive per se:[2] what stopped a Greek-language court from authorizing translations of acts drawn up in Coptic that had given rise to disputes, and interpreters for those who

[1] Except the very isolated use of *P.Kellis* VII 123 (cf. *supra*, chapter 1, pp. 18–20).

[2] Cf. Cotton 2003, 49: "Is it true that the language of documents dictated the nationality of the courts, and the law to be applied? Does the existence of documents necessarily imply the existence of formal jurisdiction, that is, of courts endowed with formal jurisdiction, for which they were presumably intended? What is the relationship between the existence of private documents and the legal and administration organs . . . ? Should one not consider the possibility of an alternative procedure, namely, that of informal arbitration by bodies lacking formal jurisdiction in the Roman sense of the word—a subject with wide ramifications?" On the latter point, see chapter 3.

were not literate in Greek? That is indeed what must have happened at the end of the Ptolemaic period and at the beginning of the Roman period, when legal acts continued to be drawn up in Demotic, even though the courts of *laocritai* had disappeared since the end of the second or the beginning of the first century BC.[3] Even if we agree that the exclusivity of Greek in courts of law implied the obligation to draw up acts exclusively in Greek, this does not explain why these acts written in Greek could not be signed (subscribed) in Coptic by the parties and witnesses who did not know Greek letters. A subscription in Coptic ("I, so-and-so, agree with that which is written above") by no means detracted from the understanding of the document by a Greek-speaking judge, who was moreover capable of reading the names of the parties and witnesses in the subscriptions, since Coptic used the same alphabet as Greek (with the exception of the few added letters). Yet, as we have seen, no subscriptions in Coptic have been found from the first three centuries of the history of the language.

Some scholars argue that the absence of legal documents in Coptic is the result of the fact that "there seems not to have been a registry office, where such documents could be deposited."[4] Apart from the fact that we know relatively little about the archiving of documents during Late Antiquity, the absence of the official registration and public submission of legal acts would seem also to concern Greek documents following the Early Roman Empire. This is therefore an explanation of scant value.[5]

The question of the absence of Coptic is raised, moreover, not only for legal acts but also for administrative documents (letters, receipts, etc.). It is legitimate to wonder why, during this period, people avoided using Coptic down to the level of the most local administration (namely, at the level of villages, which were primarily Coptophone, and where Demotic had remained in administrative use for much of the early Ptolemaic period).

---

3 The last certain evidence of *laocritai* is found in *P.Tor.Choach.* 12, VII, 3 (117 BC). On the end of the *laocritai*, cf. Anagnostou-Canas 1998, 14n76, who cites more recent yet dubious Demotic texts (the text from 96 BC that she cites according to Modrzejewski, *P.TestiBotti* I 11, does not mention any *laocritai*).

4 Alcock and Sijpesteijn 2000, 2, referring to Steinwenter 1955, 15–16.

5 Note that this argument was also put forward by Cotton 1999, 230, to explain the adoption of Greek in Judea: "An additional reason could be the need to deposit the deeds in a public archive."

In short, the institutional explanation must make way for a broader, linguistic, historical, and sociocultural approach.

The Obstacle of Multidialecticism

Let us start by considering whether there may have been a reason internal to the Coptic language that can explain the delay in its competing with Greek. In fact, what first characterizes Coptic is its multidialecticism, in direct contrast with Greek. For a long time, there were no Greek dialects, as Greek had become a common language (*koinē*) in all areas of the Hellenistic East in which it was spoken. With the exception of rare lexical features (topolects),[6] it was the same throughout Egypt. Contrary to what the term *Coptic* might have us believe in theory, there is no *single* Coptic language but rather a scattering of dialectal variations, the most important and most well-documented of which are, from north to south, Bohairic, that is, the "northern dialect" (B), Fayyumic (F), Mesokemic or Middle Egyptian (M), the dialects from Lycopolitan area (L dialects), Akhmimic (A), and as the standardized dialect of the Nile Valley, Sahidic, that is, the "southern dialect" (S) [Fig. 13].[7] What needs to be asked is whether this diversity could have been an obstacle to the development of Coptic as a language equally comprehensible by all, and therefore usable in administrative or legal acts, which had to be understandable across the entirety of the Egyptian territory. As a legal act often stipulated in its conclusion, it "will be valid and operative wherever it is produced."[8]

Due to the elongated shape of the country, there has always been significant diversity between the north (the Delta) and the south (the Nile Valley) of Egypt—I will have the opportunity to return to this in chapter 3.[9] Hori's satirical letter to Amenope, known by the name of *Papyrus*

---

[6] Cf., for example, Fournet 2000b and 2009a.

[7] I have put in parentheses the abbreviations that are still commonly used (Kasser 1990), some of which are derived from those found in Crum's dictionary (Crum, *CD*)—except for M, which is not included in it, and L, which Crum calls A^2 (we now speaks of L dialects and not just of L). For a general overview of Coptic dialects and their subvariants, cf. Kasser 1966, 1991a, 1991b; and Funk 1991. On dialects used in documents, see now Boud'hors 2018.

[8] Κυρία οὖσα καὶ βεβαία ἁπανταχοῦ προφερομένη. The expression, which is common in contracts from the sixth to seventh centuries in Egypt, appears much earlier in Near Eastern documents, as shown by *P.Dura* 31, 41–43 (Ossa, 204).

[9] Cf. *infra*, pp. 89–94.

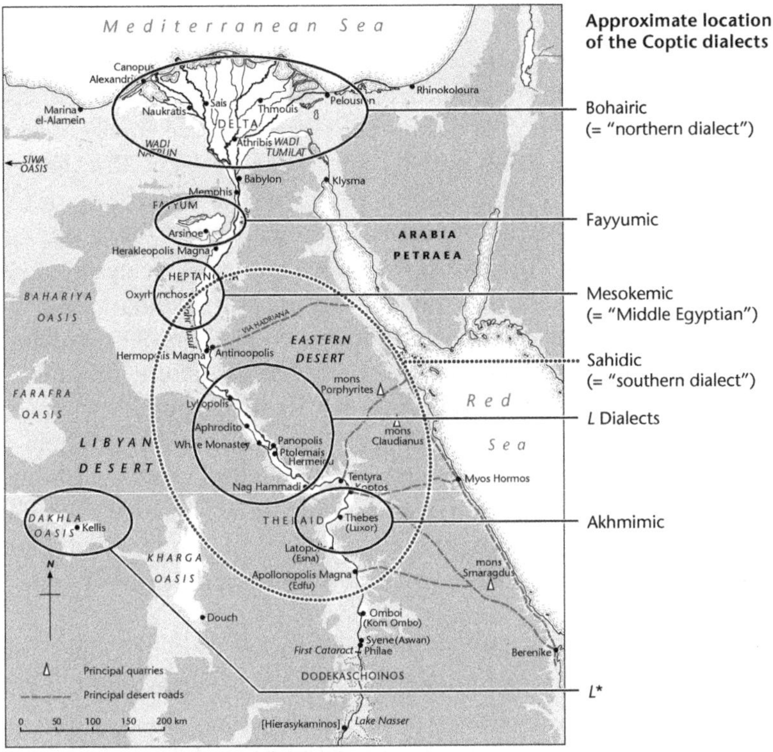

Fig. 13. Approximate location of the main Coptic dialects. (Background map courtesy of R. S. Bagnall and D. W. Rathbone.)

Anastasi 1 and dating from the nineteenth dynasty (thirteenth century BC), already stigmatized the communication difficulties between the north and south, saying that incomprehensible words are "like the talk of a man of the Delta with a man of Elephantine."[10] This famous phrase, which echoes a passage from *The Story of Sinuhe*, in which Sinuhe, exiled in Palestine, feels as foreign "as when a Delta-man sees himself in Elephantine,"[11] is often cited as evidence of the limited mutual understanding of Egyptians from the north and the south. Yet this has been called into question by Antonio Loprieno, who sees it both as a literary *topos* and as a claim of little linguistic relevance.[12]

---

[10] *P.Anastasi* 1, 28, 6.

[11] B 225–26: Gardiner 1916, 174; or more recently, Parkinson 1997, 38.

[12] Loprieno 1982, 76.

The fact remains that Coptic is characterized by formal variety across the regions. This may, however, result in two interpretations that we can schematize as follows:[13] on the one hand, there would be a phonological unity of Coptic. "In pushing this hypothesis to its extreme consequences, one would have to admit that despite the orthographical appearances, this language is by no means divided into a plurality of dialects. The differences that orthography seems to manifest would be only superficial, or to put it simply, the various schools of scribes would make use, in certain cases, of different graphemes to express the same phonemes.[14] One should then observe in Coptic not various dialects but various 'orthographic codes' applying to a language that is 'one' and not divided on the phonological level." Despite its economical and partially verified nature, this approach runs into innumerable impossibilities. It is thus indisputable that, for example, the grapheme ⲗ in Fayyumic corresponds with the grapheme ⲣ in Sahidic, without the two covering the same phonetic reality. This clearly demonstrates a dialectal diversity whose scope is not easy to evaluate, but which may have hindered the use of Coptic in nonprivate documentary usage, in other words, beyond an individual's family or sphere of relations.

Conversely, the opponents of the phonological unity of Coptic postulate that "there is for each phoneme (. . .) a single corresponding grapheme that can never serve to express another phoneme." In this case, orthographic diversity would correspond to a phonological and therefore dialectal diversity in the strict sense of the word.[15] How could it have been otherwise for a country with such an elongated territory and such geo-

[13] Cf. Kasser 1991a, 33–35. I am borrowing the following three citations (except the footnote, which is mine) from this author, which summarize the two extreme positions regarding the issue of dialects. See also Peust 1999, 33–34.

[14] For example, ⲉⲃⲟ (L-B), ⲙ̄ⲡⲟ (S), and ⲉⲃⲟⲟ (A) are three forms of the word that means "silent" and that is the result, according to Loprieno 1982, 85, of different scribal traditions ("Schreibtraditionen"), without constituting true phonological differences. The orthographic hypothesis may easily be verified through Greek words, certain phonemes of which were rendered by equivalent graphemes according to a distribution by dialects; consequently, we have ⲁⲓ S, L, M (ⲇⲓⲕⲁⲓⲟⲥ, ϩⲁⲓⲣⲉⲥⲓⲥ) compared to ⲉ B, F (ⲇⲓⲕⲉⲟⲥ, ϩⲉⲣⲉⲥⲓⲥ). Cf. Kasser 1991b, 219.

[15] The Egyptian names transliterated into Greek in the Greek papyri are a good proof of this phonological diversity, as Quaegebeur 1975 brilliantly showed. This diversity was not only phonological but also lexical: see Peust 1999, 327–28, for lexical variations between Sahidic and Bohairic.

graphical contrast as Egypt?[16] But the pluri-dialectal approach may also lead to exaggerations, and, in the past, it has established itself through the analysis of taxonomies that are so complex and based on such tiny written samples that we can doubt their truth, and at the very least, their effectiveness.

While "one must resign oneself to some compromise to be negotiated and determined from case to case," there were unquestionably multiple dialects at the same time as multiple phonetic transcription systems (or alphabets). One of these was promoted by Sahidic, which became the "vehicular" or "bridge langage" in the Nile Valley (Upper Egypt) and was shared by other dialects or subdialects, while another was promoted by Bohairic, the vehicular language of the Delta (Lower Egypt) [Fig. 13].[17] The reality of formal differentiations found in Coptic texts is therefore complex and still far from being fully understood. It is nevertheless indisputable that the inhabitants of Egypt perceived these differences. This seems to be manifest in one of the rare pieces of evidence on the subject, the *Letter on Pachomius and Theodore* of Ammon (fourth century) in which the author, a Greek-speaker who learned Coptic in the monasteries,[18] speaks of the "language of the Thebans," in other words, Sahidic.[19]

Even if we posit that there was an essentially orthographic differentiation, it seems reasonable to assume that these variations may have hindered the development of Coptic as a legal and administrative language. They detracted from its precision, a cardinal virtue in these types of documents, and necessarily resulted in the narrowing of its sphere of use to those areas in which it was perfectly intelligible. This would explain why Coptic long remained confined to an epistolary function that allowed the exchange of writing within a small circle.

We may, however, object that the multiplicity of dialects was counterbalanced by the development of supradialects or supraregional dialects, such as Sahidic in the Nile Valley, according to a dynamic of standardization that supposedly marginalized smaller dialects to the benefit of the large vehicular ones, in the fifth century or even as early as the fourth

---

16 Cf. the modeling of the "'filiform' dialectal conception" in Kasser 1966, 109–12.

17 A comparative table of these different systems can be found in Kasser 1991a, 38–39. It should be added that the Fayyum occupied a very special position, as it was not within the area of influence of Bohairic or Sahidic.

18 Dummer 1968, 40–41; Goehring 1986, 247, disagrees with this opinion.

19 See chapter 3, n. 51 for the texts and another interpretation of them.

century, as the Kellis papyri would seem to demonstrate.[20] This is possibly, mutatis mutandis, what happened in the Syro-Mesopotamian region. Despite the diverse dialects at work,[21] its papyrological and epigraphical documentation presents a remarkable linguistic uniformity in which "it is almost impossible to detect any dialectal influence,"[22] and which would have strengthened the success of Syriac as an appropriate language for recording transactions or transmitting literature.

This objection must, in turn, be nuanced. First of all, we do not know if Lower Egypt (the Delta) participated in this standardization movement. It is a region whose dampness is unfavorable to the survival of papyri, and whose linguistic situation is therefore largely unknown to us. The dialect associated with it is Bohairic, which imposed itself starting with the Arab Conquest and, in the eighth to ninth centuries, undermined the monopoly of Sahidic, becoming the only Coptic dialect and therefore the official language of the Church in the eleventh century. All that remains of it from the ancient period are a small number of biblical fragments dating from the fourth to fifth centuries, the most important of which is *P.Bodmer* III,[23] and a manuscript in the Vatican of the Twelve Minor Prophets,[24] and only one documentary text.[25] This is however the result of the disappearance of texts.

Moreover, while Sahidic quickly became the standard language in Upper Egypt, as literary manuscripts show, letters, which are the documents closest to the language spoken by populations, attest at a later date to numerous divergences from the Sahidic norm.[26] To use an example dating from the end of the period that we are discussing here, the dossier of letters from Aphrodite, a village in Middle Egypt, which was recently

[20] Cf., for example, Gardner and Choat 2004, 497–98 (with bibliography). For the contribution of the Kellis papyri to this issue, cf. *P.Kellis* V, introduction, 84.

[21] On this dialectal diversity, see the testimony of Theodoret of Cyrus in the fifth century, who, in his *Quaestiones in Judices*, XIX, distinguished between the dialects of the Osrhoenians (*Osrhoēnoi*), the Syrians (*Syroi*), the Euphratians (*Euphratēsioi*), the Palestinians (*Palaistinoi*), and the Phoenicians (*Phoinikes*). Despite being derived from Aramaic, these could present very marked differences: Ὀσροηνοὶ καὶ Σύροι καὶ Εὐφρατήσιοι καὶ Παλαιστῖνοι καὶ Φοίνικες τῇ Σύρων χρῶνται φωνῇ, πολλὴν δὲ ὅμως ἡ διάλεξις ἔχει διαφοράν.

[22] Taylor 2002, 325.

[23] = TM 107758, ed. Kasser 1958 and 2001.

[24] Biblioteca del Vaticano Copt. 9 (= TM 107766). Cf. Bosson 2012.

[25] *P.Mich.Copt.* 3 (= TM 86541; fourth/fifth century?), ed. Worrell 1935. The numerous inscriptions found in Kellia postdate for the most part the Arab Conquest.

[26] Cf. Richter 2006.

edited by Loreleï Vanderheyden, is riddled with dialectal features that reveal the outline of a hybrid language, a combination of Sahidic, Akhmimic, and Lycopolitan, and which served as an intermediary between the dialects of the north (Bohairic, Fayyumic, and Mesokemic) and those of the south (Sahidic and Akhmimic).[27] The differences that emerge in these texts are not only between the language of documents and that of literary manuscripts, but also between the users of this language of documents, who communicate with one another in a very heterogeneous Coptic, the irregularities of which fluctuate widely with respect to the supposed Sahidic norm, and which border on an idiolect.[28] The situation is therefore by no means standardized to the extent that literary papyri may lead us to believe, and effectively demonstrates in a general way, that "non-literary Coptic texts (. . .) usually represent linguistic non-standard varieties."[29]

This dichotomy between the supradialects at work in literary manuscripts and in some of the letters, and dialects, used in documents less constrained by the norm, is above all the index of a situation of diglossia. In other words, it signals the coexistence of two varieties of the same language, one of which is felt to be superior to the other, with the two fulfilling different functions.[30] As J. van der Vliet writes, Sahidic, as documented by literary texts and taught today in universities, "is to a large degree a constructed language [which] has quite likely never been spoken by anybody."[31] It is an artificial language, which, like Greek, played the role of an "elite language," except for the fact that, unlike Greek, it was not spoken and therefore contrasted with vernacular Egyptian. For these reasons, Coptic did not lend itself to becoming a language suited to the writing of

[27] *P.Bal.*, p. 48–192 (chap. VIII); Vanderheyden 2015, I, 87–115 (chap. III). One of the best examples is *P.Aphrod.LettresCopt.* 1 (ed. Vanderheyden 2015, II, 8–24) written by an official working for the *dux* or for the *praeses* [see Fig. 27 and text in chapter 3, pp. 106–7]. "Bien que ce secrétaire fût probablement très habitué à écrire le grec (ce qui explique la fluidité de son écriture), il connaissait sans doute très peu de copte standard" (ibid., 11).

[28] The term is used by Boud'hors 2008, 73, regarding *P.Aphrod.LettresCopt.* 1 (cf. the preceding note).

[29] Richter 2006, 314.

[30] Here I am using the term *diglossia* in its restricted definition as developed by Ferguson 1959. Regarding the diglossic situation of Coptophone Egypt, cf. Zakrzewska 2017, 136–38.

[31] Van der Vliet 2013, 195. Later, I will return to the exaggerations that this observation has recently produced.

legal acts or administrative documents. Since Coptophones had no choice but to use an artificial language, Greek was a lesser evil for them. Even if this meant resorting to a language not naturally employed for the writing of regulated documents, Greek actually did the job very well, all the more so in that it was possible to use an interpreter (a role that the notary most often played), and that it presented certain advantages that, as we will see, came to magnify the handicap of multidialecticism.

The Advantages of Greek, an "Inhibiting" Competitor

Greek had a long and continuous tradition as a legal language, contrary to Egyptian, which experienced a long period of eclipse in this role, as I have remarked in chapter 1.[32] Since the fourth century BC (if we look only at its history in Egypt), it could develop a complete lexical and formulary arsenal for the legal transactions and administrative processes that persisted, with the inevitable and necessary changes and adaptations following the institutional mutations caused by the Roman conquest, and thanks notably to its body of officials and the tradition of its notarial profession, which was soundly established at the local level. While it was initially competing with Egyptian, it held, for these uses, an exclusive position starting at the end of the first century AD, which marked the terminal decline of documentary Demotic, and a dominant position from a much earlier time.

Above all, Greek was the only language that adapted itself to Roman law, which was in force for the entire population since the promulgation of the Antonine Constitution by Caracalla, which made all Egyptians citizens of the Empire (212). Rapidly allowed by Rome as an acceptable substitute for Latin, it established a lexicon capable of rendering the concepts of Roman law and the terms specific to Roman institutions.[33] In 212, as noted above, written Egyptian (i.e., Demotic) was actually no longer being used by the secular population, and was therefore unable to follow this transformation or to adjust to the new political and legal conditions. It was not until the emergence of a new written medium, Coptic, that Egyptian could fully adapt and develop an autonomous language in line with

[32] Cf. *supra*, pp. 3–5.

[33] Cf. Mason 1974. It is worth noting that Greek was a language that, from an early time, displayed a general tendency to adopt Roman idioms into it, even in epistolary language. It was quick to pick things up from Latin, in contrast to how Egyptian behaved with respect to Greek in the Ptolemaic period.

the legal-administrative situation. Yet acquiring autonomy in this domain required time:[34] the task was not only to transform a preexisting linguistic heritage but also, following the rupture between the end of Demotic and the emergence of Coptic, to recreate this heritage by adapting a thoroughly renewed language[35] to the complex and therefore overwhelmingly foreign world of Roman law.

This process of developing autonomy was in fact not specific to legal-administrative writing; it also left its marks in the domain of literature. In fact, I would be tempted to compare the interval separating the first attempts to use documentary Coptic (for letters) from the first legal documents in Coptic (second half of the sixth to the beginning of the seventh century), to the interval we observe in the domain of literature between the first examples of literary Coptic (glossaries, translations) and the development of an original Coptic literature. With the noteworthy yet above all singular and for the moment marginal exception of Shenoute, the latter was mainly deployed in the late sixth and early seventh centuries.[36] It was under the Patriarch Damian (569/578–605) that we find the first production of works belonging to what we could call a large-scale "literary movement," which, to use the words of Tito Orlandi, attest to a language "which has at last become independent of the Greek model and self-sufficient in its syntactical and stylistic elements." "One does note," he added, "the ability of the authors of this period to express various concepts in Coptic with great precision. This development represents the natural progress in the language and its growing independence from Greek."[37] It was also during the same period (sixth to seventh century) that Greek liturgy started to give way to Coptic for prayers, which is an additional sign that the Egyptian language was starting to gain independence.[38]

---

[34] Even though "the old Egyptian language was supple enough and rich enough to be able to face up to these diverse new situations to answer these 'modern' needs and adapt itself, as it did several times in the course of a history of several thousand years" (Kasser 1991b, 218).

[35] Later in this chapter ("Coptic as a 'Victim' of Its Origins") we will see how.

[36] Orlandi 1986, 75–78; Emmel 2007, 95–99; Papaconstantinou 2008, 83. Regarding the beginnings of literary Coptic, cf. also Smith 1998.

[37] Orlandi 1986, 76.

[38] Greek was maintained for a longer time in hymns and above all acclamations—even in the ninth century—due to their more established form, which was difficult to translate and endowed with the literalist prestige of tradition. Regarding this fossilization of portions of liturgy in Greek, cf. Mihálykó 2019.

In other words, the process by which Coptic tried to gain its autonomy and become not only a mere medium of private communication but an "institution" crystallizing a number of values shared collectively stimulated fairly synchronously all areas of writing, whether legal, literary, or liturgical.

This process took a particularly long time because it had to free itself of Greek, which benefited from considerable prestige owing to its ancientness and wide-ranging diffusion throughout the East, and its status as the official language of Egypt for seven centuries. The prestige of Greek hindered Coptic, which had undergone profound innovations following the recent creation of a new writing system, and which had never exerted any influence outside the borders of Egypt. The prestige that one language may have to the detriment of another is a phenomenon that should not be underestimated in ancient societies with low or disparate literacy. People readily adopted a language that was not their own if it had proved itself and was endowed with more appeal and authority, without however feeling that they were betraying their own culture.[39] The same process was at work in the religious domain when foreign deities were adopted because they were deemed to be more reliable.

This *accepted* authority of Greek could lead to situations that may seem surprising to us. This is the case, for example, with a papyrus from the end of the fourth century, *P.Herm.* 7 [Fig. 14]: it is a letter from a certain Psoïs to Apa John of Lycopolis, whose archive was discussed in chapter 1.[40]

---

[39] I have trouble understanding why the concept of prestige has been severely criticized by certain linguists (cf., for example, Oréal 1999, 300–302) as if it were perverted by a colonialist vision. It is necessary to dissociate this concept from that of hierarchy. The prestige from which Latin benefited in modern Europe did not prevent national cultures from conceiving of themselves as being innovative and not necessarily enfeoffed to ancient cultural models for which Latin had formerly been the natural language of expression. Coptic's lack of prestige with respect to Greek, far from being a modern invention, is partly supported in the sources—and, on this view, I share Papaconstantinou's nuances (Papaconstantinou 2008, 84). Regarding the need not to exaggerate the nationalism of Egyptians faced with the Greek-speaking Roman-Byzantine state, cf. Wipszycka 1992b. Nonetheless, we cannot completely deny it: in certain milieus, the hegemony of Greek could contribute to developing an alternative solution, as we will see in chapter 4.

[40] The text that I give here (established on the basis of an image) and the translation differ somewhat from those of the edition.

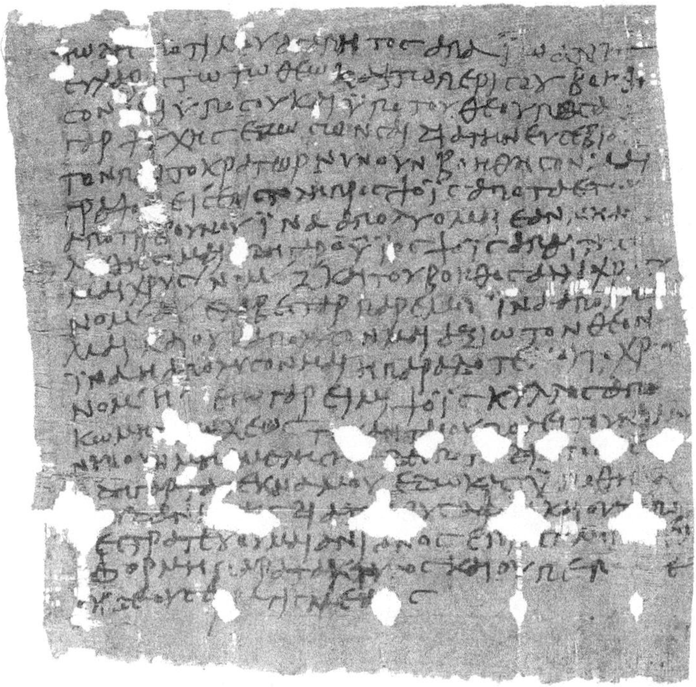

Fig. 14. Psoïs's "letter" to Apa John (*P.Herm.* 7 [Lycopolite, ca. 375–400]). (Photograph courtesy of the John Rylands Library.)

→ Τῷ δεσπ̣ότι μ̣ου ἀγ̣απητος Ἄπα Ἰωανης. Εὐχαριστῶ τῷ Θεῷ καὶ τῷ περὶ σοῦ βοηθή̣σον μα̣ι ὑπὸ σοῦ καὶ ὑπὸ τοῦ Θεοῦ· πα̣σας̣ γὰρ ψυχης ἐζωσων σαι διὰ τὴν εὐσέβια̣ν̣ τὸν πα̣ν̣τοκράτωρ. Νῦν οὖν βοήθησόν μαι· γράψον̣ εις ἐπιστολη πρὸς Ψόϊς ἀπὸ Ταετῷ̣ ἀπὸ τριβουνου, ἵνα ἀπολύομαι ἐαν μὴ ἀπ̣ο̣λυθήσομαι. Ἤ̣δη γὰρ ὁ υἱὸς Ψόϊς ἀπαίτησέ̣ μαι χρυσ(οῦ) νομ(ισμάτια) ζ´ καὶ τοῦ βοηθὸς ἄλλα̣ χρυ̣σ̣(οῦ) νομ(ισμάτιον) α´· ἔλαβες γὰρ παρ' ἐμοῦ ἵνα ἀπολ̣ύωμαι καὶ οὐκ ἀπόλυσόν μαι. Ἀξιῶ τὸν Θεὸν ἵνα ἢ ἀπόλυσόν μαι ἢ παραδοτε μ̣οι το χρυσ(οῦ) νομ(ισμάτια) η´. Ἐγὼ γάρ εἰμι Ψόϊς Κύλλος ἀπὸ κώμης Π̣ώχεως το̣ῦ̣ Ἀνταιουπολείτου νο̣μοῦ. Νῦν οὖν μὴ ἀ̣μελήσ̣ης, δέσποτα̣, διὰ̣ τ̣ὸ̣ν̣ Θ̣εό̣[ν]. Ἤδη γὰρ τὰ τ̣έκνα μου ἔδωκας ὑποθήκ̣α̣ς̣ [το]ῦ δανι̣[σ]τ̣η̣ς διὰ τ̣ὸ χ̣ρ̣υσάφι̣ν̣. Καὶ οὐτ̣έ̣πο[τ]ε στρατευου μαι Ἀνιανός, ἐπί̣ ἐ̣σ̣τί̣ μ̣ο̣ι̣ [πλ]έα ἀ̣φορμὴ π̣αρὰ τακτυλος καὶ οὐ πεπ . [.] . ε οὐδὲ οὐ σφρ̣α̣γισμένο̣ς.

verso
→ Ἀπόδῳ̣ς̣ τῷ δεσ̣π̣ό̣της ἀναχωρη̣[τῇ Ἰ]ω̣[άννη̣].

1 l. δεσπότῃ, ἀγαπητῷ, Ἰωάννῃ ‖ **2–3** l. βοηθήσοντί ‖ **3** l. μοι?, πάσας? ‖ **4** ψυχὰς?, ἔσωσέ μου?, εὐσέβειαν ‖ **5** l. ὁ?, l. μοι ‖ **6** l. μίαν ἐπιστολὴν, Ψόϊτα, Τοετῶ ‖ **7** l. τριβούνων, ἀπολύωμαι, εἰ ‖ **8** l. Ψόϊτος, ἀπήτησέ ‖ **9** l. με, ὁ βοηθὸς αὐτοῦ, ἄλλο ‖ **10** l. ἔλαβον ‖ **11** l. ἀπέλυσάν με ‖ **12** l. ἀπολύσωσί με, παραδῶσι, τὰ ‖ **13** l. Κύλλου ‖ **14** l. Πούχεως, Ἀνταιουπολίτου ‖ **16** l. ἔδωκα ‖ **17** [το]ῦ ego : [τ]ῷ ed. ‖ l. τῷ δανειστῇ, χρυσάφιον ‖ **17–18** l. οὐδέποτε ‖ **18** l. ἐστράτευσέ με Ἀννιανός ‖ **19** l. δακτύλου ‖ πεπυ̣[ι]μ̣ε (l. πεποίημαι) vel sim. propono: πεπύ̣[ωτ]ε ed. ‖ **20** l. οὐδὲ ἐσφραγισμένος ‖ **21 (verso)** ἀπόδῳ̣ς̣ (l. ἀπόδος) ego: ἀπόδο̣ς̣ ed. ‖ l. δεσπότῃ.

To my master, the beloved Apa John. I give thanks to God and whoever will assist me for your sake (?) through you and through God; for the Almighty saved all souls because of your piety (?).[41] So now help me: write a letter to Psoïs from Toeto, ex-tribune,[42] that I may be released—if I have not (by then) been released. For Psoïs' son has already demanded of me 7 gold *solidi* and his assistant another gold *solidus*; for they took (this sum) from me so that I might obtain my release, and they have not released me. I ask God that they either release me or give back to me the 8 gold *solidi*. For I am Psoïs son of Cyllus[43] from the village of Pouchis in the Antaeopolite nome. Now then do not neglect this, master, for God's sake; for I have already given my children as securities to the money-lender on account of the gold. And Annianos has never approved me for military service since I have a complete excuse for this by reason of

[41] The syntax of the first lines is so incorrect that the translation is no better than a guess.

[42] This Psoïs is a different person from the writer of this letter.

[43] P. Schubert (*P.Yale* III 137, l. 152n.) proposed to keep the text of the papyrus and understand "Psoïs the club-footed" (Ψόϊς κυλλός = *BL* XII 88). But if he were club-footed, Psoïs would not have to use his finger injury as an excuse for avoiding military service (see chapter 2, n. 44). Moreover, we expect here the name of his father so that his identity may be complete. Indeed, his father's name is a nickname derived from κυλλός "club-footed."

> my finger;[44] I have not been [drafted (?)][45] nor have I been sealed[46] either.
>
> *Verso*: Deliver to my master, the anchorite John.

We are struck by the abnormally large number of mistakes (indicated in the apparatus criticus), which consist of, in addition to the omission of words and letters, morphology and syntax errors, as well as phoneticisms (spelling errors) testifying to an inability to distinguish properly between vowel sounds and the difference between voiced and voiceless consonants—problems typical of Egyptians. This text, which must have been difficult to understand, was therefore undoubtedly written by an Egyptian, which is moreover confirmed by his Egyptian name (Psoïs < Egyptian *Pꜣ-šy* "He who belongs to Shai," in other words, Destiny). Given that his Greek language abilities were scant, we can expect that Psoïs would have resorted to using this language mainly so as to be understood by his correspondent, who must have been Greek. The latter had a New Testament name (preceded by the Hebrew title Apa), which, at the time, was used by both Greeks and Egyptians, and which is therefore of absolutely no use in determining the ethnic profile of its bearer. Nonetheless, this man is also known through another text in the same archive, *P.Amherst* II 145, a Greek letter addressed by the same Apa John to a man named Paul. Now, the final salutation serving as a signature is in Coptic,[47] indicating that Apa John simply dictated the message, which was translated into Greek and written down by a third party, and that he had "signed" in the only language he knew, Coptic [Fig. 15]. This conclusion, which certain scholars have contested,[48] is confirmed by the fact that the Greek-speaking Palladius, author of the *Lausiac History* (418–19), met with Apa John, as he recounts, through the intermediary

[44] "Be it to make oneself unable to hold a sword or to handle a gun, cutting off a finger was and remains the most economic self-mutilation which disqualifies a recruit for service" (Zuckerman 1995, 186).

[45] I would propose a form of πεποίημαι here with the meaning "to be appointed, to be drafted."

[46] "Since the first Tetrachy, recruits approved for the draft were marked with a special sign, *signaculum*" (Zuckerman 1995, 184).

[47] L. 27–31: ϯϣινε εροκ πⲁcοn πⲁγⲗε ⲙⲛ ⲛⲁ πεκηει τηρογ ϩⲙ̄ πϫοειc "I greet you, my brother Paul, as well as all your household in the Lord."

[48] Van Minnen 1994, 84, who maintains that the Greek text is written by the same hand as the Coptic subscription. In my opinion, nothing guarantees this. Camplani 2015, 138n26, also does not agree with this conclusion.

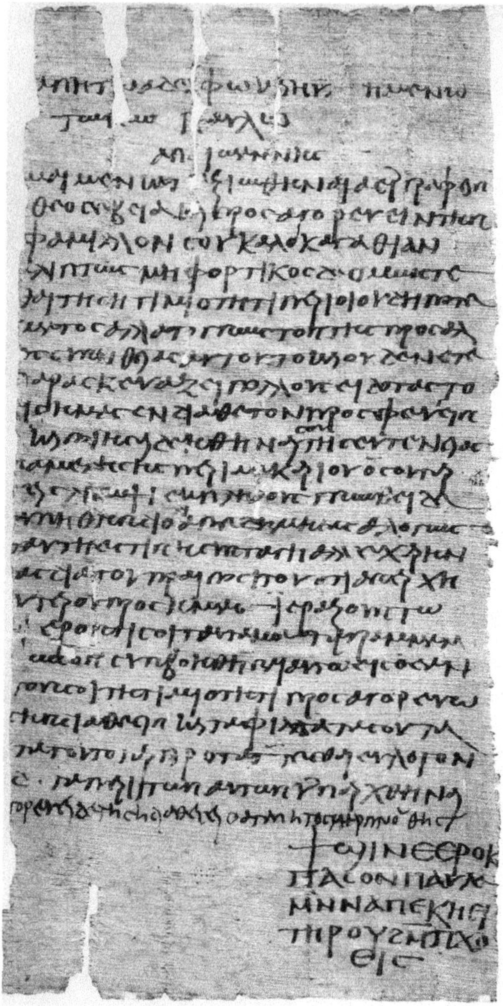

Fig. 15. Greek letter addressed by Apa John to Paul with his subscription in Coptic in the last five lines (*P.Amh.* II 145 [Lycopolite, ca. 375–400]). (From B. P. Grenfell and A. S. Hunt, *The Amherst Papyri*, London 1901, Pl. XXI.)

of an interpreter.[49] In light of this information, which also corresponds to what we know about other Egyptian anchorites,[50] we cannot help but be intrigued by the fact that Psoïs, an Egyptian with poor Greek skills, resorted

[49] Palladius, *Historia lausiaca*, XXXV 5: ἀσπασάμενος οὖν με ἔλεγε δι᾽ ἑρμηνέως κτλ. "After greeting me, he said through an interpreter . . ."

[50] Cf. the anecdote about Poemen recounted by the *Apophthegmata patrum* (*collectio systematica*), XVIII 21 (= *collectio alphabetica*, *Poemen* 183, *PG* LXV, col. 365, 48–52),

to writing in Greek to an Egyptian who knew no Greek! How can we explain this aberration, which is verified through other letters addressed to Apa John?[51] The reason is precisely the aura of the Greek language, which was charged with prestige and authority.

Let us imagine for a moment the context in which Psoïs's letter was written. Apa John—about whose profile we know more through two hagiographic works, Palladius's *Lausiac History*, which we have already mentioned, and the *History of the Egyptian Monks*[52]—was a holy man whose sainthood and gift for prophecy, known to the Emperor himself, attracted crowds of pilgrims and beggars of all types from afar: monks,

---

ed. J.-C. Guy, Sources chrétiennes 498, Paris 2005: Παρεβάλομέν ποτε ἀπὸ Συρίας τῷ ἀββᾶ Ποιμένι, καὶ ἠθέλομεν ἐρωτῆσαι αὐτὸν περὶ τῆς σκληρότητος τῆς καρδίας. Ὁ δὲ γέρων οὐκ ᾔδει ἑλληνιστὶ οὐδὲ ἑρμηνέα ηὕραμεν "We went to Syria one day to see Abba Poemen and we wanted to ask him about purity of heart. But the old man did not know Greek and no interpreter could be found" (trans. Ward 1975, 192). Likewise, the *dux Aegyptii*, Artemius must communicate with the monks of Pbow through an interpreter (Pachomius's *Vita prima*, 118 ed. Halkin 1932, 86; trans. A.-J. Festugière 1965, 236; see other Pachomian examples in Papaconstantinou 2014). We can compare the monolingualism of the anchorite Apa John to that of Antony according to the portrait painted of him by Athanasius, *Vita Antonii* 74, 2 (ἔλεγε δι᾽ ἑρμηνέως, τοῦ καλῶς τὰ ἐκείνου διερμηνεύοντος "he told them through an interpreter who faithfully translated his words"; see also ibid., 16; 72 and 77 as well as Jerome, *Vita Hilarionis*, 30, who speaks of *Isaac interpres Antonii* and the *Historia lausiaca*, XXI 15: Τῶν λόγων τούτων ὅλων ἑρμηνεὺς γέγονα, τοῦ μακαρίου Ἀντωνίου ἑλληνιστὶ μὴ εἰδότος· ἐγὼ γὰρ ἠπιστάμην ἀμφοτέρας τὰς γλώσσας, καὶ ἡρμήνευσα αὐτοῖς, τοῖς μὲν ἑλληνιστί, ἐκείνῳ δὲ αἰγυπτιστί "For all these speeches, I was the interpreter, since the blessed Antony did not know Greek. For I knew both languages and I served as their interpreter, for some in Greek, for him in Egyptian") despite the Graeco-Egyptian bilingualism that seems to be implied by the letters attributed to him (regarding this problem, see Camplani 2015, 132–33, who concludes that antique evidence of multilingualism is not exempt from ideological intentions; cf. also Dummer 1968, 34–35 and 47–48; Papaconstantinou 2014, 19–20). Nonetheless, we know plurilingual anchorites such as—to limit ourselves to the fourth century—the bilingual Hierax (Epiphanius, *Panarion*, 67), the trilingual (Greek, Latin, Egyptian) Theon (*Historia monachorum in Aegypto*, VI 3), or the trilingual monks evoked in the same work (VIII 62)—not to mention the figure, without historical consistency (cf. recently Wipszycka 2009, 22 and 198–99), of Paul of Thebes, regarding whom Jerome, *Vita Pauli*, 4, tells us that he was *litteris tam graecis quam aegyptiacis apprime eruditus*. For the linguistic situation of Egyptian monasteries in the fourth and fifth centuries, see Torallas Tovar 2003.

51 See also *P.Herm.* 17, a letter addressed by a certain Leuchis (daughter of?) Malamos to Apa John, written in a bad Greek.

52 *Historia monachorum in Aegypto*, I (ed. Festugière 1961, trans. Festugière 1964).

soldiers, senior officials, and ordinary individuals.[53] He was approached by visitors during audiences where people had to push and shove, and which must have been as impressive as the hearings of governors rendering justice, for those lucky enough to be admitted to them. We know from literary sources that they were received by Apa John while he was standing behind a window through which "he blessed and greeted his visitors, talking to each one of his own concern."[54] The letters that people gave to him at this time even looked like petitions, similar to those that the governor received during his own hearings; with the exception of their prescript, the formulary that they followed was very similar.[55] Under such conditions, we can understand why Psoïs, very impressed (he did not even want to put his name on the prescript as was customary!), wanted to rise to the occasion by writing his request in Greek. In his opinion, as the language of administration and of the Church, Greek seemed to be a requirement for the "petition" that he was going to submit to the holy man, considering also that Coptic was used during this period for private correspondence of an informal nature only. The language that Apa John actually spoke was of little importance. The formal context, the weight of the legal procedure, and the aura of the saint transcended his person and his linguistic limitations. Besides, his secretariat could manage petitions in Greek. In one word, we are in a typical situation of *diglossia*—and this time I am using the term in its broad sense of the coexistence of languages that are not necessarily related.[56] Greek played the role of the "High Language" compared to the "Low Language" constituted by Coptic; for any procedures outside of

---

[53] Van Minnen 1994, 80–84.

[54] *Historia monachorum in Aegypto*, I 5 (ed. Festugière 1961, trans. Festugière 1964): ηὐλόγει γὰρ μόνον διὰ θυρίδος καὶ ἠσπάζετο τοὺς προσιόντας ἑκάστῳ ὑπὲρ τῆς οἰκείας σπουδῆς διαλεγόμενος. See also Palladius, *Historia Lausiaca*, XXXV 4: Καὶ παραγενόμενος ὥραν δευτέραν ἐν τῇ συντυχίᾳ εὗρον αὐτὸν ἐν τῇ θυρίδι παρακαθεζόμενον, δι᾽ ἧς ἐδόκει παρακαλεῖν τοὺς παρατυγχάνοντας "And having come at the second hour for an interview I found him sitting by the window, through which he seemed to be comforting his visitors." The crowd was so big that "the brethren built on later a very large vestibule holding about one hundred men" (ὕστερον γὰρ προσῳκοδόμησαν οἱ ἀδελφοὶ προεισοδικὸν μέγιστον, ἐν ᾧ χωροῦσιν ἄνδρες ὡς ἑκατόν, ibid.).

[55] They start with an introduction in which the petitioner praises the recipient, followed by the grounds for the complaint, and concludes with the request. In spite of their epistolary form (and the address in the endorsement), they were not sent but most likely submitted in person to Apa John (or handed over to his secretariat).

[56] Fishman 1967.

the ordinary and involving formality, people were tempted to give priority to the former as far as possible.[57]

This prestige of Greek, endowed with the radiance of authority and tradition, persisted for a long time, long after the Arab-Muslim Conquest, even though that event broke the link with the Greek-speaking Byzantine regime. It was maintained as the language of liturgy; in documents that came to be written in Coptic from that point on, Greek continued to be used for the most official and formal parts, those which reinforced the authority of the text (such as the initial divine invocation, the regnal dating,[58] the "signature" of the notaries); in funeral inscriptions, which would become more and more frequently carved in Coptic, it slipped into the first position in the form of an invocation to God, prior to the anecdotal information regarding the deceased, which was written in Coptic.[59] To sum up, it occupied an overarching position in all senses of the term.

The Church Was Also Greek-Speaking

The fact that Greek, in addition to being the language of the state, was also the language of the Church of Egypt since its origins, helped it consolidate its privileged position.[60] The Church actually did not contribute much to the development of Coptic, as is often thought, even though the latter was an offshoot of Christianity. The Church was born before the advent of Coptic and, after the Empire became Christian, it developed in

[57] I also believe that it is excessive to conclude, as does Camplani 2015, 144–45, that "non possiamo interpretare la collocazione sociolinguistica reciproca del greco e del copto nei termini di una differenziazione funzionale netta. (. . .) Avremmo una differenziazione funzionale in senso proprio se tutte le lettere private d'Egitto fossero redatte in copto e non in greco." Coptic-speaking communities used Coptic, in the epistolary domain, for informal communication, and Greek for communication requiring a larger degree of formality, whereas Greek was systematically used for regulated writing. The quasi-exclusivity of Coptic for private letters in Kharga (cf. chapter 1, p. 20) is a good indicator of this functional differentiation. The latter is at work to an even greater extent, given that we are dealing with less Greek-speaking communities.

[58] Let us mention an interesting exception in a Coptic graffito from 609/610 found by H. Burton in the Theban Mountain (edited in *P.Mon.Epiph.* I, p. 11, and discussed by Worp 1990): the regnal dating is expressed in Coptic. It is worth noting in passing that it contains a strange mistake: the Greek term of Latin origin Αὔγουστος, often spelled Ἄγουστος is translated with the verb ⲥⲱⲧⲙ "to listen" because the redactor probably connected Ἄγουστος with ἀκούω "to listen"!

[59] Fournet 2018a, 72–73 and 80.

[60] Camplani 2015, 145–53.

coexistence with the Greek-speaking state, which came to influence it in a number of areas—we will see examples of this in chapter 4. It promoted a religion of the book whose sacred texts were written in Greek (the Septuaginta, the Greek version of the Old Testament, and the New Testament written in Greek), and whose theologians, fathers of the Church, were, for the eastern portion of the Empire, Greek-speaking, and made use of an intellectual toolkit that came from Greek philosophical culture. These same theologians had promoted Greek to the rank of a sacred language, like Hebrew and Latin.[61] This language was also adopted for the liturgy, and would remain the language of worship for a long time in the most traditional parts of the service, as many papyri attest.[62] Based in Alexandria, a city that was linguistically and culturally mono-Greek,[63] the ecclesiastical institution established, throughout the *chōra*, a hierarchy with which it communicated in Greek. The best-known examples of these writings are the festal letters that circulated from diocese to diocese, veritable treatises with doctrinal and disciplinary content sent by the bishop of Alexandria to the other bishops of Egypt each year to announce the date of Easter [Fig. 16]. This is evidenced in the last known example, dating from 713 or 719[64]—even though these letters may subsequently have been translated into Coptic.[65] Monumental ecclesiastical epigraphy provides even later

[61] Isidore of Seville, *Etymologies*, IX 1: *Tres sunt autem linguae sacrae: Hebraea, Graeca, Latina, quae toto orbe maxime excellunt. His enim tribus linguis super crucem Domini a Pilato fuit causa eius scripta. Unde et propter obscuritatem sanctarum Scripturarum harum trium linguarum cognitio necessaria est, ut ad alteram recurratur dum siquam dubitationem nominis uel interpretationis sermo unius linguae adtulerit* "There are three sacred languages—Hebrew, Greek, and Latin—which are preeminent throughout the world. On the cross of the Lord the charge laid against him was written at Pilate's command in these three languages (John 19:20). Hence—and because of the obscurity of the Sacred Scriptures—a knowledge of these three languages is necessary, so that, whenever the wording of one of the languages presents any doubt about a name or an interpretation, recourse may be had to another language" (trans. Barney, Lewis, Beach, and Berghof 2006).

[62] Cf. chapter 2, n. 38.

[63] See, for example, Wipszycka 1992b, 103–4; or Fournet 2009a, 67. Let us recall that this city has not yet yielded any written examples of Coptic, which does not mean that Coptic was not used by some of its inhabitants: cf. Fournet 2009a, 75.

[64] *BKT* VI 5 (= TM 59099), a festal letter from Alexander II. See also *P.Heid.* IV 295 (= TM 65417), anonymous festal letter, datable to the eighth century (according to P. Orsini, cf. TM). Regarding festal letters, see Külzer 1998.

[65] P.Ryl., Coptic Suppl. N. 47–48 (= TM 108317; ed. Camplani 2004). See also P.Berol. 11346 (TM 108227; ed. Camplani 2012), a pastoral epistle from the seventh century.

Fig. 16. A copy of the festal letter sent by Cyril of Alexandria in 421 (PSI inv. 3779, ed. Bastianini-Cavallo 2011). (Photograph courtesy of the Istituto papirologico "G. Vitelli.")

evidence of the use of Greek with the carved lintel of the church of Al-Muʿallaqa ("Hanging church") of Cairo, which dates from 735 [Fig. 17]![66]

The fact that this state of affairs lasted long after the Council of Chalcedon (451), which began the process of creating fissures inside the Egyptian Church and later caused it to break away from Byzantium, demonstrates the extent to which Greek transcended political-religious dissent. Above all, it shows how it would be erroneous, as scholars have sometimes ventured to do in the past, to make of the opposition between Chalcedonians and anti-Chalcedonians a framework of analysis for understanding the linguistic rupture—if we can indeed talk about a *rupture*—between Coptophones and Greek speakers.[67]

[66] Coptic Museum (Cairo), Inv. 753 (=*I.Lefebvre* 69). See Fournet 1993 (with bibliography), in which I show that this inscription did not contain Coptic elements, as MacCoull 1984 had previously claimed.

[67] Cf., for example, Wipszycka 1992b, 120–25.

Fig. 17. The Greek inscription of the church of Muʿallaqa, now in the Coptic Museum, Cairo (735). (Photograph courtesy of Alain Lecler [IFAO].)

The Church, certain dignitaries of which, like Athanasius, may have known Coptic[68] and would later encourage its use—as we will see in chapter 4—was therefore of Greek expression during the centuries of interest to us here. It nevertheless remained aware of the non-Greek-speaking component of its flock, for whose benefit it provided certain types of assistance, such as interpreters. In the book of prayers that is attributed to him,[69] Serapion, Bishop of Thmuis in the fourth century, included interpreters along with subdeacons and readers in the category of church staff.[70] These liturgical interpreters were by no means specific to Egypt and were found in other Eastern churches as well. During her journey to Jerusalem in around 380, the pilgrim Egeria describes them at work in a passage that allows us to understand, better than any other, their fundamental place at liturgical celebrations in the eastern provinces (*Pilgrimage of Egeria*, XLVII, 3–4):

> Now, forasmuch as in that province some of the people know both Greek and Syriac, while some know Greek alone and

[68] Dummer 1968, 24–29. Lefort 1933 went too far in his claims for Athanasius's Coptic abilities: cf. Wipszycka 1992b, 112–14.

[69] Attribution challenged by Botte 1964. But a date in the fourth century and an Egyptian provenance seem rather sure.

[70] Serapion of Thmouis, *Euchologium*, 25, ed. Maxwell Johnson 1995: παρακαλοῦμεν δὲ ὑπὲρ τῶν ὑποδιακόνων καὶ ἀναγνωστῶν καὶ ἑρμηνέων· πάντας τοὺς τῆς ἐκκλησίας <λειτουργοὺς> ἀνάπαυσον "Let us pray for the subdeacons, readers and interpreters. Give rest to all the church servants."

> others only Syriac; and because the bishop, although he knows Syriac, yet always speaks Greek, and never Syriac, there is always a priest standing by who, when the bishop speaks Greek, interprets into Syriac, that all may understand what is being taught. And because all the lessons that are read in the church must be read in Greek, he always stands by and interprets them into Syriac, for the people's sake, that they may always be edified. Moreover, the Latins here, who understand neither Syriac nor Greek, in order that they be not disappointed, have (all things) explained to them, for there are other brothers and sisters knowing both Greek and Latin, who translate into Latin for them. (trans. McClure and Feltoe 1919)[71]

However, more so than was the case for Aramaic dialects, Coptic remained quite negligible in the life of the Church of Egypt during the first centuries of its history.

The Crushing Weight of the Past: The Institutional Marginalization of Egyptian

The advantages of Greek combined with the handicaps of Coptic are, it seems to me, not sufficient to explain the long time that it took Coptic to become autonomous and to free itself of Greek dominion. These causes were also amplified by the historical situation experienced by the Egyptian language since the Ptolemaic period and above all during the Roman period. Here, I think it is necessary to go back in time.

Egyptian was not always so dependent on Greek and relegated to private letters. The number of documents written in Demotic was actually greater than that of the documents written in Greek during the first fifty years of Greek domination. The trend was later reversed, although Demotic continued to be commonly used for a multitude of acts: not

[71] *Et quoniam in ea prouincia pars populi et grece et siriste nouit, pars etiam alia per se grece, aliqua etiam pars tantum siriste, itaque quoniam episcopus, licet siriste nouerit, tamen semper grece loquitur et nunquam siriste: itaque ergo stat semper presbyter, qui episcopo grece dicente siriste interpretatur, ut omnes audiant [ut omnes audiant] quae exponuntur. Lectiones etiam, quecumque in ecclesia leguntur, quia necesse est grece legi, semper stat, qui siriste interpretatur propter populum, ut semper discant. Sane quicumque hic latini sunt, id est qui nec siriste nec grece nouerunt, ne contristentur, et ipsis exponitur eis, quia sunt alii fratres et sorores grecolatini, qui latine exponunt eis* (ed. Maraval 1982). About this text, see Scott Johnson 2015, 5–7.

only private letters, but also legal acts between individuals (marriage or divorce contracts, sales, cessions, exchanges, donations, divisions of property, leases, loans, acknowledgments of debt, receipts, service contracts), acts involving religious institutions (hierodule contracts,[72] oaths to gods, documents relating to the administration of temples, sanctuary inventories, the regulations of religious associations), and, last of all, documents established between the state and individuals (censuses, divisions of land parcels imposed by the state, tax registers, tax receipts, sureties, legal proceedings): in short, a large range of documents, which, far from being restricted to private relations between individuals, also formalized legal transactions and bore evidence for the communication between the government and individuals. In any case, during the first generations, the administrative system implemented by the Ptolemies was based on established structures authorizing the use of Demotic on the local level (consequently, almost 20 percent of Ptolemaic census documents are written in Demotic, and this was still the case up until the second century BC).[73]

Greek was nonetheless imposed as an administrative language, and documentation from the Ptolemaic period clearly demonstrates its unstoppable rise to power. Egyptians were increasingly pressured into abandoning Demotic and using Greek instead when performing their administrative duties. The more a person ascended in the ranks of the administration, the more exclusive Greek became. To go back to the example mentioned just above, census declarations could be written in Demotic, depending on the village officials taking them; however, when the registers were summarized at the level of the nome before being sent to Alexandria, only Greek was used.[74] A fortiori, all requests sent to the king were necessarily written in Greek.

The situation was more flexible for contracts between individuals, which could be either in Greek or in Demotic. Rather than seeking out Greek notaries (the *agoranomoi*, who appeared at the end of the third century BC), Egyptians had the freedom to have contracts drawn up in Demotic by priest-notaries or *monographoi*, or later by notaries practicing at bilingual offices independent of the temples. This choice was all the more legitimate if they wanted to make a claim based not on Greek law but rather on Egyptian law (οἱ τῆς χώρας νόμοι "the laws of the Country") and, in the event of a dispute, to deal with the court of the *laocritai*, which

[72] A personal commitment by which a person places him- or herself in the service of a god and declares him- or herself to be its "slave" in exchange for its protection.

[73] As demonstrated in *P.Count.* 53 and 54 from the Lycopolite nome.

[74] Cf. *P.Count.* 1 (254–231 BC).

applied Egyptian law and gave its judgments in the Egyptian language, and not that of the *chrēmatistai*, which judged matters that were the subject of a contract in Greek.[75]

However, this freedom to establish contracts in Demotic found itself subject to increasingly more restrictive constraints. It was through the registration of contracts, which was necessary in the event of subsequent proceedings, that the Hellenophone state was able to control the Egyptian-speaking notarial profession and was therefore able, at the outset of Roman rule, to asphyxiate it to the benefit of the Greek-speaking one. Starting in 146 BC, a Demotic contract could only have a legal value if it had previously been registered in Greek[76] at the offices where Greek acts were drawn up (*agoranomia*), and therefore if it carried a Greek note on the back.

The erosion of Demotic, observable during the century preceding the Roman conquest, accelerated from the beginning of the Early Roman Empire under the effects of Romanization. The Roman authorities, who retained Greek as the language of administration, excluded Demotic from the public sphere: bilingual public notices disappeared. In transactions between individuals, and for a Demotic act to be valid and registrable, the Romans started by requiring the declarant—when he or she was not also the beneficiary—to appose a detailed subscription in Greek that recapitulated the terms of the contract.[77] Furthermore, the disappearance of the *laocritai* meant that the only judicial instance before which Demotic acts could be produced ceased to exist, as justice was rendered exclusively in Greek from then on. People nevertheless continued to draw up contracts according to Egyptian law, albeit in Greek, which explains that, from that point on, both notaries and judges had to be provided with Greek translations of Demotic customary law.[78]

These constraints could only dissuade people from using Demotic for transactions between individuals. In fact, the variety of contractual genres (outside of temples) declined to the point of containing nothing but sales during the first century AD. The few contractual documents subsequent to 100 pertain to sacerdotal milieus: for the most part, these are conventions regulating the obligations of service. The latest ones date from the

[75] At least up until the disappearance of the *laocritai* (around 100 BC): see chapter 2, n. 3.

[76] Cf. *P.Paris* 65 and Depauw 2011.

[77] The first example is *P.Tebt.* II 386 from 12 BC. Depauw 2003.

[78] For instance, *P.Oxy.* XLVI 3285 (second half of the second century AD).

beginning of the third century.[79] Note that these acts, regardless of their form, all come from the Fayyum, the only region where a body of notaries using Demotic attempted to survive, despite the region's high degree of Hellenization, and that they reveal an increasingly uncertain knowledge of writing, language, and formulary.

It was in the domain of taxation that Demotic put up the most resistance: in Upper Egypt, and particularly in the region of Thebes, the custom of issuing tax receipts in Demotic was maintained. Following a strong increase during the first quarter of the first century AD, their number underwent a drastic decline in the following two quarters. In the Memnonia (Western Thebes), this went so far as a complete stoppage: whereas up to the year 41 at the least, receipts were exclusively in Demotic, starting from 43 they were only in Greek. This was probably the effect of an administrative decision.

This brief historical survey shows that Egyptian was not only hindered by the competition of Greek, the language of the conquerors, but also that it was the victim of a genuine policy implemented by Greek-speaking authorities (whether Ptolemaic or Roman) to restrict the field of action of Egyptian and to exclude it from the sphere of regulated writing. Completely absent from the government, which was strictly Greek-speaking, and increasingly limited to unregulated private communication, written Demotic ended up dying out in the company of the decline of the temples that ensured its teaching.

When it started to make its appearance during the third century, Coptic was therefore born under a sign that was doubly unlucky: following a period of interruption during which Egyptian had no longer been naturally used in writing, it had to find its place in a written culture that had been completely occupied by Greek from that point on. And, above all, it had to recover the official status that had formerly allowed Egyptian to play a legal and administrative role, and which had been progressively denied by the authorities.

The task was all the more difficult, given that the centuries of collective "agraphia" into which Egyptians had been plunged[80] marked a break in the legal-administrative tradition that the Egyptian language had hith-

[79] *P.Louvre* I 61–64 r° (unedited). The last dated document known, P.dem.Leconte 7 (unedited, currently at the British Museum classified under number 76675), from 244 to 249, is probably from a clerical context (it mentions the "great gods"); nonetheless, its reading is too problematic for Demotists to be able to derive a consistent meaning from it. I thank Didier Devauchelle for the information on this text he gave me.

[80] Cf. chapter 1, p. 4.

erto enjoyed. Certain scholars, such as Arthur Schiller, have nonetheless advanced the hypothesis of a continuity that was maintained either underground in an oral manner, or through the intermediary of Greek documents, which supposedly allowed Coptic not to start once again from ground zero but rather to establish a link between the ancient Demotic notarial tradition and the development of a Coptic practice.[81] Detailed research on the lexicon and the formulary of Coptic documents has, however, shown that there was in fact a break between the two.[82]

Coptic as a "Victim" of Its Origins

I believe that the obstacles related to multidialecticism and the diglossic situation of Egypt, which were reinforced by the authoritative role of Greek, do not however address the entire problem, and do not sufficiently account for the delay suffered by Coptic in its quest for official recognition. What needs to be asked is whether, beyond the constraints specific to the language and the weight of history, this quest for recognition by Coptophones or more precisely Coptographs did actually take place; or whether, on the contrary, these milieus forsook, at least initially, the promotion of Coptic in domains other than literature or private communication, by recognizing Greek as having a natural authority and legitimate hegemony in other sectors. In that case, the first hindrance would have been the users themselves. This question plunges us into the heart of the sociology of this language and the conditions of its emergence.

Despite the large amount of papyrological documentation and ancient literary works covering this period, we have relatively little information on the mechanisms that governed the invention of Coptic in the milieus that instigated it.[83] Admittedly, the emergence of Coptic was part of the general trend in the East during Late Antiquity, to create new forms of writing for local languages that were needed for the translation of the Bible and for establishing more firmly a Christian production in the vernacular, breaking with pagan traditions.[84] But the phenomenon in Egypt is manifestly not as precisely documented as in other regions. We would like to know as much about it as we do about other languages: Ethiopian, which morphed from the writing called *Ge'ez* into *abugida* (with the notation of vowels in the form of diacritics) at the time that King Ezana of Axum

---

[81] Schiller 1957, 211.

[82] Richter 2008b, 31–36.

[83] For a recent summary of the question, cf. Choat 2012.

[84] Signes Codoñer 2014.

(ca. 320–60) converted the country to Christianity, making Ethiopian the official language of this new Christian state; Armenian, Georgian, and Albanian, which were supposedly invented by the monk Mesrop Mashtots (360/361–440), once again as a part of the Christianization of the Caucasian countries using these languages; or Glagolitic, which was invented much later by Cyril and Methodius in ninth-century Slavic Moravia.[85] This is, however, not the case, as the Church of Egypt retained no memories of the invention of Coptic, and we are thus confined to venturing with mere speculations.

It is indeed a hypothesis—and I am aware of this—that I advanced in chapter 1 while examining the first written examples of Coptic, and specifically those dating from the first fifty years of its history. We were able to note that they were all bilingual texts in which Coptic was combined with Greek in the form of annotations to a Greek main text, of glosses on Greek lemmas, or of a text among other Greek texts. In other words, Coptic made its entrance into our documentation while closely being linked to Greek and, as it appears, emanating from the Hellenized milieus of cities or from the Fayyum, unlike documentary texts, which massively appeared only during the following century. This strange discrepancy, provided that it is not only the result of our sources, which are still too limited in number, leads us to postulate that there was a change in profile between the first users of Coptic—perhaps its inventors, and in any case its promoters—and those of the next generations. Following this hypothesis, Coptic would have developed among the former not to fill a void, to compensate for ignorance of the Greek language, or a fortiori through the desire to compete with the latter, but rather as an auxiliary to the Hellenization process or as a complement to Greek training.

However, the best evidence of this "consubstantiality" and complementarity, rather than being found in its first written manifestations, is seen in Coptic itself, the genes of which contain these elements at a deep level. We may even go so far as to say, without entering into a paradox, that Coptic is a product of Hellenism.

This is demonstrated above all by its writing [Fig. 18], which is not only Greek but also adopts a graphic style specific to a certain type of Greek book production. Certain sounds that were not represented or were poorly represented by Greek letters required the creation of a few additional letters (six in Sahidic), which, despite being derived from Demotic, were nonetheless adapted to the Greek writing system by borrow-

[85] Dagron 2012, I, 245–48.

ing an analogical form of similar Greek letters:[86] for example, *shai* (ϣ) is an omega with a tail; *fai* (ϥ) reuses the form of *koppa* from papyri (Ϥ); *djandja* (ϫ) is a delta with an additional prolongation; *ti* (ϯ) is no more and no less than a psi—only *hori* (ϩ) and *k^y^ima* (ϭ) are independent of the Greek graphic system.

It could be argued that the "Old Coptic" already used the Greek alphabet while originating from pagan circles deeply rooted in the ancient Egyptian tradition (Egyptian sanctuaries). This might be true, yet these attempts, in addition to testifying to the deculturation of milieus that started to lose their command of the ancient pharaonic scripts and therefore needed to resort to the use of Greek,[87] did not grant such a large place to Greek loanwords (as we are going to see) and did not conform to such a large extent to Greek graphic usage. Coptic did more than borrow letters from Greek; it also appropriated its diacritic signs—in other words, signs that facilitated reading by separating syllables and words more easily [Fig. 18]. The function of some of them, such as the circumflex accent, is modified;[88] that of others remains the same, like that of the umlaut, which signals both the beginning of a word starting with ⲓ or ⲩ (ⲓ̈ⲱϩⲁⲛⲛⲏⲥ) or a phonetic diaeresis (ⲙⲱⲩ̈ⲥⲏⲥ);[89] likewise, the apostrophe or the period are used to mark the end of a word, according to modalities that are somehow different from what they are in Greek, even though they remain little known.[90] The most encroaching diacritic sign in Coptic is the supralinear

[86] See recently Milizia 2016, 183–84.

[87] See the Demotic ostraca from Narmouthis (third century), which used Old Coptic to give the phonetic value of certain hieroglyphic ideograms (*O.Narm.Dem.* II 37–41) [Fig. 3]. Others (for example, *O.Narm.Dem.* II 60 or 90–99) are riddled with Greek words in Greek writing which seem to testify to a restricted Hellenization.

[88] Layton 2011, § 11.

[89] Layton 2011, § 12. On two uses of the umlaut, cf. Fournet, forthcoming. As for Greek, certain Coptic message writers, who lost sight of the primary function of the umlaut as a graphical separator, ended up endowing all ⲓ or ⲩ signs with one regardless of their position.

[90] It should be noted that the use of the apostrophe in the Isaiah codex (cf. chapter 1, p. 7) is very similar to that of the same sign in Greek: it marks the end of words ending with a consonant (and rarely ⲥ or ⲛ). Yet the words ending with other consonants than ς or ν may be problematic for Greek readers who were not accustomed to such endings. That is why they developed the habit of marking them with a "diastolic" apostrophe that signals the break between words (cf. Fournet, forthcoming). As a result, the use made of this sign in the Isaiah codex seems to be justified only if the writer of the Coptic annotations or the reader for whom it was intended was a Hellenophone accustomed to Greek morphology.

Fig. 18. An example of Coptic script from the fourth century (*P.Kell.* VII 83 [Kellis, ca. 355–80]). (© Dakhleh Oasis Project and C. A. Hope.)

stroke, which appeared at a very early date. What the latter owes to Greek, however, is not yet fully understood.[91] It is found above consonants that are not accompanied by a vowel, to indicate that they have a syllabic value and do not form a unit with the preceding consonant: for example, ⲙⲛ̄ for /m^{e}n/ and not for /mn/.[92] This is a particularity of the Coptic syllabic system, which is totally foreign to Greek, and which is potentially upsetting for a reader accustomed to reading according to the Greek syllabic system. It happens that the supralinear stroke was also used in Greek to signal ambiguous sequences and to avoid the incorrect breaks that they could cause in the *scriptio continua* in use at the time.[93] In this sense, they were used above a letter with a numeric value—letters also served as numerals in Greek—so as to prevent readers from granting it an alphabetic value, or above a foreign word or proper noun without a Greek flexional ending—so that the reader did not hesitate about how to delimit them within the sentence. Mutatis mutandis, the Coptic supralinear stroke has the same anti-amphibolic function, insofar as it neutralizes the potential trap constituted by a consonant without a visible vowel support *for a reader accustomed to the Greek system.* If I am not mistaken, this observation is ripe with consequences: not only is it an additional example of the dependence

[91] *Pace* Paola Buzi, cited by Camplani 2015, 133, who sees this as an innovation. I will show that this is not the case. I do not mention the function of the supralinear stroke above the *nomina sacra* because the latter are directly borrowed from Greek: by using the same sacred names, people reused the same internal abbreviation system and the supralinear stroke that visually signalled abbreviations.

[92] Layton 2011, §§ 35 and 38.

[93] Fournet, forthcoming. It may be recalled that the ancient Greeks did not separate words when writing.

of the Coptic graphic system on Greek, but above all it demonstrates that Coptic was created by readers who were accustomed to Greek and who were attempting to inscribe this new writing within a model for which Greek was the norm and the reference. In short, Coptic was invented by Hellenographs for Hellenographs.

In addition to its writing, the lexicon of Coptic is striking for its eminently Greek nature. Loanwords from Greek to Coptic constitute a phenomenon that has long attracted attention[94] and that, through its scope, has aroused surprise, although it was not until recently that a team undertook the compilation of a *Database and Dictionary of Greek Loanwords in Coptic*[95]—"a long-term project with a projected lifespan ranging through 2024," which shows the complexity of the phenomenon and the extent of the undertaking! While awaiting the results of this program, which will produce precise statistics for the first time,[96] we must limit ourselves to noting the strong presence of Greek words in Coptic texts from all periods, which contrasts strikingly with their very low number in Demotic.[97] With the exception of the few sequences that are purely and simply taken from Greek,[98] these words are adapted to the Coptic morphology and phonology to such an extent that it is more appropriate to speak of "Copto-Greek" terms.[99] The proportion of Greek words within a Coptic text, which clearly fluctuates depending on the time period, the type of writing, and the personality of the author, revolves around 20 percent,[100] but may

---

[94] Cf., to limit myself to a few recent studies, Kasser 1991b; Oréal 1999; Reintges 2001; Richter 2008b, 72–76; Clackson 2010, 77–84; Zakrzewska 2015, 194–96; Zakrzewska 2017, 117–19.

[95] http://research.uni-leipzig.de/ddglc/index.html.

[96] While waiting, it is possible to consult Förster 2002, who lists the Greek words in Coptic documents.

[97] Clarysse 1987.

[98] See appendix 2, **1**, 20–21: ⲫⲩⲥⲉⲓ/φύσει "by nature, naturally." Here, the term is declined, which indicates—since Coptic did not have declensions—that it is a loaned Greek expression not adapted in Coptic. Compare the English usage of *par excellence*.

[99] This is the term used by Kasser 1991b. The same author, in his French publications, uses the word "grécopte," which he coined. Richter 2008b, 72–76, speaks of "Graeco-Coptica."

[100] This number, which is very approximate, is given by Kasser 1991b, 217, and reused by Fournet 2009c, 431; and Clackson 2010, 77. According to Kasser, the total number of Greek words within the Coptic vocabulary is around 40 percent. Oréal 1999, 290, speaks of "un cinquième du vocabulaire copte attesté," although it is likely that she is reusing the number given by Kasser for the proportion of loanwords within a text.

climb to above 70 percent in certain texts.[101] To use the example of the first texts that benefit from an assured date and context, in the Kellis papyri, Greek words represent 25 percent of the vocabulary in documents and 18 percent in literary texts.[102] The significance of this proportion, which seems impressive, was nonetheless downplayed recently by Ewa Zakrzewska, who, based on the Kellis materials and the comparative research of the *World Loanword Database*,[103] concluded that Coptic "could qualify as an 'average borrower,' comparable to Dutch (with 19 percent loanwords) rather than a 'high borrower' like English (41 percent). This is clearly at odds with some rather 'impressionistic' assumptions of an exceptionally high degree of Greek lexical influence on Coptic."[104]

In reality, quantitative analysis should leave room for qualitative analysis. What is striking in the loanwords from Greek to Coptic is not so much just their number, as their nature. Above all, we find very few "necessary" loanwords (whose function is to fill lexical "gaps" in the recipient language), that is, words that most often denote material or institutional realities (weights and measures, currencies, functions, titles[105]) that were imposed on society. Rather, the large majority of loanwords concern lexemes for which Coptic had an equivalent of Egyptian origin: for example, in letters from Kellis or those sent to Apa John, we find words as ordinary as ψυχή "soul," instead of which we would have expected to encounter the Coptic ϩⲏⲧ "heart" or κοσμός "world," which the Coptic ⲧⲟ communicated equally clearly.[106] These loanwords therefore appear to be arbitrary. Scholars have attempted to attribute their number to the decisive role that translation of Greek texts played at the beginning of its history.[107]

---

[101] One example is given by Kasser 1991b, 217, with a passage from Clement's *First Epistle*. Richter 2008b, 74, calculated the proportion of Greek words in the legal acts of the notary David (first half of the eighth century): it is 45.45 percent.

[102] Zakrzewska 2015, 195.

[103] http://wold.clld.org/.

[104] Zakrzewska 2015, 195.

[105] See, in appendix 2, ἀναχωρητής "anchorite" (**4**, 1; 2–3); πρεσβύτερος "priest" (**3**, 1); διάκων "deacon" (**3**, 2; 6); μακάριος "blessed," title used for the deceased (**5**, 23).

[106] See appendix 2, **2**, 8; **4**, 14; 22 for the first one, and **5**, 27 for the second one. On the equivalence between ψυχή/ϩⲏⲧ and κοσμός/ⲧⲟ, cf. Crum, *CD*, respectively col. 714a and col. 396b.

[107] Kasser 1991b, 217: "This very evident and massive presence of the Greek element in the Coptic language (as an Egyptian language) has no doubt some relation to the fact that the majority of the Coptic texts preserved today were translated from the Greek."

However, this does not account for the situation in documentary texts, which have shown a pronounced propensity to use terms of Greek origin from the beginning. In documents, even more so than in the translations of the Scriptures, the use of a Greek word rather than an Egyptian word must be considered an indicator of a personal intention or the acceptance of conventions or modes of expression that translate a collective state of mind. Therefore, these loanwords come close to what linguists call the "linguistic imaginary"[108] or the symbolic function of language; they are vehicles for the expression of a social and cultural identity.[109] In the context at hand, the high proportion of such words in our texts likely demonstrates the desire, on the part of the writer, to lay claim to a Greek cultural identity or in any event to demonstrate his active participation in this identity in more or less personal forms. Already in the earliest collections of Coptic documents available to us, the presence of these loanwords is very obvious—which indicates that a vocabulary of Greek origin established itself and was canonized, borrowed not only from Greek epistolography,[110] the rhetoric of Greek petitions,[111] and the lexicon of legal acts,[112] but also from the Greek language's Christian or philosophical literature.[113] This vocabulary testifies to a profound Hellenization and to the simultaneous desire to make this Hellenization visible in the language that was being developed.

This Hellenization goes significantly beyond the use of nouns and verbs, which could have allowed us to support the hypothesis that Coptic was an "average borrower." It touches the very framework of the Coptic language through grammatical words directly borrowed from Greek, such as negations,[114] interrogatory words,[115] conjunctions or conjunctive

[108] Regarding this concept, cf. Simonin and Wharton 2013, 112–13 and 377.

[109] Zakrzewska 2015, 194.

[110] I will limit my examples to the texts given as samples in appendix 2: ἐπιστολή "letter" (**1**, 38; **4**, 17); χαίρειν "greetings" (lit. "rejoice!") (**4**, 3–4; **5**, 2); ἀξιόω "request" (**4**, 42); ἀμελέω "neglect" in the phrase μὴ ἀμελήσῃς "don't neglect to do such and such" (**3**, 8); σπουδάζω "be zealous, make haste to do such and such" (**3**, 4) and σπουδή "zeal" (**3**, 8); maybe πιστεύω "believe" (**4**, 11) and συντομία "brevity" (**2**, 17).

[111] θλίβω "oppress" (**4**, 28); ταλαίπωρος "miserable" (**5**, 8).

[112] ὁμολογέω "acknowledge" (**4**, 21); πληρόω "complete" (**4**, 33); ὑπομένω "wait, submit to" (**4**, 32).

[113] Besides ψυχή "soul" and κοσμός "world" (cf. chapter 2, n. 106), see βοήθησις "help" (**4**, 37), ἐλπίς "hope" (**5**, 22), αἰσθάνω "feel" (**2**, 13).

[114] οὔτε . . . οὔτε "neither . . . nor" (**1**, 7).

[115] ἆρα (**1**, 10).

adverbs,[116] subordinating conjunctions,[117] and prepositions[118]—not to mention adverbs.[119] It is somewhat as though the logical toolkit and the demonstrative framework of the Egyptian language had been Hellenized.[120] These types of loanwords are the most striking proof of the profound Hellenization of the inventors and first users of Coptic, and have led certain scholars to see this language as being "a bilingual language variety,"[121] in other words, a "pidginized" language.

The degree to which Egyptian was in fact Hellenized has nonetheless been called into question by Ewa Zakrzewska: far from the product of the coexistence of Egyptian and Greek, "early Coptic," on her account, is "a deliberately constructed literary idiom" created "to discuss new ideas with like-minded, well-educated 'counter-culturists.'"[122] She believes that loanwords are "more likely an expedient for constructing novel literary conventions than a reflection of actual bilingual speech."[123] Can we therefore conclude that we are dealing with a semblance of Hellenization, in other words, an artificial Hellenization? While she is right to caution us against confusing a language (*Sprache*) with its written expression (*Schriftsprache*), which is nothing but a restricted and often very deceptive manifestation of it, I believe that this analysis goes too far. First of all, it comes up against the statistics that she herself provides: if we are dealing with a "constructed literary idiom," how is it possible that, to use the case of the Kellis texts, Greek words are less numerous in literary texts (18 percent) than they are in documents (25 percent), which are more likely to resemble actual speech than literary texts? The documents in question are private letters, which must not be completely severed from the oral uni-

---

[116] ἀλλά "but" (**2**, 14; **3**, 8), γάρ "for" (**3**, 3; **4**, 21; **5**, 5; 17); μέν "on the one hand" (**4**, 34); δέ "and, on the other hand" (**1**, 29; **5**, 8); οὖν "so" (**3**, 4); ὅμως "nevertheless" (**1**, 13; **5**, 8).

[117] ἐπειδή "since" (**2**, 14; **4**, 34; **5**, 12; 16; 19); εἰμήτι "except" (**2**, 21).

[118] κατά "according to" (**1**, 4; **3**, 7; **4**, 5; 38; **5**, 3).

[119] μάλιστα "most of all, especially" (**1**, 8); ταχύ "quickly" (**1**, 31); καλῶς "well" (**5**, 13); ἀληθῶς "truly" (**3**, 3).

[120] Cf. Lefort 1948. This conclusion is criticized by Oréal 1999, 293–94, whose argument only takes into consideration literary sources. However, even if these types of words are "just as likely to be borrowed as other elements of the lexicon" ("tout autant susceptible[s] d'être emprunté[s] que d'autres éléments du lexique," 294), it is the number that is surprisingly high in Coptic. The fact that these types of loanwords pertain more to vocabulary than syntax does not decrease their significance.

[121] Reintges 2001, 233.

[122] Zakrzewska 2015, at 188 and 192. Cf. also Zakrzewska 2016.

[123] Zakrzewska 2015, 197.

verse, despite the inevitable epistolary rhetoric and the artifice implied by all written communication. Around ten years ago, Sebastian Richter attempted to unearth sequences in documents that were likely to belong to the spoken register; but the latter too were riddled with "arbitrary" loanwords.[124] Even though the Hellenization of Coptic must have been embedded much deeper in its written manifestations than in the spoken language, it is nonetheless a phenomenon that must have had an effect on the different forms of the language, at least among certain population segments. Moreover, we must not underestimate the impact that a "deliberately constructed idiom" may have over time and on all speakers, from the moment that it is diffused and becomes standard. Yet the phenomenon is sufficiently omnipresent, regardless of the varieties of texts, their contexts, and their period,[125] for this not to be interpreted as the reflection of language practices standardized at the collective level. And these were profoundly marked by Greek.

To return to written practice, the mark of Hellenization is also observed in the diplomatics (or external and structural aspects) of the documents that we have. The structure and the formulary of the first-generation letters (fourth century) show that people did not attempt to break the link with Greek culture nor to compete with it; rather, they forged a Coptic epistolography by molding it on the Greek one: the prescript (the initial part of the letter that gives the name of the writer and the recipient) was often written in Greek, as was the final closing formula (which played the role of our signature), with the addresses written on the reverse side, visible only once the letter had been rolled up.[126] In cases when the prescript was not entirely in Greek, it was written in Coptic adopting the Greek

---

[124] Richter 2006. In these sequences, note the Greek words σκεύη "recipients," γνώμη "approval," χρεία "need," μέρος "part," χολή "wrath," ἀπολογίζω "pay," κωλύω "hinder," οὐ δίκαιον "it is not fair." It can also be noted that grammatical words are absent from them. Nonetheless, the sequences are too short and devoid of their context.

[125] Compare the percentages given by Richter 2008b, 73, for the diverse categories of loanwords in a discourse by Shenoute (who was nonetheless a champion of Copticity and sworn opponent of Greek culture, despite having practiced it) in the fifth century and in a legal act written in the eighth century: they are almost identical. In them, we find between 7 and 9 percent grammatical words (prepositions, conjunctions, particles).

[126] Cf. letters **1** and **2** in appendix 2. The addresses on the back are in Greek in the letters from Kellis, from the Hathor monastery, and perhaps from the Apa John archive: that of *P.Neph.* 15 (**3**) is unquestionably in Greek, but that of *P.Lond.* VI 1921 is not clear (it could be understood as Greek: π(αρὰ) Παειοῦς Δικαίου); that of *P.Lond.* VI 1920 is Copto-Greek: ⲁⲡ(ⲁ) ⲡⲁⲓⲏⲩ ϩⲟⲙⲟⲗⲟⲅ(ⲏⲧⲏⲥ) παρὰ Ἀ[τρῆτος). The only

model to varying degrees: it calqued the Greek formulary, or alternatively, following a formulation typical of Egyptian ("A (is) who writes to B"),[127] used the verb χαίρειν "greetings! (lit. rejoice!),"[128] typical of the Greek formulary. It is interesting to note that the latter construction is found in letters from the Hathor monastery, Nag Hammadi, or Douch, places that are quite distant from one another, which shows that a formulary created at an earlier stage and that had spread in competition with other formularies was standardized. However, even in their attempts to forge an epistolary diplomatics specific to the spirit of the Egyptian language, by maintaining the χαίρειν from Greek letters, the first Coptographs wished to set it within the long tradition of Hellenism.

As we can see, Coptic certainly constitutes the best proof of the in-depth Hellenization of the people who developed it and used it during its first stage. In a departure from the language of pagan Egyptians and its writing, which was practiced from time to time in the still operating sanctuaries, these people developed—according to coordinating mechanisms and instances that are yet unknown—a writing that owed almost everything to Greek and that gave form to a language that claimed to have a Greek dimension. Their aim was not to forge a new instrument for themselves with which to proselytize non-Greek-speaking populations, as has often been thought—this would not come until later—but rather to construct, in their own language, a cultural heritage that would be experienced as an extension and complement of the Greek heritage, while providing themselves with a specific communication tool that, just like Greek, would be "a prestige variety," a language that would also serve as a reference without competing with Greek. The profile of these inventors and promoters of the first version of Coptic is fundamentally bicultural and directs us toward those Christian Egyptians who started to establish themselves as elites in villages and cities. While fully participating in Greek culture (in which they were trained by receiving a literary, rhetorical, and philosophical education via the Greek method, and to which they

endorsement in Greek from the Apa John could be that of *P.Ryl.Copt.* 275 () *locus sigilli* ιωνηc θεολω[]).

[127] I do not believe, as does Choat 2007b, 676, that the creation of this formula has something to do with any type of pagan milieu. In this case, it is a structure specific to Egyptian, one of those particularities of language that correspond to a mindset (*ingenium linguae*!) and that did not require the continuity of a written tradition to re-emerge after an interruption.

[128] For instance, letters **4** and **5** in appendix 2. Cf. Choat 2007b and 2010. See more generally Biedenkopf-Ziehner 1983.

contributed by financing the copying of Greek manuscripts), these elites wished to appropriate it for themselves, within their own language.[129]

These first Coptographs were sufficiently Hellenized to continue to adapt to the traditional context without difficulty and not to attempt to lay claim to a broader use of Coptic in society. Considering that they were bilingual, the use of Coptic in legal acts must have appeared to be perfectly useless—especially since these acts were written by professionals who were accomplished in Greek and who had mastered the intricacies of Roman law, in a state context confined to the exclusive use of Greek. Coptic nevertheless "escaped"—dare I say—from its first users, and later spread to other milieus, the same ones that are documented by the monastic archives from the fourth century. Its social facies was modified at the same time as the institutional framework started to shift, making the official use of Coptic possible one day or another.

[129] On these elites, cf. chapter 1, n. 45.

CHAPTER 3

The Rise of Legal Coptic and the Byzantine State

In 549/550, Callinicus son of Victor, an inhabitant of a large village in Middle Egypt, Aphrodite, arbitrated in a dispute between a man named Dioscorus and Joseph the currier: the former rented fields to the latter, who did not use them, thus depriving Dioscorus of the income that he was expecting. After each of the parties had made a statement and the plaintiff, Dioscorus, had provided proof to support his accusations, the arbitrator pronounced his decision, ruling in favor of Dioscorus and requiring Joseph to compensate him. This settlement was put into writing and ends with the arbitrator's subscription in his own hand: "I, Callinicus son of Victor, have issued this decision."[1] This act, transmitted by a still unedited papyrus that I noticed in the Berlin collection [Fig. 19],[2] may seem trivial—just another conflict between farmers! Yet it is exceptional in its language: while Callinicus's subscription is in Greek, as one would expect, the report of the settlement that precedes it is entirely in Coptic. This papyrus is the first Coptic text lying outside of the narrow domain of epistolary communication or of accounts—if we exclude Kellis's failed attempt at an acknowledgment of debt, which is in fact subordinated to the epistolary scheme[3]—and it inaugurates a long series, initially with a certain degree of discretion during the period preceding the Arab Conquest of 641–42, and then ostensibly and increasingly systematically following it.

The proliferation of legal and administrative documents in Coptic is not surprising after the Arab-Muslims severed the link between Egypt and the Greek-speaking Byzantine state. From then on, nothing prevented the

[1] P.Berol. 11349, l. 51–52: Καλλίνιḳ[ος]| [Β]ịκτọρος ἐπειδέδωκα τοῦτ[ο]ν τὸν ὅρον.

[2] Cf. Fournet 2010b, 130–32. Its date may also be, with less likelihood, 534/535. The papyrus will be edited with the other settlements from the archives of Dioscorus by Anne Boud'hors and myself.

[3] Cf. chapter 1, pp. 18–20.

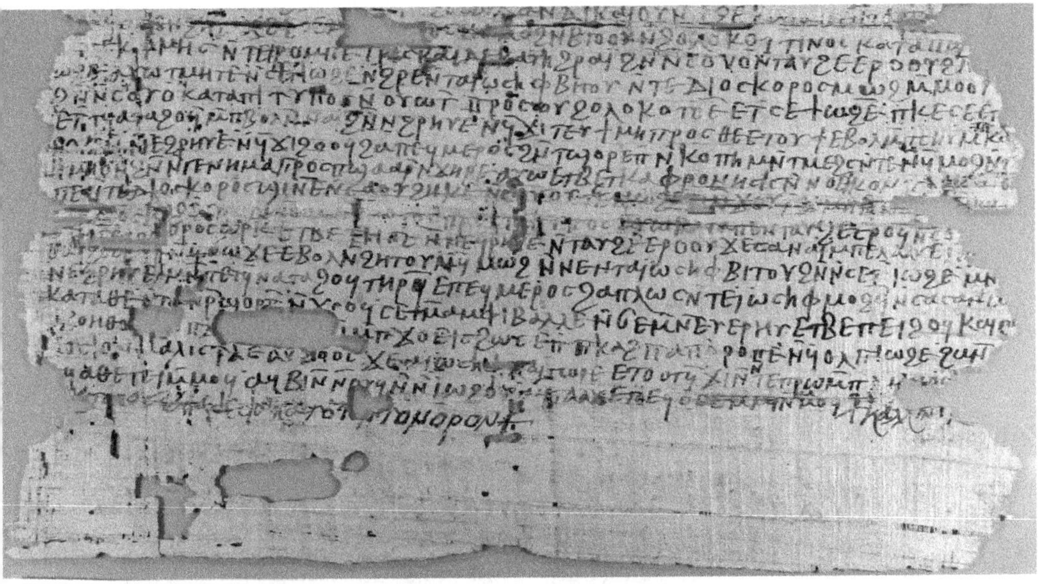

Fig. 19. The end of a settlement in Coptic with the subscription of the arbitrator in Greek (P.Berol. 11349): this is the oldest Coptic text that is not a letter. (Reproduced by permission of the Staatliche Museen zu Berlin—Ägyptisches Museum und Papyrussammlung [photo: Jean-Luc Fournet].)

more visible use of Coptic in society. However, the question is, why did this movement begin almost a century earlier, and in particular following the three centuries of silence that I discussed previously?[4]

Coptic Legal Documents Finally Come into Being!

Legal acts in Coptic prior to the Arab Conquest are not so numerous. If we stick to documents that are dated or are more or less precisely datable, we obtain around fifteen of them.[5] Rather than going over them one by one, which would be tedious, I will seek to present this corpus according

[4] "How are we to explain the appearance of these texts which pose the thorny problem of the legal status of the Coptic language?" I raised this question in my conclusion to the section that I dedicated to the relations between Coptic and Greek in Fournet 2009c, 441, venturing a few hypotheses, but without proposing real answers to them. The question was also raised by MacCoull 2007b, but the answers provided are somewhat impressionistic, and are not based on in-depth analysis of the sources.

[5] Cf. appendix 3. From this point on, I will cite papyri based on the bold number that they are given in this appendix.

to several criteria, that is, their type, the transaction that they enact, their writer, and their provenance.

Diplomatic Types: Notarized Documents That Are Not Actually Notarized

What types of documents are these? The oldest three (**1–3**) are of a somewhat particular genre, because they are not legal acts *stricto sensu* but rather reports of private settlements under the authority of an arbitrator chosen by opposing parties. I have already presented the oldest of these texts at the outset of this chapter (**1**). The other two come from the same archive, that of Dioscorus of Aphrodite, and are written by the latter, who, after having been a party to the oldest dispute, acted as an arbitrator in the others. One of them dates from 566/567 (**2**), the other from 28 October 569 (**3**). Insofar as these texts, as well as possibly **9** (from the seventh century), do not stipulate penalty clauses that would be binding on the parties, they are not true dispute resolutions (*dialyseis*), and it is questionable whether they had legal validity.[6] It has been stated on numerous occasions that they did, but without any supporting evidence.[7] Out of precaution, I will limit myself to seeing them as semilegal texts, given that they are contained within the framework of the legal system without being provided with mechanisms to permit their proper execution. The obligation that they impose—we will have the chance to return to it—is of a psychological and social nature.

The following examples (**4–8** and **10–16**) appear to be genuine documents modeled on Greek documents, from which they borrow Greek denominations, and frequently are referred to by the Greek word *asphaleia*, "guarantee," a vague term that nonetheless insists on the binding nature of the act for the declarant. They also follow the structure of such acts, with, depending on the case, an initial Christian invocation, dating according to the reign of the emperor, a protocol presenting the parties, the transaction

[6] The penalty clause is undoubtedly absent from **1**, which is completely preserved, and **3**, the end of which is complete. The case of **2** is more doubtful: its end (and therefore the arbitrator's decision) has been lost. The penalty clause is nevertheless present in dispute resolutions (*dialyseis*): see, for instance, Gagos and van Minnen 1994, 45–46. For the *dialysis*, cf. Gagos and van Minnen 1994 with a list of texts, 121–27, to be supplemented with Kreuzsaler 2010, 23n27.

[7] For example, Papaconstantinou 2008, 82: "[les arbitrages] avaient donc potentiellement une validité juridique, et celle-ci ne devait pas être fondamentalement altérée lorsqu'ils étaient rédigés en copte," but nothing supports this claim.

itself, the subscription of the declarant and those of the witnesses, and finally the writer's subscription. In some of them, the writer's subscription follows the model of a notarial *completio* (subscription by which a notary concludes an act and assumes responsibility for its writing): it is written either in Greek[8] or in Coptic, at times following the Greek formulary.[9] The majority of documents provided with these *completiones* have thus been considered notarized acts. Yet, with the exception of a land lease contract from the 580–90s that I recently coedited,[10] in which the writer of the document, George, signs as a tabellion (= notary), the others are never signed by notaries in the strict sense of the term: when they specify their function, they refer to themselves as scribes (of the village)[11] or deacons.[12] In other words, contrary to what may have been thought, these are pseudonotarial private acts.[13] This can be demonstrated by the *completio* of two wills drawn up within a short time of one another, by two superiors of the Monastery of St. Phoebammon (to which I will return in chapter 4), one written in Greek and the other in Coptic:

- *P.Mon.Phoib.Test.* 1, 89 (end of the 610s): δι᾽ ἐμοῦ Πέτρ̣ο̣υ̣ νομ̣ικ(οῦ) Ἑ̣ρ̣μώ̣νθ(εως) ἐγένετο "Done by me, Peter, notary of Hermonthis."
- *P.Mon. Phoib.Test.* 2 (**14**), 183–85 (634): ± 8 ⲡⲡⲣⲉⲥⲃⲩⲧⲉ]ⲣ̣ⲟⲥ ⲛ̅ⲁⲡⲁ ⲕⲟⲗⲗⲟⲩⲑⲟⲥ ϩⲛ̅ ⲉⲣⲙⲟⲛⲧ ⲡⲁⲓ̈ ⲉⲧⲟ̅ ⲛ̅ⲅⲣⲁⲙⲙⲁⲧ(ⲉⲩⲥ) ⲉⲡⲕⲁⲥⲧⲣⲟⲛ ϫⲏⲙ̣ⲉ [ⲕⲁⲧⲁ ⲡⲟ]ⲩ̣ⲉϩ ⲥⲁϩⲛⲉ ⲙ̅ⲡⲛⲟⲩⲧⲉ ⲁϥⲕⲉⲗⲉⲩⲉ ⲛ̅ϭⲓ ⲡⲑⲉⲟⲫⲟⲣⲟ̅ⲥ̅ ⲛ̅ⲉⲓⲱⲧ ⲉⲧⲟⲩⲁⲁⲃ ⲁⲡⲁ ⲃⲓⲕⲧⲱⲣ ⲡⲁⲛⲁⲭⲱⲣ(ⲏⲧⲏⲥ) [ⲁⲓⲥⲙⲛ †]ⲇ̣ⲓⲁⲑⲏⲕⲏ ⲁⲩⲱ ⲁⲓ̈ⲥϩⲁⲓ̈ ϩⲁⲣⲟ̅ϥ̅ ϫⲉ ⲙ̣ⲛ̅ ϣϭⲟⲙ ⲙ̅ⲙⲟ̅ϥ̅ ⲡⲣⲟⲥ ⲧⲉϥⲕⲉⲗⲉⲩ̣ⲥ̣ⲓⲥ "[Done by me, . . .], priest of Apa Kollouthos in Ermont, scribe of Djeme

[8] See **4**: δι᾽ ἐμοῦ Γεωργίου σὺν Θ(εῷ) ταβελλ(ίωνος) ἐγρ(άφη); **5**: δ̣ι̣ ἐ̣μ̣ο̣ῦ̣ Ἰωσὴφ ἐγρ(άφη); **16**: δι᾽ ἐμοῦ Ἀγάθωνος γραμμα(τέως) ἔγρ(αψα) κατὰ τὴν κέλευσιν τοῦ ἐνδοξ(οτάτου) Βαραχια βασιλεισκος (l. βασιλίσκου).

[9] **12**: ϩⲓⲧⲟⲟⲧ ⲇⲁⲛⲓⲏⲗ ⲁⲡⲓ̈ⲉⲅⲅⲣⲁⲫⲟⲛ ϣⲱⲡⲉ; **13**: ϩⲓⲧⲟⲟ̅ⲧ̅ ⲇⲁⲛⲓⲏⲗ ⲁ†ϩⲟⲙⲟ[ⲗⲟⲅⲓⲁ ϣ]ⲱ̣ⲡⲉ, modeled on the Greek formula διὰ τοῦ δεῖνος . . . ἐγένετο, also attested in Edfu (cf. *Byz.Not.* 16).

[10] **4** (see chapter 3, n. 8).

[11] **6** (γραμμ(ατεύς)); **11** (ⲡⲥⲁϩ ⲛⲧⲓⲙⲉ); **14** (ⲅⲣⲁⲙⲙⲁⲧ(ⲉⲩⲥ)); **16** (γραμμ(ατέως)).

[12] **9**.

[13] Kovaric 2014, 489: "explizit 'private' Dokumente"; 491: "'pseudo-notariellen' Urkunden." Technically, we are dealing with *cheirographa* "chirographs" (lit. "note of hand"), documents drawn up in an epistolary form by the party contracting the obligation. The latter is supposedly required to write himself, but often the writing was entrusted to a third party. The advantage of the chirograph is its simplicity, and without the intervention of a professional scribe, the fact that it can be freely implemented. Its disadvantage is its mediocre value as legal documentary evidence.

> according to the commandment of God, the theophoric Holy Father Apa Victor, the anchorite, asked me to write this will and I wrote for him because he is unable, at his request."

The writer of the Greek will is a notary (*nomikos*), whereas that of the Coptic one is a village scribe. This difference is too systematic to be the result of chance. It could be interpreted as evidence of a difficulty in finding professional notaries capable of writing in Coptic, as did the tabellion George, at a time when the Coptic notarial profession was not yet well established. Yet it may also be due to a difference in status between a Greek and Coptic legal document, which is not easy to assess, precisely because of the counterexample of the land lease contract drawn up by the tabellion George, which shows that at a very early date, there did exist Coptic acts drawn up by real notaries.

Even though these documents were not written by notaries, they nonetheless attempted to copy Greek notarial acts by seeking, as we have seen, to follow their diplomatics, to the point of introducing the elements most typical of a notarized act, which are the initial divine invocation,[14] the regnal dating,[15] and the notarial-type *completio*.[16] This propensity for mimicry is not easy to interpret either: does it contribute to an acknowledgment of the legal inferiority of Coptic acts, attempting to compensate for it through the imitation of Greek acts?[17] Or, as is more likely, is it evidence of a notarial practice that was in the process of finding and establishing itself, naturally by basing itself on the Greek model?

Types of Transaction: Restraint Was Still Necessary!

Let us take a look now at the types of transactions that are established by our documents. The majority of them consist of relatively unimportant transactions: a land lease, a sale on delivery (a type of loan where people

---

[14] **7**, **13**, **14**. On these invocations, see *CSBE*², 99–109.

[15] **7**, **10**, **14**. The obligation of the tabellions to start their acts with regnal dating (and not just indictional dating) was legislated by Justinian in his *Novel* 47 from 537: cf. Feissel 1996 and *CSBE*², 43–54.

[16] Cf. just above.

[17] Likewise, the frequent use of the *asphaleia* "guarantee" to designate these acts could be motivated by a desire to lay claim to a validity superior to that which they truly had or which people recognized them to have, according to a process that pertained mutatis mutandis to a Coué method (which uses the repetition of self-fulfilling prophecies, supposed to lead the subject's adherence to the positive ideas that he imposes on himself).

commit to make repayment in kind), an acknowledgment or settlement of debt, and an agreement concerning a former deed. They concern quantities of goods of little value, with the noteworthy exception of a sale of flax for future delivery (**11**), for an amount of thirty-six golden *solidi* (a large amount!) [Fig. 25]; a declaration concerning an inheritance (**13**), which involves the house and other properties owned by the declarant; and a marriage contract (7), the subject of which is no less than the daughter of the declarant [Fig. 21]! The first two exceptions can be explained by their date—I will come back to this point. It is more difficult to justify the third, but it must be acknowledged that this document also presents singular irregularities (the father giving his daughter did not appose his subscription, which theoretically makes the act illegal). The fact that the transaction is of a family nature, in other words, the fact that the parties (the father and the son-in-law) were, from that point onward, bound by strong family ties, could be the beginning of an explanation. Lastly, note the exception that an act from Pathyris (**16**) could constitute, and which was believed to be the freeing of a slave. This text is actually entirely singular, starting with the figure of the declarant: he is the "King of the nation of the Blemmyes,"[18] a nomadic population that originated in Nubia, a community of which established itself for a time in Pathyris, whence this papyrus originated. The content of the text is, moreover, quite enigmatic.[19]

Coptic was also used for the first time for another type of legal act, of a slightly different nature: wills. Our only example of a will prior to the conquest is that of Victor, the elder of the Monastery of St. Phoebammon [Fig. 34], who left nothing less than the monastery and its outbuildings to his successor (**14**). The monastic context of this will, to which the act of acknowledgment of ownership rights for the same monastery (**6**) is also tied, explains the exceptional nature of these texts, the discussion of which I will keep for the last chapter.

Barring these exceptions, none of our texts constitute legal acts with a definitive scope. It was not until the Arab Conquest that the first genuine property sales and other documents regarding property transfers appeared.[20] Before that time, Coptic was normally used for temporary transactions (leases, loans), and somewhat timidly. We clearly have the impression of a transitional phase. Yet we must avoid thinking that the legal use of Coptic during this transitional phase is explained through

---

[18] ⲡ̄ⲣⲣⲟ ⲙ̄ⲡϩⲉⲑⲛⲟⲥ ⲛ̄ⲛⲃⲉⲗϩⲙⲟⲟⲩⲉ.

[19] See commentary in *FHN* III, 1212–13.

[20] **19** (sale of a plot of land); **20** (sale of a plot of land); **21** (exchange of properties). The first two could also date from the Persian period (see below).

the infrafamilial nature of transactions, as some scholars have claimed in the past regarding some of these transactions,[21] and as the marriage contract that I discussed above (7) may lead us to believe.[22] Despite their small number, our texts clearly demonstrate that this is not the case and that Coptic was used for professional transactions or for transactions between parties, which did not belong to the same family.

The Writers: Digraphic Scribes

The profile of the writers of these texts is informative. One might assume that people used Coptic due to their inability to write in Greek. Admittedly, we have seen that the first legal documents were almost never drawn up by real notaries, who, as we know, had the habit of switching constantly between the two languages, translating the information provided by the Egyptian client into Greek and retranslating it into Egyptian for the latter once the act was finalized.[23] By contrast, our documents were written by professional scribes who were not notaries or who were ordinary individuals acting as scribes. These scribes, and above all the latter group, might not have had the same bilingual capabilities, and were reduced to using Coptic. Yet this is not the case. The first legal acts were produced by truly bilingual people—more specifically, digraphs—as the profile of three of them illustrates.

The most ancient of these is Dioscorus of Aphrodite (sixth century), who, as we have seen, officiated in two settlements that he also put into writing (**2–3**) [Fig. 20]. Dioscorus is well known by papyrologists through the archive that is named after him and which, in addition to these Coptic texts, has provided many texts notarized by him,[24] as well as Greek

[21] MacCoull 1995, 346, on Coptic papyri in the archive of Phoebammon and Kollouthos.

[22] We note that 7 is written in Coptic, whereas the same writer would use Greek for four other transactions of a professional nature (cf. chapter 3, n. 27).

[23] See *P.Oxy.* LXIII 4397, 188–88; *P.Münch.* I 13, 71; and *P.Mon.Phoib.Test.* 1, 13–15 and 70 (= *P.Lond.* I 77, 12–14 and 69 [p. 231]), cited in chapter 1, nn. 57–58.

[24] Although he never subscribes them as a notary. As a result, he probably worked at a notary office in Antinoopolis without having had real notary status. The position he occupied was given to him during his "exile" in the provincial capital. In order to get it, he wrote a poem to the governor with the following conclusion: ψῆφον δọ́ṭε γẹ τὴν π̣αροῦσαν, δέσποτα· | σ̣[τ]ῆσọν ṭọ̀ṿ [οἰ]κ̣έτην νομικὸν τῇ πόλει "Give this following order, O master: give your servant a job of notary in the city" (*P.Aphrod.Lit.* IV 12, 31–32).

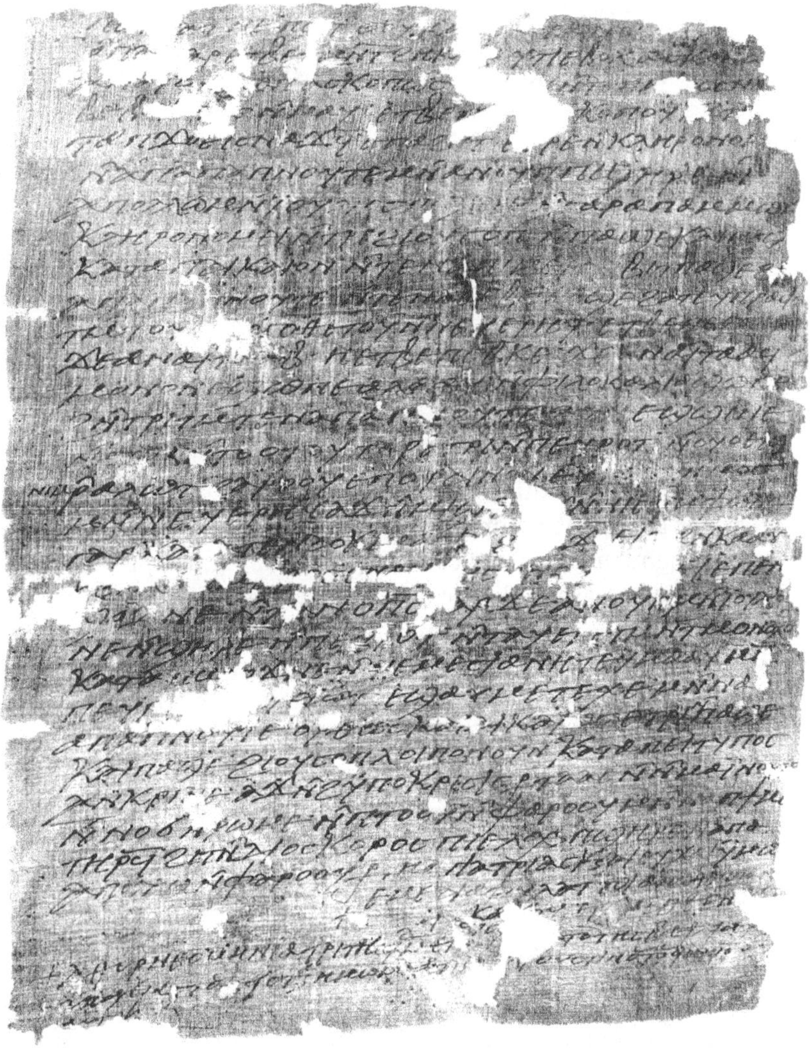

Fig. 20. End of the settlement written in Coptic by Dioscorus of Aphrodite in 569 (P.Alex. inv. 689). The last lines are in Greek ("May the holy Trinity and your prayers protect me from all harm. Greetings in the Lord" followed by the date), which is evidence of Dioscorus's bilingualism. (Photograph courtesy of Alain Lecler [IFAO].)

poems.[25] He is considered to be one of the best examples of bilingualism and biculturalism in Egypt during Late Antiquity, capable as he was of switching from Coptic to Greek with such ease—even though his poems bear witness to the limits of his poetic talents, which have triggered the

[25] For a recent summary of these archives, cf. Fournet 2008. His poems and part of his library are edited in Fournet 1999.

irony of modern scholars. I will not dwell on this figure, who has already been thoroughly analyzed.

The second is Paul son of Megas, originally from This.[26] Not only is the Coptic marriage contract (7) written by him [Fig. 21], but also four other contracts in Greek.[27] His literacy was far from perfect: he must have been more at ease with Coptic, given the numerous errors that he makes in Greek. Furthermore, he had a poor grasp of the graphic conventions regulating the use of Greek, which he confused in a way that a professional scribe would not do.[28] He was nevertheless deemed to be sufficiently bilingual by his acquaintances for them to use his services as a scribe in both languages.

Our last digraph is Daniel son of Heracleides, who wrote, in Coptic, an agreement concerning a former deed (**12**) and a declaration about inheritance (**13**), as well as, in Greek, the sale of a house.[29] Unlike Paul, Daniel had a perfect grasp of both languages,[30] their formulary,[31] and the graphic conventions governing them in this type of text. Consequently, for Greek he used upright cursive, which was required during this period for legal documents, whereas for Coptic he used sloping uncial, which was also typical of contemporary documents [Fig. 22]. Therefore, when switching from one language to the other, he knew how to adapt the style of writing based on convention, demonstrating equal abilities in both languages, as Dioscorus of Aphrodite had sixty years earlier [Fig. 7].[32]

---

[26] *Byz.Not.*, 95. Cf. MacCoull 1995, 347–49.

[27] *SB* I 4503 = *P.Paris*, p. 254, *P.Berl.Schmidt* 1 (This, 605 or 607 [*CSBE*², 125]), service contract; *SB* I 4543 = *P.Paris*, p. 256, *P.Berl.Schmidt* 2 (Panopolis, 613), sale on delivery; *SB* I 4505 (This, 606 or 608 [*CSBE*², 125]), sale on delivery; *P.Paris* 21 (This, 616), house sale contract.

[28] For example, for Greek, he uses straight cursive (*SB* I 4503), sloping cursive (*SB* I 4504, 4505), and sloping uncial (*P.Paris* 21); for Coptic, sloping uncial (*CPR* IV 23). We do not expect the use of sloping uncial in a Greek legal text. Was it because he was more comfortable with this style of writing and preferred to use it for the text that required the most care and attention due to its importance (sale contract)? This explanation would confirm his unequal bilingualism, with a better grasp of Coptic.

[29] *SB* I 5112 (Edfu, 618) [*P.Lond.* II, *Facsimiles*, pl. 120–23].

[30] The mistakes that we observe in the three texts are, apart from minor phoneticisms, *lapsus calami*.

[31] We saw, chapter 3, n. 9, that he adapts the formulary of the Greek notarial *completio* in Coptic.

[32] Cf. chapter 1, p. 16.

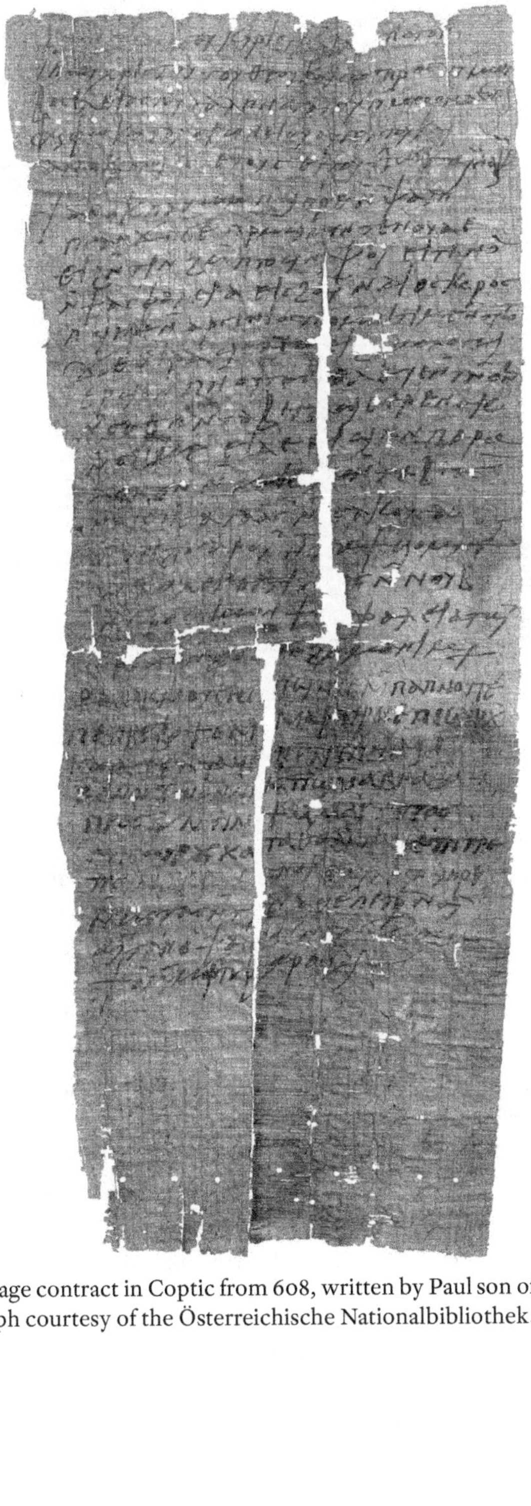

Fig. 21. A marriage contract in Coptic from 608, written by Paul son of Megas (*CPR* IV 23). (Photograph courtesy of the Österreichische Nationalbibliothek.)

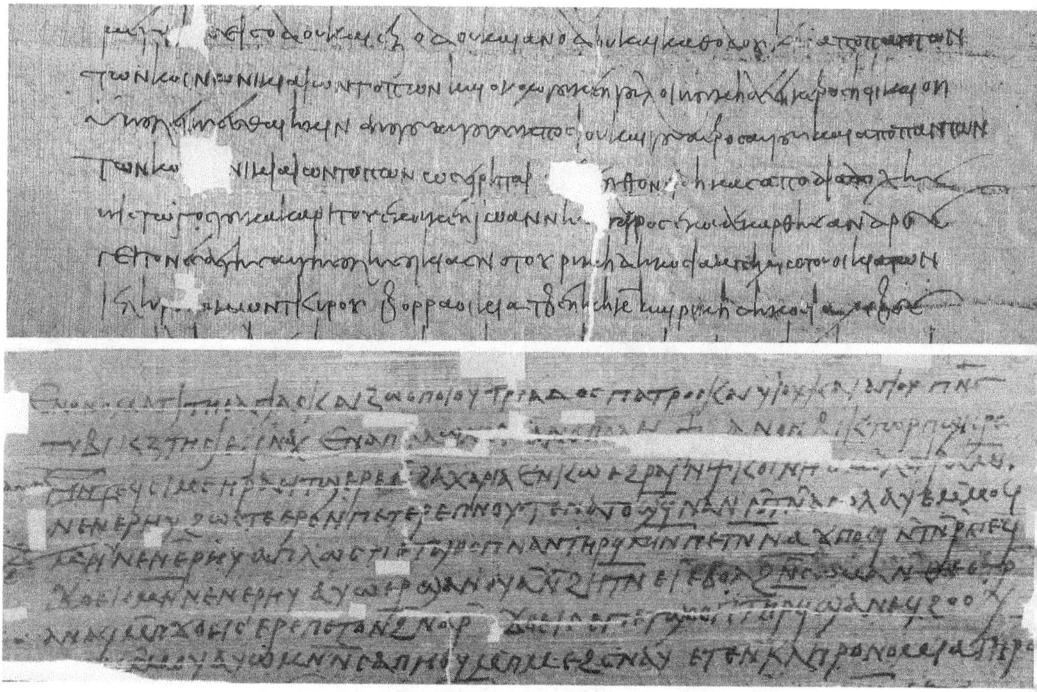

Fig. 22. The two scripts of Daniel: the upright cursive used for Greek documents (top: *SB* I 5112 [Edfu, 618], extract from *P.Lond.* II, *Facsimiles*, pl. 121) and the sloping uncial used for Coptic documents (bottom: extract from Salomons and Sijpesteijn 1987, pl. 7 [Edfu, 618]).

These three figures[33] provide information on this milieu of digraphs, which must have continued to grow, and in which they played the role of mediators capable of transferring Greek forms and models into Coptic. This process of transfer is particularly visible in the work of Paul [Table 1].

He begins the two documents with a divine invocation and regnal dating in Greek (the prestige of Greek was a requirement for these sections, as they placed the document under divine and imperial oversight), introduces the transaction with the same Greek verb, and adds a penalty clause whose Coptic version is modeled on the Greek. The only differences are related to the prescript (the nominative-dative sequence cannot be ren-

---

[33] I also could have added Damianus, the writer of **6**, who we know translated texts into Greek according to *P.Stras.Copt.* 24, or, as an example of someone active following the conquest, Apa Rhasios (*Byz.Not.*, 31), the writer, in Coptic, of **21**, an exchange of properties, and in Greek, *P.Mich.* XIII 662 (Aphrodite, 645 [Bagnall and Worp 2004, 249, 252 correcting *BL* VII 116]).

TABLE 1

	Greek (*SB* I 4503)	**Coptic (7)**
invocation + regnal dating	ἐν ὀνόματι τοῦ κυρίου καὶ δ[ε]σπότου Ἰησοῦ Χριστοῦ τοῦ Θεοῦ καὶ σωτῆρος ἡμῶν, βασιλείας τοῦ γαληνοτάτου ἡμῶν δεσπ(ότου) Φλ(αουίου) Φωκᾶ τοῦ αἰωνείου Αὐγούστου καὶ Αὐτοκράτορος ἔτους ἕκτου, Θὼθ α, ἰνδ(ικτίωνος) ῑδ	ἐν] ὀνόματ[ι] τοῦ κυρίου καὶ δεσπότου Ἰη[σοῦ Χριστοῦ] τοῦ Θεοῦ κα[ὶ σ]ωτῆρος ἡμῶν, βασιλείας το[ῦ γαλη]νοτ(άτου) ἡμῶν δεσπό[του] τῆς οἰκουμέ(νης) Φλ(αουίου) Φωκᾶ τοῦ αἰωνείου Α[ὐ]γούστου καὶ Αὐτοκράτορος ἔτους τρίτου, Τῦβι ιε, ἰνδ(ικτίονος) δεκάτης.
prescript	ὁ δεῖνος τῷ δεῖνι χαίρ(ειν)	ⲁⲛⲟⲕ X ⲉⲓⲧⲁⲛⲟ̄ ϯⲁⲥⲫⲁⲗⲉⲓⲁ ⲉⲓⲥϩⲁï ⲛ̄-Y
body	ὁμολογῶ . . .	ⲉⲓϩⲟⲙⲟⲗⲟⲅⲉⲓ . . .
penalty clause	ἐπὶ τῷ ἐμὲ παρασχ(εῖν) σοι ὑπὲρ λ[όγ]ῳ προστίμου χρυσ(ίου) ν[ο(μισμάτιον)] α	ⲉⲡⲓ ⲧⲱ ⲁⲣⲟⲓ ⲛ̄ⲧⲁϯ ϣⲟⲙⲛ̄ⲧ̄ ⲛ̄ϩⲟⲗⲟⲕⲟⲧⲧⲓⲛⲟⲥ ⲛ̄ⲛⲟⲩⲃ ⲛ̄ⲡⲣⲟⲥⲧⲓⲙⲟⲛ
final clause	*stipulatio* clause (εἰς τ(ὰ) προγεγραμμ(ένα) πάντ(α) ἐ[περωτ(ηθεὶς)] ὡμο(λόγησα))	validity clause (ϯⲁⲥ̣ⲫⲁⲗⲉⲓⲁ ⲧⲁï ⲟⲣϫ̄ ⲥⲟ ⲛ̄ϫⲟⲉⲓⲥ ϩⲙ̄ ⲙⲁ ⲛⲓⲙ)

dered similarly in Coptic, which must articulate the names of the two parties with a verb, as in letters) and the final clause (the former Roman clause of *stipulatio*,[34] which no longer meant anything for an Egyptian, was replaced in Coptic by the validity clause, which emphasized what could be considered to be the weak point of Coptic legal acts[35]).

Based on their bilingualism, these digraphs, who were veritable transmitters, played a decisive role in reinventing a legal language following a three-century break. As in the transition phase from 550 to 642, this reinvention necessarily went through the imitation of Greek forms before becoming more autonomous.[36] It also must have become more established

[34] Cf. chapter 1, p. 26.

[35] Cf. chapter 3, n. 17.

[36] In Fournet 2016, 124, I give an example of this emancipation from the domination of Greek through an expression that we find in Coptic acts from Aphrodite with an interval of approximately sixty years: ϩ́ⲙⲧⲡⲉⲇⲓⲁⲥ ⲛ̣ⲛⲉⲙⲛⲧ ⲙⲡⲓⲧⲓⲙⲉ ⲛⲟⲩⲱⲧ ϫⲕⲱⲟⲩ | [ϩⲙⲡⲕ]ⲗⲏⲣⲟⲥ ⲛⲁⲛⲟⲩⲡ "in the western *pedias* of the (aforementioned) village

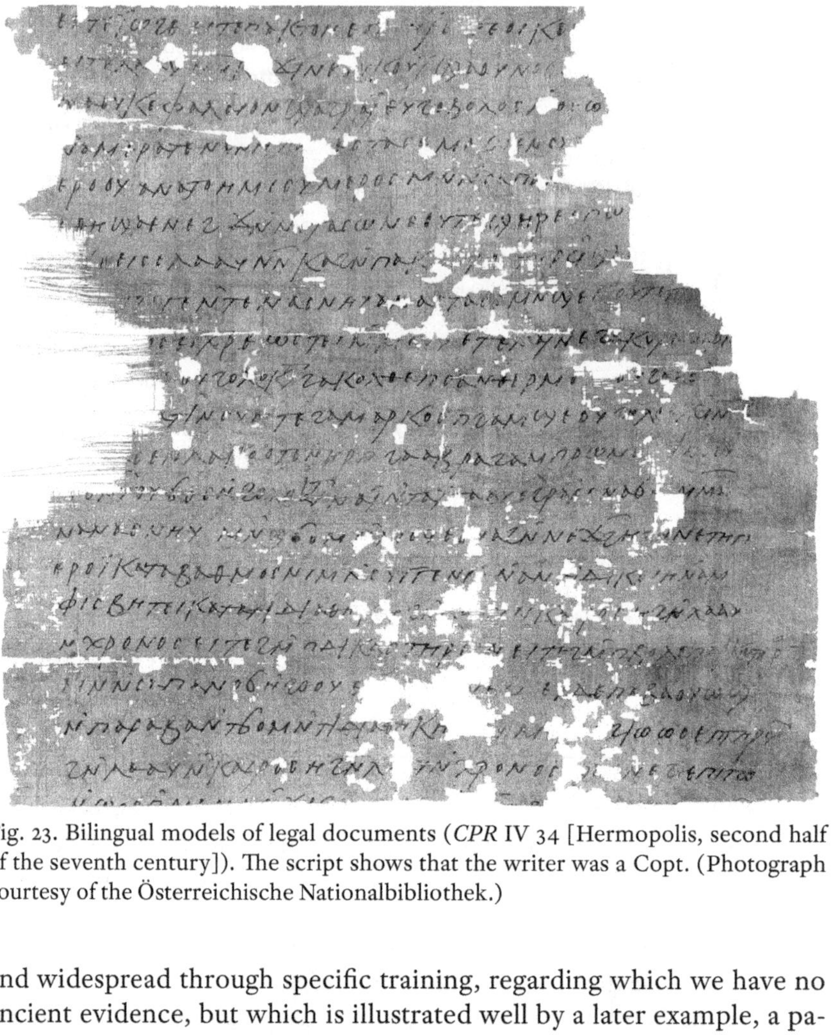

Fig. 23. Bilingual models of legal documents (*CPR* IV 34 [Hermopolis, second half of the seventh century]). The script shows that the writer was a Copt. (Photograph courtesy of the Österreichische Nationalbibliothek.)

and widespread through specific training, regarding which we have no ancient evidence, but which is illustrated well by a later example, a papyrus from Hermopolis written in the second half of the seventh century [Fig. 23].[37] This sheet contains a Coptic will on the recto, in a writing that suggests that it is an exercise and not a real document. This is confirmed

of Djkōou in the *klēros* of Anoup" (P.Lond. inv. 2849, 13–14 [4]) becomes, in *SBKopt.* III 1369, B, 12–13 (**21**), ϩⲛ ⲧⲕⲟⲓⲉ ⲛⲛⲉⲙⲏⲛⲧ ⲛⲡⲧⲓⲙⲉ ⲛϫⲕⲱⲟⲩ | ϩ̣ⲛ̣ⲡ̣ⲉⲕⲗⲏⲣⲟⲥ ⲛⲁⲛⲟⲩⲡ: the Greek word πεδιάς is replaced by its Coptic equivalent.

[37] *CPR* IV 34 + 177: the front side, *CPR* IV 177 (= *SBKopt.* IV 1808), gives a will in Coptic; the reverse side, *CPR* IV 34 (= *P.Rain.Unterricht* 112 descr.; *P.Rain.Unterricht Kopt.* 223; *SBKopt.* IV 1806), the excerpt of multiple documents. Till has dated the front side to the seventh century and the reverse side to the eighth century—dates that were accepted in *P.Rain.Unterricht* 112 and *P.Rain.Unterricht Kopt.* 223. It is likely

by the other side, which gives a series of excerpts from three legal documents[38] in the Greek and the Coptic versions. It was through these types of exercises that bilingual scribes were trained, and it was also through these bilingual models that a Coptic legal *koinē* copying the Greek model and developing a common terminology was forged.

Provenances: The Exclusivity of the South

To what milieus did these digraphs belong? The majority of our documents originate from villages, but a third of them—which is not negligible—were written in urban milieus: the second settlement (**2**) was drawn up in Antinoopolis, the capital of the Thebaid province, a city moreover known for the vibrancy of its Hellenism;[39] the two documents by Daniel (**12**, **13**) were written in Apollonopolis (Edfu); and two other acts (**8**, **9**) were produced in Syene in the far south of the Thebaid. This shows that, at the time, and contrary to the image that epistolary documentation from the fourth and fifth centuries has conveyed, Coptic was no longer restricted to the countryside and monasteries; it was also used among the urban upper classes. For example, one of the two parties to the Antinoopolis settlement was a certain Phoebammon and his sister Victorine, the children of the deacon John, who was the steward of the large estate of Athanasius, Duke of the Thebaid (the supreme authority in that province).[40] Victorine is also known for the copy of her marriage contract (in Greek), with her comfortable dowry being listed across more than ten lines (jewelry, clothing, upholstery fabrics, furniture, and multiple ceremonial objects).[41] However, the small size of our corpus cautions against overusing these scant pieces of information.

---

that the two sides are more or less contemporary. The use of the *gentilicium* Αὐρήλιος (*CPR* IV 34, 15; 43) rather favors the seventh century, a date that I retain along with M. R. M. Hasitzka (*SBKopt.* IV 1806, without argument). On this papyrus, cf. Richter 2010, 50–51; and MacCoull 2002–3.

[38] These probably contain two sales on delivery, a genre whose success we saw among the first Coptic legal documents.

[39] Cauderlier 1978; Bagnall 1993, 104.

[40] *P.Lond.* V 1709 (**2**), 3–5: ⲓ̈ⲱϩⲁⲛⲛⲏⲥ ⲡⲇⲓⲁⲕⲱ[ⲛ]| ⲡⲁⲡⲟⲡⲣⲟⲛⲟ̣ⲏⲧⲱⲛ ⲛ̄ⲡⲏⲓ̈ ⲉⲧⲧⲁⲓ̈ⲏⲩ ⲛ̄ⲡ`ⲡ´ⲁⲛⲉⲩⲫⲏ̣[ⲙⲟⲥ]| ⲛ̄ⲡⲁⲧⲣⲓⲕⲓⲟⲥ ⲁⲑⲁ̣ⲛ̣ⲁ̣ⲥ̣ⲓ̣ⲟ̣ⲥ̣ "John the deacon, the ex-superintendent of the honoured house of the famous patrician Athanasius." On Duke Athanasius, see Fournet 1999, I, 330–32; and Kaiser, forthcoming.

[41] *P.Cair.Masp.* I 67006 v° (Antinoopolis, after 566 [cf. *P.Lond.* V, p. 131]), trans. Russo 1998, 150–51.

One point is nevertheless striking for its exclusivity and the fact that it is unlikely to have been the result of chance discoveries: all of our documents come from the Thebaid province, that is, the south of Upper Egypt. The fact that there is nothing from the northern provinces of *Aegyptus* and *Augustamnica* that form the Delta is normal, given that papyri were destroyed by the humidity of this region. Yet there is also nothing from the province of *Arcadia*, which has provided so many papyri from the villages of the Fayyum and the city of Oxyrhynchus. The latter holds the record, by far, for the most papyrus discoveries, with tens of thousands of texts.[42] Our texts start to appear to the south of Oxyrhynchus: Hermopolis and its district (**5**, **11**, **15**), Antinoopolis (**2**), Aphrodite (**1**, **3**, **4**), Panopolis and its district (**7**, **10**), the Theban area (**6**, **14**), Pathyris (**16**), Apollonopolis/Edfu (**12**, **13**), and Syene (**8**, **9**). It may be hazardous to seek a single explanation for this exclusivity of the south, given that our documents come from so many different milieus (cities, towns, monasteries), which each pose varied problems. Yet we cannot ignore the fact that southern Egypt has a certain specificity, which could at least partially explain this gap in the distribution of the languages in our documentation. For a long time, the south had cultivated much deeper roots in Egyptian tradition than the north, which was more quickly and more fully Hellenized and subjected to the influence of Alexandria. Without going so far as to say, as some scholars have done, that "in the north of Egypt, Hellenism reigned, and in the south, pure Egypt,"[43] and without overlooking what certain cities such as Hermopolis, Antinoopolis, and above all Panopolis contributed to late Hellenism,[44] we are forced to recognize that the south, more so than other parts of Egypt, constituted a hotbed for opposition to the state (it was responsible for

[42] Note that since Diocletian, the province of Egypt had been divided into two provinces or eparchies (Gr. *eparchia*), with *Aegyptus* being governed by a prefect sitting in Alexandria and the Thebaid governed by a *praeses* sitting in Antinoopolis. These two provinces were subdivided into seven provinces during the sixth and seventh centuries: *Aegyptus* I and II (the western half of the Delta), *Augustamnica* I and II (the eastern half), *Arcadia* (Fayyum and the upper portion of the Nile Valley, formerly *Heptanomia*), and the Upper and Lower Thebaid (lower part of the Valley), without counting the two Libyas.

[43] C. D. G. Müller cited by Wipszycka 1992b, 105n65 ("Souvent on a dit qu'au nord de l'Égypte règne l'hellénisme et au Sud l'Égypte pure").

[44] For Hermopolis, cf. Drew-Bear 1992; van Minnen and Worp 1993; or *P.Sorb.* II 69, 63–65; for Antinoopolis, cf. Cauderlier 1978; Bagnall 1993, 104; for Panopolis, cf. Cameron 1965, 472; Miguélez Cavero 2008, 198–210. These last two studies show more generally the role taken on by the Thebaid in Greek poetic culture during Late Antiquity.

the large-scale rebellions that Egypt had undergone since the Hellenistic period). Moreover, outside of the large cities, it was the source of a form of anti-Hellenism or indifference to Hellenism, symbolized in the figure of Shenoute († ca. 465[45]), the famous abbot of the White Monastery not far from Panopolis [Fig. 24]. "It is your idiotic poets," wrote Shenoute with regard to Greek culture and its literary heritage, "who have learned pointless things and songs that are not useful and demonic teachings that make us stray far from the truth, and not only them, but those who make the voice of birds, having filled books, for them and you, with fluttering words, like: *tigs, tigs* and *kouax, kouax* [here, he is citing *The Frogs* by Aristophanes while thinking of *The Birds*!]."[46] Although such a vision of Egypt, which can quickly descend into caricature, has been contested by Ewa Wipszycka, in that it can, if taken too literally, validate the erroneous idea of the existence of Egyptian nationalism,[47] there are numerous signs, if not of antagonism, then at least of a discrepancy between the north and south in terms of Hellenism and Romanization. This discrepancy is also present at the linguistic level—even more so given that the ambiguity of the term *hellēn,* which means both "Greek" and "pagan," does not always help to distinguish between linguistic and religious identities. This aspect still has to be studied, although for the Theban area, the rarity of Greek documents and their high degree of idiomatic expression with respect to the remainder of Egypt has already been noted.[48] An illustrative example, despite its much later date than our first Coptic legal documents, seems to me to be provided by a papyrus from the Theban village of Djeme from 711/712.[49] This "legal agreement" written in Coptic is subscribed by the parties (the abbot of the Monastery of St. Phoebammon and the officials

[45] Emmel 2002, 97–98; and Emmel 2016.

[46] Amélineau 1907, 386. Cf. ibid., ccxl–ccxli; and Erman 1894. However, it is necessary to keep in mind that all the while criticizing Hellenism (above all as a catalyst of paganism), Shenoute knew Greek, and "his style, which has no Coptic precedent, is clearly based on a careful study of the scholastic rhetoric of his times, i.e., the Greek rhetoric of the 'second sophistic' " (Orlandi 1986, 69).

[47] Wipszycka 1992b, 105.

[48] Garel 2015, I, 173. The latter remarks that legal documents involving transfers of ownership were "rédigés en copte, sur un modèle grec qui ne se rencontre que très peu au même endroit" (176). She links *P.Herm.* 25 and 31 to the Theban region, stating that they are exceptionally written in Greek because "des personnes extérieures à la région de Memnonia sont impliquées" as opposed to *P.KRU* 105 (**6**) written in Coptic, "qui est à peu près contemporain mais dont la validité est restreinte à une échelle locale" (175–76).

[49] *P.CLT* 5. Till 1962, 43–44.

Fig. 24. Portrait of Shenoute in the north lobe of the church of the Red Monastery (sixth century). (Reproduced by permission of the American Research Center in Egypt, Inc. [ARCE]. This project was funded by the United States Agency for International Development [USAID]. Photograph: Arnaldo Vescovo)

of Djeme) and eleven witnesses. All signed in Coptic, except for one who preferred to do so in Greek ("I, Jacob son of Isaac, *pragmateutēs*, from Justinianopolis in Lower Egypt, I am witness (to this document)"[50]), and he is from the Delta!

[50] L. 159: Ἰακὼβ υἱὸς Ἰσὰκ πραγματευτὴς ἀπὸ τῆς Ἰουστινιανῆς (l. Ἰουστινιανοῦ) πόλεως τῆς κάτο (l. κάτω) χώρας μαρτηρῶ (l. μαρτυρῶ). This Justinianopolis is known by another papyrus from the sixth century (*CPR* I 30, 37: τῆς Ἰουστινιαν[οῦ] πόλεως τῆς κατὰ Ἀλεξ(ανδρείαν)). It is very likely necessary to identify it with the Cynopolis

Although this issue still awaits full scholarly treatment, I am inclined to think for the moment that the Thebaid province, and above all its southern portion, which had always been distant from the nerve center of official Egypt, Alexandria the Greek, and which, with the exception of its large towns, was less profoundly subjected to its influence in institutional, religious, and cultural matters than were Lower Egypt or Arcadia, might have been the breeding ground for a cultural affirmation, which has, among other things, expressed itself at the level of language through the more rapid and more intensive use of Coptic. It is significant that in texts from the Pachomian corpus (fourth century) presenting monks of Alexandrian origin or from a Greek-speaking culture, Coptic seems to be called "the language of the Thebans,"[51] whereas Greek continued to be considered "the language of the Alexandrians" long after the Arab Conquest. We find this stated in the colophon of a Coptic manuscript copied in Edfu in 951.[52] The development of the "monastic Thebaid" and the major intellectual

---

from the Busirite nome, which, under Justinian, took the name of Nova Justiniana (Mansi 1743, 391 to compare with 175; reference omitted by Calderini, *Diz.*, *s. v.* Κυνῶν πόλις 2, but given by Jones 1937, 557).

[51] Cf. Ammon, *De sanctis Pachomio et Theodoro epistula* 17 (ed. Halkin 1982, 105): καὶ λοιπὸν νοοῦντά με τὴν Θηβαίων γλῶτταν καλέσας ὀνομαστὶ καὶ πλησίον ἑαυτοῦ στήσας ἔλεγέ τινι Θηβαίῳ μονάζοντι Ἀμμαῒ τοὔνομα "and he called me by my name as I know the Theban language and, getting closer, he said to a Theban monk named Ammaï (. . .)." See also *Vita prima*, 94 (ed. Halkin 1932, 63), which tells of how Theodore the Alexandrian, staying in the Pachomius monastery, learned the "Theban language" from an old man: καὶ οὕτως ὑποδεξάμενος αὐτὸν ἐποίησεν εἶναι ἐν οἰκίᾳ παρά τινι ἀρχείῳ ἀδελφῷ εἰδότι τὴν ἑλληνικὴν γλῶσσαν εἰς παραμυθίαν Θεωδώρου, ἕως μάθῃ ἀκοῦσαι τὴν Θηβαϊκήν "After having welcomed him, Pachomius placed him in a house close to an old brother, who knew the Greek language, as a guide for Theodore, until he learned to understand the Theban language" (trans. Torallas Tovar 2010, 40). Cf. also *Vita tertia*, 146: καὶ ἐσπούδασε Θηβαϊστὶ μαθεῖν αὐτὸν τῇ χάριτι τοῦ Χριστοῦ "he tried dutifully to learn the Theban language in the grace of Christ" (trans. Torallas Tovar 2010, 40n95). However, the expression Θηβαίων/Θηβαϊκὴ γλῶττα is ambiguous: some scholars believe that it just means "Coptic" (Festugière 1965, 208: "jusqu'à ce qu'il pût comprendre la langue thébaïque (copte)"; or Torallas Tovar 2010, 39: "Coptic, called here 'Theban language' "—nonetheless, the latter, 40n97, considers that the "Theban language" is equivalent to "Sahidic Coptic").

[52] British Museum Or. 7022 fol. 59 verso: "Pourot [. . .] is responsible for the production of this book and gave it to the church of St Mercurius of Edfu, Apollonia in the language of the Alexandrians" (trans. A. Alcock, "Colophons of Coptic Manuscripts. Part Two: Upper Egypt," 8, downloadable from https://www.academia.edu/30978332/Colophons_of_Coptic_Manuscripts_Part_Two_Upper_Egypt; text in Budge 1914, 100, trans., 355).

role played by Shenoute in the region, who, from the fifth century, sought to establish an original literary production in Coptic, may nevertheless be enough to explain the zeal driving this language in this part of Egypt.

Chronology: Coptic and the Political Situation

Nonetheless, the geographical explanation alone is not sufficient. We need to take a closer look at the chronological distribution of our first texts, in particular those that represent transactions whose importance seems to set them apart from the others. All the while remaining conscious of the somewhat random nature of the distribution of such a small amount of textual evidence, we may venture to observe a clear increase in 600–610, which was maintained at more or less the same level during the decade of 620–30. Moreover, it was during these two decades that transactions with a much greater value than the other documents were established (**7**, the marriage contract from 608; **11**, the sale of flax for future delivery from 625 for an amount of thirty-six golden *solidi*; **13**, the declaration about the inheritance of a house and other properties in 627). I am inclined to relate these two peaks and the writing of these three acts to the political situation in Egypt: the first decade of the seventh century was marked by the overthrow and assassination of the emperor Maurice by Phocas (602), inaugurating a period of instability that had a direct effect on Egypt. In 608, Nicetas was sent to Alexandria by his uncle Heraclius the Elder, exarch of Africa, to win Egypt over to his cause, which meant removing the usurper Phocas, before he could send out troops under the command of the *comes Orientis* Bonosus to retake Egypt. If we are to believe the *Chronicle* of John of Nikiu, these events sowed disorder in Egypt, kindling rivalries between factions, which "gave themselves shamelessly to pillage and murder."[53] Concerning the second period, it was marked by the Sasanian Conquest (619–29), which removed Egypt from Byzantine authority. The sale of flax for future delivery from 625 (**11** [Fig. 25]) even directly alludes to the new masters, because the beneficiary is a man named Perēs Kōsrōi (a very Persian name, Pērōz Xusrō), and the parties to the contract were required to swear an oath to respect the contract "on the health of the King of Kings."[54]

[53] John of Nikiu, *Chronicle*, CVII–CIX, esp. CIX, 15: "Taking advantage of the war between Bonosus and Nicetas the artisan guilds of Egypt (i.e. the Greens) arose (and) perpetrated outrages on 'the Blues,' and gave themselves shamelessly to pillage and murder" (trans. Charles 1916, 175).

[54] L. 20: [ⲡ]ⲉ̣ⲩ̣ⲭ̣ⲁ̣ⲓ̣ ⲙⲡⲉⲣⲟ ⲛⲉⲣⲱⲟⲩ.

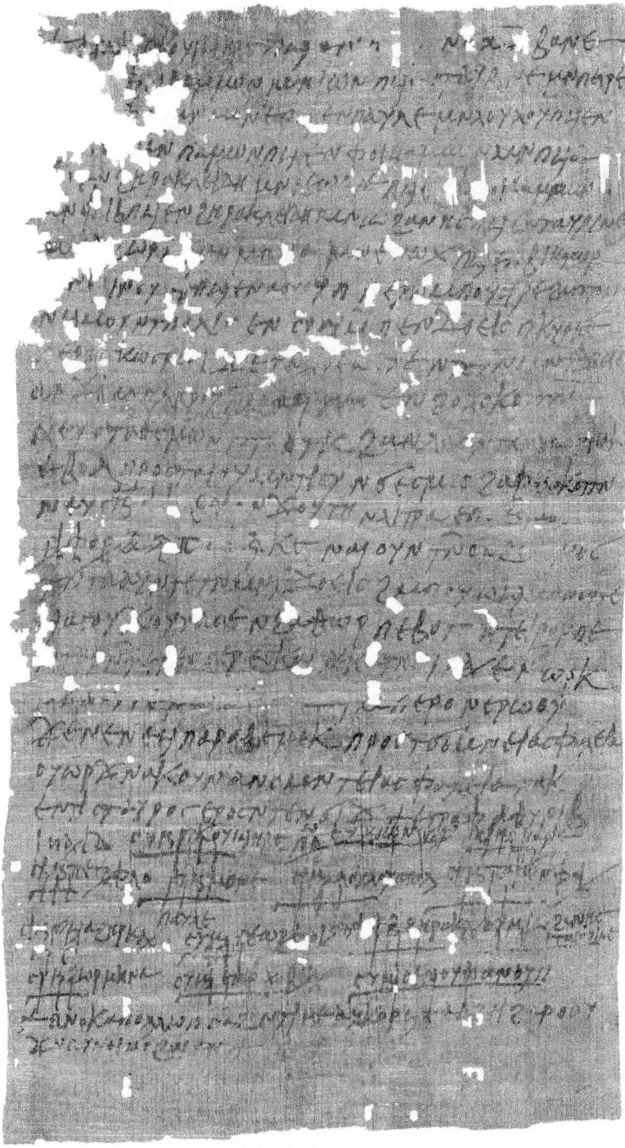

Fig. 25. A sale of flax for future delivery from 625 contracted between the inhabitants of the village of Pousire and the Persian Perēs Kōsrōi (*CPR* IV 48). (Photograph courtesy of the Österreichische Nationalbibliothek.)

The political instability that led to the undermining of the state apparatus and of its grip on the country, and above all, during the Sasanian period, the break with the Greek-speaking Byzantine state—which relaxed the burdensome obligation that the prestige of Greek as the language of the state represented—contributed to widening the gap that had been timidly opened. It encouraged the population who so desired to make more intensive use of Coptic for contracts that did not need to be limited to confidential or minor transactions.

In the end, the geographical and chronological approaches share the fact that they are both oriented toward an explanation that attributes the development of Coptic legal documents to the withdrawal, weakening, or failure of the state, and therefore to a reduction in the pressure that it could exert on the population in terms of linguistic constraints in the domain of legal writing. While there is a certain truth to this analysis, in reality the problem is more complex and must be reconsidered within the cultural and institutional context of the sixth and seventh centuries.

Greek Culture Losing Its Momentum

Is it possible that the ascendance of legal documentation in Coptic fits more generally within the context of the decline of Greek and more broadly of Hellenism (by that word, I mean Greek-language culture in all its forms)? This question is all the more difficult to answer in that, if there was indeed a decline to the benefit of Coptic, it cannot easily be observed in looking at the proliferation of the archives of large estates and churches during the period of interest to us, and later, starting in the mid-seventh century, of administrative archives. Both of these sources document very restricted milieus, where Greek was required, and are not indicative of the more general situation. Moreover, the slower development of Coptic papyrology, whose sources have not been edited at the same pace as Greek papyri, makes statistical analysis a highly uncertain undertaking, to say the least. We will nevertheless attempt such an analysis. A graph of the number of documentary and literary papyri in the two languages shows that the development of the first Coptic legal texts in 550–642 corresponds to a period that witnessed the acceleration of the increase in Coptic documents in general (which would become the majority between the seventh and eighth centuries) and the reversal of the relationship between Greek and Coptic literary texts [Graph 1]. The methodological objections that I have just mentioned also force us to consider that the documentation available to us necessarily underestimates the Coptic element, and I suspect that the two curves of Greek and Coptic documents should intersect

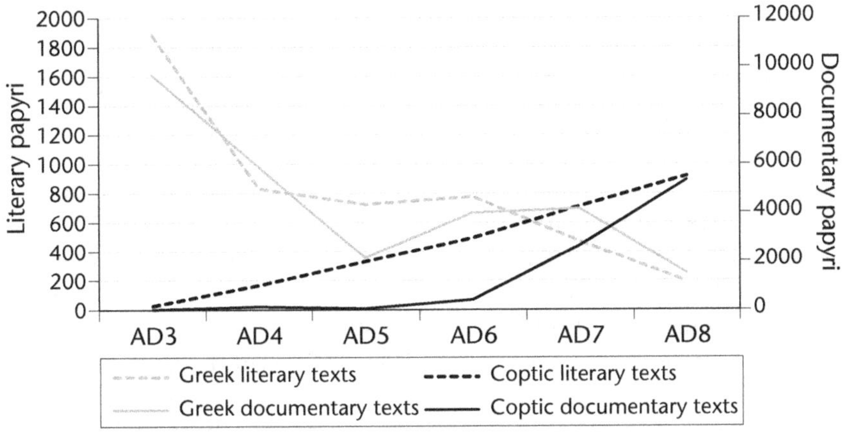

Graph 1. Quantitative comparison of literary and documentary papyri in Greek and Coptic.

earlier, between the sixth and seventh centuries.[55] Therefore, it was during that period that a change in the linguistic-cultural paradigm occurred. Of course, Greek culture continued to be a model and a benchmark, although in milieus that were receding, despite being overrepresented in the documentation.

These milieus were above all those of cities, which had always been a stronghold for Hellenism and had played the role of the promoter of a constantly renewed literary culture. However, despite their continued strategic position in the institutional framework, "we have the impression that the cities of the sixth century had difficulties functioning, and that the state had to place them under the responsibility of large landowners or under direct management or assistance. From that point on, some scholars grant them only a formal existence."[56] While the new administrators of cities still belonged to the Greek-speaking elite and continued to feed the operation of the book production market,[57] this transfer could only

[55] The discrepancy between literary texts and documents in terms of chronology is due to the fact that the former have been studied more systematically than the latter and that the datings proposed by the editors for literary Coptic texts are even more approximate than for literary Greek texts.

[56] Gascou 2004a, 419: "En somme, on a l'impression que les cités du VIe siècle éprouvent des difficultés à fonctionner et que l'État a dû les mettre à la charge des grands propriétaires ou les placer en gestion ou en assistance directe. Certains savants ne leur concèdent plus alors qu'une existence formelle."

[57] Morgan 2003.

undermine the vitality of literary creation, which was so strongly linked to municipal life and which, in turn, stimulated the remainder of written production. Furthermore, this situation was aggravated by the disappearance in the fifth century of the gymnasiums where the values of Hellenism were passed on.[58] Concretely, rhetorical or poetic works that punctuated the events and the celebrations taking place in cities became rarer after the last embers of the fourth and fifth centuries had died out.[59] We know of no other great Egyptian rhetoricians after the fifth century,[60] unlike the situation that prevailed at the same time in Gaza. As for the only Greek poet who remains accessible to us following the mid-550s, Dioscorus of Aphrodite (whom we have already discussed) used the ancient models and attempted to give his poems the character of an encomiastic production similar to that formerly produced within cities, but better to serve private interests: his praises of high officials or his poems that give the impression of having been pronounced during ceremonies[61] were in fact simply private written requests, which sometimes accompanied petitions

---

[58] Bagnall 1993, 104, believes that gymnasiums remained active for longer but recognizes that "the documentation is lacking." Moreover, we do not know what the activities of gymnasiums consisted of during the late period: cf. Meyer 1997, 695.

[59] Codex 279 from Photius's *Bibliotheca* has conserved one of the best examples of this literary production with works from the second half of the fourth century: cf. Hammerstaedt 1997 to be completed by Gascou 1998 and Miguélez Cavero 2008, 79–83. In the domain of poetry, Cameron 1965 (revised in Cameron 2016) links the decline of Greek to the Council of Chalcedon in the conclusion of his seminal article on the "Wandering Poets" of Egypt: "By then (sc. Pamprepius, born in 440) the language of Egyptian Christians had for some time been largely Coptic, and with the dominance of Schenute, who knew Greek but wrote only in Coptic, it began to supplant Greek, increasingly so after 451, when the fourth Ecumenical Council at Chalcedon condemned Miaphysitism, the religion of the Egyptian church, which signalled its severance from the Greek church by abandoning Greek as its official language. It is hardly surprising that Greek poetry could not survive the change" (Cameron 2016, 34). This is a conclusion that is somewhat outdated in its desire to attribute the decline of Hellenism to the conflict between Chalcedonians and anti-Chalcedonians (cf. chapter 2, p. 59, and chapter 4, p. 114), which does not do justice to the complexity of factors. Moreover, Colluthus of Lycopolis (fifth to early sixth centuries), the author of multiple poems, including *The Abduction of Helen*, shows that this decline occurred somewhat later.

[60] With the exception of the Alexandrines, Stephen (around 580; cf. *PLRE* III, *s. n.* Stephanus 20), and John (beginning of the seventh century; cf. *PLRE* III, *s. n.* Ioannes 254), whose works are nonetheless lost.

[61] For example, *P.Aphrod.Lit.* IV 17 (praise pronounced on the occasion of the arrival of the imperial images of Justin II), 18–20 (praise of the duke during his *adventus*).

submitted in the legal context, and which reflect a narrowing of the perspective symptomatic of the general cultural situation.[62]

Furthermore, even though a large proportion of these poems were composed in Antinoopolis, where he resided for a few years, Dioscorus was above all of rural origins. He is a characteristic example of the paradigm shift that took place during this period: villages assumed center stage in our documentation, strengthening their institutional position within the organization of the territory. At the same time, they acquired a much greater cultural significance, exemplified by hagiographic literature, which was in full development at the time: in it, saints and martyrs were often rich peasants, with Christianity "grant[ing] the rural world a new ideology and new dignity."[63] As we can see with Dioscorus, villages did not renounce Hellenism; rather, the latter progressively became more of a minority overall.

Greek culture was still very much alive, but its sphere of influence shrank as it came to be used for gradually more practical and utilitarian purposes, essentially the training of public or ecclesiastical officials. It was in the religious domain that it best survived, by renewing itself through a process synthesizing Hellenism and Christianity. However, it was also in this domain that it was the most likely to face competition from Coptic, especially since certain monastic milieus rejected the Greek *paideia*. As Ewa Wipszycka neatly sums it up, "the proliferation of churches and, consequently, of the ecclesiastical apparatus, as well as the simultaneous rise of asceticism, offered Egyptians the possibility of playing a prominent role in society without knowing Greek, something that had been unthinkable before."[64]

A Crisis of Judicial Institutions?

This cultural transformation serves as a backdrop to the emergence of Coptic legal documents, yet it fails to provide a sufficient explanation for it. Insofar as our documents have the function of affirming the rights of the individuals employing them, and therefore pertain to a legal and potentially judicial context (in the event of a breach), we can legitimately ask whether the initial cause of their appearance might lie within a change in the conditions of the functioning of justice.

---

62 Fournet 1999, I, 259–69 and 290; Fournet 2003, 108–11.

63 Wipszycka 1984, 285.

64 Wipszycka 1984, 286.

Let us consider the features of Greek papyrological documentation from the sixth to the seventh centuries, relating to the judicial domain (petitions, reports of proceedings, paralegal proceedings). The most striking phenomenon is the quite drastic drop in the number of petitions, the most prevalent documents in legal proceedings, given that it was through them that one would go to court to denounce damages suffered. During our time period, it was the governor who played the role of judge and resolved disputes in the context of the so-called *libellus* process, which was carried out, at all stages, exclusively in Greek. Very numerous during the Early Roman Empire (around 900), petitions started to disappear during the seventh century, when we find fewer than ten examples [Graph 2].[65] The last datable petition, which remains unedited at the Louvre Museum, is dated from slightly later than 629, as one can observe from an allusion to the Persians. In other words, the drop in petitions took place well before the Arab Conquest.

Moreover, reports of judicial proceedings, which constituted the procedural complement to petitions, disappeared even more rapidly than petitions: the last certain example dates from 558/559.[66]

At the same time that petitions *stricto sensu* were becoming scarcer, in the sixth century, we see a proliferation of procedures exempting the litigating parties from appearing in court—always a stressful experience. One of these corresponds to the following scenario: after having received a statement of grievances from a plaintiff (as it appears, often orally), an official sends the latter to an authority, usually at a lower level, to resolve the case through mediation or settlement. This was a less cumbersome procedure that alleviated the burden on the courts by directing plaintiffs toward an amicable resolution at a local level, by lower officials benefiting from sufficient authority to implement it.[67] Another method consisted in addressing the Bishop; this is the *audentia episcopalis*, which I will discuss in chapter 4. A farmer or an artisan could also address a petition to the owner of a large estate (called a "glorious house" in the papyri) for which he worked. These petitions, which have been categorized as "private," are explained through the semipublic status of large estates, which acquired capabilities and authority allowing their owners to be solicited, based

[65] Fournet and Gascou 2004.

[66] *P.Mich.* XIII 660 and 661 + *SB* XVI 12542 (for the date, cf. Fournet 2014, 104–5). For a list of Byzantine reports, cf. Thomas 1998, 132–33, completed by *P.Thomas*, 217n1; and Gascou 2009b, 149n1.

[67] Morelli 2007.

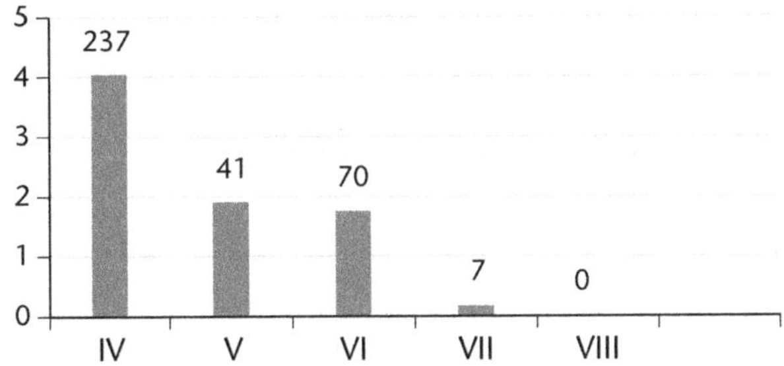

Graph 2. Petitions in Late Antique Egypt (percentages of total preserved documents).

on the mechanisms in effect for municipal magistrates or state officials.[68] Last of all, individuals in conflict could follow a completely extrajudicial route, that of amicable resolution, by contacting a mediator or private arbitrator to resolve their dispute and whose decision they would commit to observing. This was a process that suddenly became highly visible in documentation from the sixth century (there are more than twenty-five examples, compared to only five from the fourth century and nine from the fifth century) and which, as we have seen, inaugurated the use of non-epistolary Coptic around 550 (**1**).[69]

It is tempting to relate the emergence of legal Coptic to all of these phenomena, which appear to provide evidence for the retraction of state justice in favor of para- or extrajudicial processes. The use of Coptic for settlements could be direct proof of this, and the use of Coptic for the writing of contracts would be an indirect cause of it. Yet how can we relate the appearance of legal Coptic to the withdrawal of state justice? Of the two, which is the cause, and which is the effect? It could be that it was the rise of Coptic in the population and its corollary, the decline of Greek, that prompted the litigating parties to give up traditional methods (the *libellus* process) involving the obligatory use of Greek. In that case, the loss of interest in state justice would therefore be the consequence of the Egyptians' aspiration to obtain justice in their own language without going through Greek-speaking intermediaries. The opposite can also be ventured: there may have been a crisis of legal institutions forcing the population to resort to extrajudicial proceedings, which made the use of Coptic possible. In this case, the rise of Coptic in our documentation would be the result of the retraction of state justice.

[68] Gascou 2004b.

[69] List available in Gagos and van Minnen 1994, 121–27, to be completed by Kreuzsaler 2010, 23n27.

It was the second hypothesis that A. Arthur Schiller put forward in a famous article from 1971, "The Courts Are No More," in which he claimed that the courts had literally disappeared in the sixth century.[70] Even though he went too far, to the extent of situating the beginning of the phenomenon as early as the first half of the sixth century, and even though his reasoning was tainted—as was commonly the case among scholars at the time—with a "feudalist" vision of Byzantine society that accentuated the antagonism between Egyptians and Greeks, he did put his finger on the problem.

Dieter Simon fought these views in a paper that he presented the same year at the Thirteenth International Congress of Papyrology in Marburg.[71] There he provided irrefutable proof that the legal system continued to function as before, all the while recognizing the drop in the number of proceedings. This is only partially explained through the development of settlements (the number of which he underestimated[72]); other reasons probably played a more determining role, including the fact that some matters may have been dealt with by large landowners themselves, and, above all, the preference given to officials' justice without going through the costly and constraining *libellus* process. Moreover, the execution clauses in contracts guaranteeing creditors the help of the administration encouraged people to look to the administration, given that it was provided with a significant expedient, namely prison, the threat of which was more frightening than a summons before a court. Simon's reasoning, more soundly backed by documentation, is much more convincing, even if he is not always very attentive to the chronology of the documentation, which he tends to treat as a whole and thereby fails to perceive the distinct erosion of the legal system at the end of the sixth century.

It is necessary to step out of the vicious circle to which the opposition between state justice and extrajudicial proceedings is condemning us. An arbitration led to the establishment of a *dialysis* or deed of dispute settlement signed by both parties, the breach of which could be brought before the courts. Moreover, the documentation shows that attempts to resolve a conflict amicably often took place *after* initial proceedings were started, as if the legal process were a means to put pressure on the adversary into amicably negotiating or respecting the decision of a settlement.[73]

---

[70] Schiller 1971.

[71] Simon 1971.

[72] Simon 1971, 651.

[73] Kelly 2011, 271.

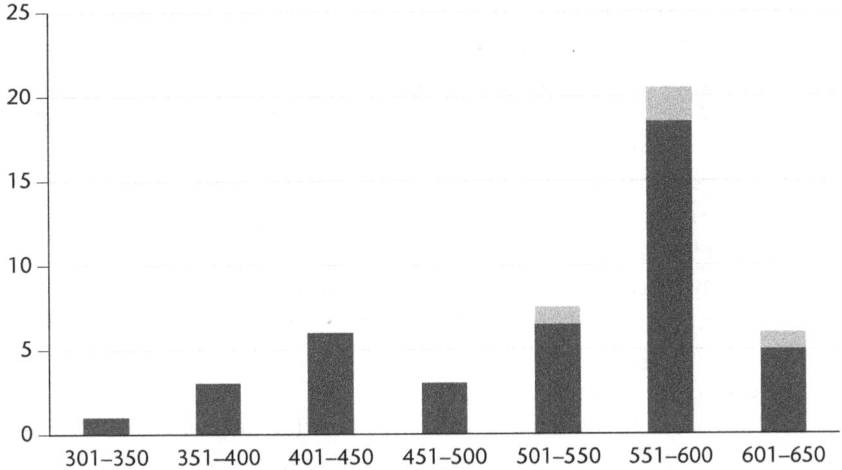

Graph 3. Settlements in Greek (dark gray) and Coptic (light gray).

I would be more inclined to dissociate the drop in the number of petitions from the increase in settlements, which is attested at the time when petitions were still numerous, attesting to the proper functioning of the *libellus* process [Graph 3]. The development of settlements is explained, on the one hand, by the very nature of this process, which was less costly and did not necessarily involve traveling. Settlements were also more discreet and better suited to the family nature of the majority of disputes (particularly during inheritances), while also being preferred by individuals who did not have a good grasp of Greek and who wished to avoid having to go through the ordinary process in which each stage (petition, hearing) involved the obligatory use of Greek. On the other hand, the disappearance of petitions is of another nature: it can be explained by the recourse to other forms of justice, not necessarily private settlements, but also the justice of large landowners, the mediation by the bishop, or settlements conducted by lower officials at the request of their superiors without a proper legal hearing. It is possible—but not inevitable—that the use of these other forms of justice resulted in a crisis in the legal system, especially during the first decades of the seventh century. The latter were marked by political instability and Sasanian domination, which, without having rendered state institutions inoperative, nonetheless modified their functioning.

The documentation and its chronological distribution seem to favor the idea of a process in two stages, each of which played a role in the development of Coptic.

(1) During the first stage, the increasingly widespread use of private settlements, starting as of the first half of the sixth century, stimulated the use of Coptic: the more informal nature of settlement hearings, where each party expressed itself freely without the intermediary of a lawyer, and at which there was only the arbitrator chosen by the parties, who was often a friend, the parties themselves, and their supporters (witnesses), encouraged the use of the language most natural to them, not requiring them to submit to the imperative of Greek, as they were "among themselves." Therefore, people experimented with the use of Coptic in contexts other than epistolary relationships. The writing up of the reports of these settlements in Coptic had a secondary consequence, that of favoring the development of a legal vocabulary and contributing to disseminating the idea that Coptic was not necessarily condemned to being used for private letters only, but rather that it could have a much larger scope of use. The phenomenon of making legal Coptic autonomous was thus born. The settlements from the archive of Dioscorus (**1–3**) bore witness to this first stage.

(2) During the second stage (end of the sixth and, above all, the beginning of the seventh century), the loss of momentum—for whatever reason—of the state normative process (the *libellus* process and its corollary, Greek proceedings before the governor), and the development of less formal state proceedings (in which the petition was presented orally) must have permitted appeals in Coptic, given that they were increasingly carried out by lower-ranking officials, close to the population, which contributed to legitimizing the idea that Coptic could be used in a state context.

Justice in Coptic

This incorporation of the indigenous language by the administration is a phenomenon that is still little known and poorly documented. However, evidence of it is already found during the first half of the sixth century, thanks to several papyri from the archives of Dioscorus. The first is an ordinance from the Duke of the Thebaid [Fig. 26], regulating the payment of court officials, which concludes with the order that it will have to "be translated into vernacular (= Coptic) and posted."[74] Yet we have no examples of these types of documents posted in Coptic. I think that in any case, it was no coincidence that the governor wanted the circulation in Coptic

[74] *P.Cair.Masp.* I 67031, 16 = *ChLA* XLI 1196, 16 (Antinoopolis, ca. 543–45 [*BL* X 33]): τῇ ἐπιχωρίῳ μεθερμηνε̣[υ]θ̣ῆναι διαλ̣έ̣κτῳ καὶ προτεθῆ[ν]αι.

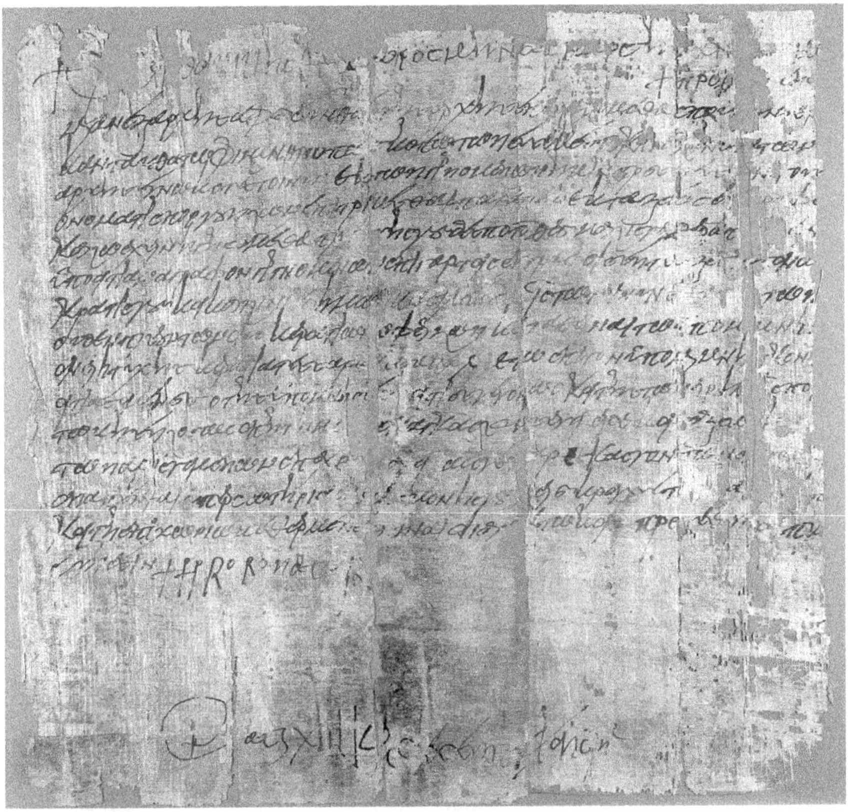

Fig. 26. Ordinance from the Duke of the Thebaid restricting the fees charged by court officials (*P.Cair.Masp.* I 67031 [Antinoopolis, ca. 543–45]). (Photograph courtesy of Adam Bülow-Jacobsen.)

of a ruling to combat the corruption of justice officials. In theory, this must also have interested the non-Greek-speaking population, which, as we saw, was already starting to abandon the courts, if only for economic reasons.

The two other texts attest to the use of Coptic in missives originating from the administration. The first, recently edited, is a letter from an official of the tax bureau (the *logistērion*) named John, datable to 566.[75] This letter addresses shepherds in the village of Phthla to give them various orders, including that of paying their taxes, which were overdue. He signed and dated the letter in Greek to make it more official,[76] but the letter itself

[75] Vanderheyden 2015, 149–56 (= *P.Aphrod.LettresCopt.* 15).

[76] L. 19: Ἰωάννης β̣οηθ(ὸς) λογι(στηρίου) σεσ̣ημ(είωμαι). ⳨ ἐγράφη Φαρμουθι̣ [. . . ⸗ ἰνδ(ικτίονος) ⸗ ιδ (?)] "I, John, assistant of the treasury office, have endorsed (this document). Written in Pharmouthi [. . . of the 14th (?) indiction]."

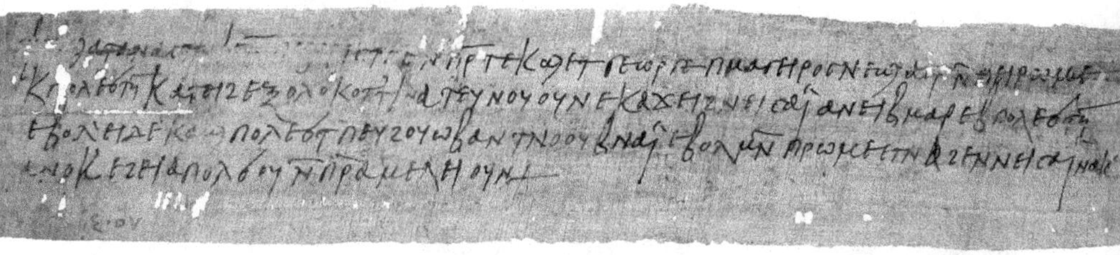

Fig. 27. A Coptic letter of an official in Antinoopolis enjoining the headman of the village of Aphrodite to settle a dispute (= *P.Aphrod.LettresCopt.* 1 [Aphrodite, first half of the sixth century]). (Photograph courtesy of Loreleï Vanderheyden.)

was in Coptic, and as it appears, was written in his own hand, despite the difference in graphic style between the two languages. This is a very early example of an administrative letter in Coptic.

The other letter, originating from the same archive, is even more interesting for the problem that interests us here [Fig. 27]:[77]

recto

+ ϣⲁ ⲧⲁⲛⲁⲥⲧ̣ⲁ̣ⲥ̣ⲓ̣ⲥ̣ ⲛ̣̄ⲡⲉ̣ⲭⲣ̣ⲓⲥⲧⲟ̣ⲥ ⲛ̄ⲡⲣ̄ⲧⲉⲕϣⲉⲧ ⲅⲉⲱⲣⲅⲉ ⲡⲙⲁⲅⲉⲓⲣⲟⲥ
ⲛⲉϣⲁⲁ̣ⲣ̣ ⲛ̄ⲡⲉⲓⲣⲱⲙⲉ
ⲕⲡⲟⲗⲉϭⲧϥ̄ ⲕⲁⲧⲉⲓ ϩⲉⲝ ⲟⲗⲟⲕⲟⲧⲧⲓⲛⲁ ⲧⲉⲩⲛⲟⲩ ⲟⲩⲛ ⲉⲕⲁϫⲉⲓϩ
ⲛⲉⲓⲥⲁï ⲁⲛⲉⲓⲃ ⲙⲁⲣⲉⲃⲡⲟⲗⲉϭⲧϥ̄
ⲉⲃⲟⲗ` ⲉⲓ ⲇⲉ· ⲕⲁϣⲡⲟⲗⲉϭⲧ ⲡⲉⲩϩⲟⲩⲱⲃ ⲁⲛ ⲧⲛⲟⲟⲩⲃ ⲛⲁï ⲉⲃⲟⲗ
ⲙ̄ⲛ ⲡⲣⲱⲙⲉ ⲉⲧⲛⲁϩⲉⲛ ⲛⲉⲓⲥⲁï ⲛⲁⲕ
ⲁⲛⲟⲕ ⲉϩⲉⲓⲁⲡⲟⲗϭⲟⲩ ⲛ̄ⲡⲣ̄ⲁⲙⲉⲗⲉⲓ ⲟⲩⲛ +

verso

ἐ̣π̣ί̣δ̣(ος) τ̣ῷ̣ θ̣α̣υ̣μ̣α̣(σιωτάτῳ̣) <Ἀ>πολ⊗ λῶτι πρωτοκ(ωμήτῃ̣)
Ἀφροδ(ίτης) π̣(αρὰ) [.] . . . .

By the resurrection of Christ, do not impose on George the butcher the financial demands of this man and obtain his agreement. You shall give six golden *solidi*: therefore, as soon as you receive this letter, bring them so that he (= this man) will be in agreement. However, if you cannot resolve their matter, let me know by means of the man who will bring you this letter. I will make them agree. Therefore do not be negligent.

[77] It was first edited, according to the transcription of W. E. Crum, by Boud'hors 2008, and later, according to the original, by Vanderheyden 2015, II, 8–24 (= *P.Aphrod. LettresCopt.* 1).

> *Verso* (in Greek): Deliver (this letter) to Apollos, the headman of Aphrodite, on behalf of [. . .].

This is the case in point that I mentioned above, namely that of a plaintiff who is sent before a local authority by a higher official, who asks the local authority to resolve the matter without going through legal proceedings. The recipient is the headman of the village of Aphrodite, Apollos, who had to resolve the dispute. The sender's name is lost, but, according to the editor, it must be an official from the governor's administration. We thus see that justice moved closer to Coptophone parties by adopting their language and organizing proceedings in which they were able to express themselves exclusively in Coptic.

In this rapprochement, one official had to play a major role: the *defensor civitatis* (Greek *ekdikos*). This was possibly the most noteworthy innovation in the domain of justice during Late Antiquity.[78] The primary vocation of this official, created by Constantine, was to defend the people "against the abuses of the powerful" (*contra potentium iniurias*).[79] In 535, Justinian reaffirmed this task by granting him more power in relation to governors. He was thus granted jurisdiction in minor criminal cases, and in matters in which the disputed amount was no greater than three hundred *solidi*, the plaintiff was required to address him rather than the governor.[80] The *defensor* was more than ever before the judge of the "small man," who could thus obtain justice at a lower cost and be protected against the abuses of the *potentiores*, as well as the judge of minor affairs, which thus relieved the courts of governors. He was therefore the justice official in closest interaction with the administration and the population, which was probably in the main not comfortable with Greek. Nonetheless, we still need proof that people could appeal to him in Coptic and that he could in turn render justice in the same language.

This proof exists but has gone unnoticed up until now. It is a Coptic papyrus from Vienna edited in 1938 by Walter C. Till as a letter.[81]

---

[78] Frakes 2001 (which stopped at the beginning of the fifth century). Otherwise, see Rees 1952; and Mannino 1984.

[79] *Cod.Theod.* I, 29, 1 (364 or 368) regarding Illyricum. For the date, which is debated, cf. Frakes 2001, 94–104, who opts for 364.

[80] *Novellae* XV, 3.

[81] *SBKopt.* IV 1709 (without provenance, seventh century). This text was recently re-edited by Alain Delattre and myself (Delattre and Fournet 2018, whose Coptic text is given here).

⳨ ⲁⲣⲓ ⲧⲁⲅⲁⲡⲏ <ⲙ̄>ⲡⲉⲟⲟⲩ ⲛ̄ⲧⲁⲡⲛⲟⲩⲧⲉ ⲭⲁⲣⲓⲍⲉ ⲙ̇ⲙⲟϥ ⲛⲁⲕ vac.
ⲛ̄ⲅⲥⲱ̣ⲧ̣ⲙ ⲡⲁϫ̄ⲛ̄ϭⲟⲛⲥ̣. ⲧⲁⲣⲉ̣ⲡ̣[ⲛⲟⲩⲧⲉ]
ⲥⲙⲟⲩ ⲉⲣⲟⲕ. ⲙⲁⲣⲉⲧⲉ̣ⲕⲙⲛ̄ⲧϫⲟⲉⲓⲥ ⲥⲱ̣ⲧⲙ̣ ⲡ̣ⲁ̣ϫ̣ⲓⲛ vac. ϭⲟⲛ̄ⲥ
ⲙⲛ̄ ⲡⲁⲩⲗⲟⲥ ⲡⲁϩⲁⲓ̣. [0–4]
ϫⲉ ⲁⲓ̈ⲙⲓⲥ ϣⲟⲙⲧ̄ ⲛⲙ̄ⲙⲁϥ ⲙ̄ⲡⲁϯⲣ̄ ϭⲱⲃ ⲡⲛⲟ̣ⲩⲧⲉ ⲥⲟⲟⲩⲛ ϫⲓⲛⲧⲁⲓⲣ̄
ϭⲱⲃ ⲁⲓ̈ⲙⲓⲥ ⲕⲉⲟⲩⲁ ⲛⲙ̣[ⲙⲁϥ.]
ⲛ̣̄ⲧⲉ̣ⲣⲉϥⲛⲁⲩ ⲉⲣⲟⲓ̈ ϫⲉ ⲁⲡⲛⲟⲩⲧⲉ ⲛ̄ ⲡϣⲱⲛⲉ ⲉϫⲱⲓ̈ ⲁϥⲛⲟϫⲧ̄ ⲉⲃⲟⲗ.
ⲁϥⲃⲱⲕ ⲙⲛ̇ ⲕⲉⲟⲩⲉⲓ̇. ⲁϥⲕⲱ ⲛⲛ̣[ϣⲏⲣⲉ(?)]
ⲉⲩⲛⲉϫ ⲉⲃⲟⲗ. ⲙⲛ̇ⲛⲥⲁ ⲡⲣⲱϣⲉ ⲙ̄ⲙⲁϫⲉ ϩⲛ ⲧⲁⲙⲏⲧⲉ ⲛⲙ̄ⲙⲁϥ ⲙⲛ̇
ⲧⲕⲉⲥⲓⲙⲉ ⲛ̣ⲧ̣[ⲁ]ϥ̣ⲃⲓⲧⲥ̄ ⲁⲥⲇⲟ̣ⲝⲓ
ϫⲉ ϥⲛⲁϯ [ⲡⲁ]ⲛ̣ϩⲁ̣ⲗ̣ⲱⲙⲁ ⲛⲁⲓ̈ ⲕⲁⲧⲁ ⲣⲟⲙⲡⲉ ⲉⲧⲉ ϥⲧⲟⲟⲩ ⲛ̄ⲣⲧⲟⲃ
ⲛ̇ⲉⲓⲱⲧ’ ⲛⲉ ⲙⲛ̇ ϥ̣ⲧⲟⲟⲩ ⲛ̄ⲝⲏⲥⲧⲏⲥ ⲛ̣ⲛ̣ⲉϩ̣
ⲙⲛ̄ ϥⲧⲟ̣[ⲟ]ⲩ ⲛ̄ⲕ̣ⲟ̣ⲗ(ⲗⲁⲑⲟⲛ) ⲛ̇ⲏ̣ⲣⲡ̄ ⲙⲛ̄ ⲟⲩϩⲟⲉⲓⲧⲉ ⲛ̇ⲟⲩⲣⲟⲙ<ⲡ>ⲉ
ⲟⲩⲣ̄ϣⲱⲛ ⲛⲟⲩⲣⲟⲙⲡⲉ. ⲁϥϩⲟⲩⲣⲱⲧ̄ ⲙ̇ⲡⲕⲉⲁⲛ-
ϩⲁⲗⲱⲙⲁ. ⲙ̄ⲡⲉϥ̣ϯ ⲛⲁⲓ̈ ϫⲓⲛ ⲥⲛⲟⲩϥ ⲛ̄ⲥⲁ ⲟⲩⲣ̄ⲧⲟⲃ ⲛ̄ⲉⲓⲟⲩⲧ’ ⲙ̇ⲙⲁⲧⲉ
ⲁⲩⲱ ⲛ̄ϯϣⲓⲛⲉ ⲁⲛ̄ ⲛ̄ⲥⲁ ⲗⲁⲩⲉ ⲛ̄ⲥⲁ
ⲡⲁⲛϩⲁⲗⲱⲙⲁ ⲛ̄ⲧⲁϥⲥⲙⲛ̄ⲧⲥ̇ ⲛⲙ̄ⲙⲁⲓ̂ ϫⲉ̣ ⲁ̣ⲓⲣ̄ ϭⲱⲃ ⲛ̣ . . ⲟϭⲥ ⲛ̄ⲧⲁⲱⲛϩ
ⲉⲣⲟϥ. ⲧⲁⲣⲉⲡⲛⲟⲩⲧⲉ ⲥⲙⲟⲩ ⲉⲣⲟⲕ̣.

Have the goodness, <by> the glory that God has granted to you, to listen to my misfortune, and may God bless you! May Your Lordship hear of the misfortune (that I have been enduring) with Paul, my husband. I had three children by him before falling into suffering and God knows that as of the moment that I was suffering, I had another child by him. When he saw that God had afflicted me with disease, he chased me away. He left with another woman. He left the children abandoned. Following the copious dispute between him, myself, and the other woman that he took, it was decided that he would pay me alimony each year, of an amount of four *artabae* of barley, four *sextarii* of oil, four *kollatha* of wine, one overcoat per year, and one blanket per year. <Nonetheless,> he has stripped me of my alimony itself. Since last year, he has only given me one *artaba* of barley. And I am asking no more than the alimony that he established with me because I am in suffering, [. . .] so that I may live from it. May God bless you.

This text does rather give the impression of being a petition, but it is true that during this period, letters often tended to be contaminated by the rhetoric of petitions, especially when they communicated a request. The absence of a prescript prevents us from knowing whom this poor woman (whose name was probably Merkouria[82]) was addressing, but on the other hand, it shows that this request was placed directly in the hands of its recipient, which was typical of petitions, for they were always personally placed in the hands of the judge. It happens that the reverse side contains capital information that the editor did not see: in a script that attempts to imitate the style of the addresses inscribed on the back of letters, it reads, in Greek, between two columns of a subsequent account, "Aurelius John, *defensor* by the grace of God."[83] We would expect this to be the name of the recipient of this petition, and the fact that he is a *defensor* makes it very likely that our unfortunate woman was addressing him.[84] This address is repeated on the front side upside down with respect to the text of the petition, with additional information added by another person: "Aurelius John, *defensor* of Apollonos Ano,"[85] in other words, Edfu.

However, that is not all: once again upside down with respect to the petition, we can see the end of another text, only the last line of which is visible: "[. . .] that was how I was able to resolve (μεσάζειν) the matter between them."[86] In other words, we have the end of the decision of the *defensor*.

Therefore, this is what we can reconstruct regarding the progress of the matter at hand: Merkouria claims alimony from her husband, who left the marital home. This provokes a dispute that is initially resolved by a settlement, requiring the husband to pay alimony to his wife. He does not respect his commitments, and Merkouria decides to call upon the justice of the *defensor* by submitting a petition to him. He renders a decision.[87] Moreover, as we see, everything was done in Coptic.

---

[82] See chapter 3, n. 85.

[83] Αὐρήλιος Ἰωά(ννης) σὺ̣ν Θε(ῷ̣) | ἔκδι̣{. . .}κ̣ο̣ς |. . ἔκδικο̣ς ε̣.

[84] It is surprising that the name is in the nominative and not the dative, but the awkwardness of the hand shows that we are dealing with someone who had very poor Greek skills and who may have confused the cases (unknown in Coptic, as we have noted earlier).

[85] Αὐρήλιος Ἰωά(ννης) ἔκδ<ι>κος τῆς ἄ̣ν̣ω Ἀπ̣όλλωνος. We read, just below it, to the right, Μερκο( ). This may possibly be the name of the plaintiff, Μερκο(υρία). In that case, we would have a sort of address starting with the name of the recipient (despite the nominative case) and ending with that of the sender.

[86] ⲧⲁⲓ ⲧⲉ ⲑⲉ ⲛⲧⲁⲓⲉϣ ϭⲙϭⲟⲙ ⲙⲙⲉⲥⲁⲥⲉ ⲙⲙⲟⲟⲩ.

[87] We could also argue that the matter was delegated by the *defensor* to another authority, to which he would have sent Merkouria's petition (which would explain the endorsement in the nominative case). This authority would have noted its decision on the papyrus containing the petition and then would have sent back the entirety to the *defensor*. This seems more complicated to me, and we resolve the difficulty of the

This is the first known petition in Coptic. It does not have a date, but I believe the writing to be from the beginning of the seventh century, and in any case, it seems to me and Alain Delattre to date prior to the Arab domination.[88] Another petition, also published as a letter and quite similar in its form, although in this case addressed from a widow to a bishop, clearly dates to the Sasanian period (619–29), as can be seen from allusions to the Persians.[89] There are certainly others still to identify within the vast corpus of Coptic letters.

I would have liked the evidence regarding the legal use of Coptic to be datable without question to the Byzantine regime, but this is not the case of the widow's petition, and there is doubt surrounding that of Merkouria. However, I think it likely that the aspirations of a Coptophone population with limited Greek skills were increasingly taken into consideration by the administration, which developed or allowed the development of alternatives to the normative process allowing the use of Coptic.

This context could but favor the use of Coptic, including for the drawing up of legal acts. The validity of the latter as proof in investigations carried out in Coptic, like those of our village headman Apollos or our *defensor* John, leaves no room for doubt. In more formal proceedings, where Greek was required, or with Greek-speaking officials, translations could be used. This is what we understand from a recently edited Coptic ostracon in the Strasbourg collection.[90] This letter, probably written by the secretary of Bishop Abraham († 621[91]), whom I will discuss in greater detail in chapter 4, concerns a legal matter (possibly an inheritance) and mentions a

---

nominative case only by adding another difficulty: if the *defensor* had sent the petition to another person, we would expect the name of this person to be mentioned, which is not the case.

88 Allusions to the *defensor* after the Arab conquest are rare and are limited to the beginning of the Arab period: *P.Apoll.* 46 (Edfu, 2nd half of the seventh century) and *SPP* X 252 (Arsinoite, eighth century according to the ed., but the seventh century seems possible to me)—as for *CPR* XIV 17 (Arsinoite, 652 or 636) and *SB* I 4490 (Arsinoite, 656 or 641), a Byzantine date is possible (*CPR* XIV 17, intr.). Note that they are nonexistent in the Coptic documents. On the *defensor* after the Arab conquest, see Rees 1952, 97; *P.Apoll.* 46 intr.; and especially *CPR* XIV 17 intr. and 7 n., where the editor concludes that "it is not known what legal or administrative functions the *defensor civitatis* retained in the Arab period because references to the ἔκδικος in the period are all of unofficial nature."

89 *SB Kopt.* I 295 (Thebes, Sasanian period).

90 *O.Stras.Copt.* 24.

91 See chapter 4, n. 40.

document (ⲭⲁⲣⲧⲏⲥ) that was translated into Greek for the occasion and probably served as documentary proof.

Therefore, conditions were established that no longer constituted an obstacle to the use of Coptic in legal or judicial contexts. Yet there is no evidence that the Coptophone population massively rushed into the gap thus opened. The prestige of Greek was still very powerful, sustained as it was by the administrative machine that was (almost) exclusively Greek-speaking, and by the possibility of an appeal before the governor, whose rulings were certainly considered to be more effective than other decisions rendered in less formal proceedings by lower-ranking officials. The archive of Philemon and Thecla (622–47) clearly demonstrates the ambivalent attitude of urban Egyptian milieus.[92] It is composed of four documents, one Coptic (a settlement[93]) and three Greek (a marriage contract, a sale contract, and a *dialysis* or dispute resolution[94]). Coptic was used for the settlement, given that writing up the debates held in Egyptian, which took many days and filled 286 lines (despite being summarized!), would have been labor-intensive had they been translated into Greek. On the other hand, for contractual documents, which were intended to be legally binding, Greek was used exclusively. This clear distribution seems to be proof that there was reluctance to use Coptic when it was a matter of stepping out of the private or informal context. It could not yet be entirely trusted.

With Philemon and Thecla, we are on the fringes of the first years of the Arab regime, which profoundly modified the situation by theoretically cutting the organic tie that had linked the law, justice, and administration to the Greek language under Byzantine domination—even though, in practice, the prestige of Greek was not swept away overnight. Long before the Arabs arrived, other milieus had had fewer scruples or reluctance than Philemon and Thecla, and had not hesitated to use Coptic much more systematically. We will discover them in the next chapter.

---

92 MacCoull 1995, 350–51; Richter 2010, 40–43.

93 *SBKopt.* I 36, also known as *P.Budge* (Edfu, ca. 647), currently being re-edited by T. S. Richter.

94 *SB* VI 8986 (Edfu, 640/641); 8987 (Oxyrhynchos, 644/645); 8988 (Edfu, 647).

CHAPTER 4

The Role of the Church and Monasticism in the Growth of Legal Coptic

"One day Abba Arsenius consulted an old Egyptian monk about his own thoughts. Someone noticed this and said to him, 'Abba Arsenius, how is it that you, with such a good Latin and Greek education, ask this peasant about your thoughts?' He replied, 'I have indeed been taught Latin and Greek, but I do not know even the alphabet of this peasant.' "[1] This excerpt from the *Apophthegms* (or *Sayings*) *of the Desert Fathers* is one example among many others of the figure of the uneducated Egyptian monk that we so often encounter in the sources, who knew no Greek and did not even know how to write. For a long time, this passage and those like it were thought to validate the idea that monastic milieus, which were illiterate and a fortiori non-Greek-speaking, or even somewhat rebellious with respect to Greek culture, were very largely Coptophone. Without delving into the edifying anecdotes of the Desert Fathers, it is true that the texts often present monasteries as being inhabited by Egyptians unable to understand Greek, integrating Greek-speakers only if they made the effort to learn Coptic. For example, the Greek-speaking Theodore of Alexandria, admitted by Pachomius into his monastery, had to learn Coptic, which then allowed him to become

[1] *Apophthegmata patrum (collectio alphabetica)*, Arsenius 6 (*PG* LXV, col. 89A): Ἐρωτῶντός ποτε τοῦ ἀββᾶ Ἀρσενίου τινὰ γέροντα Αἰγύπτιον περὶ ἰδίων λογισμῶν, ἕτερος ἰδὼν αὐτὸν εἶπεν· Ἀββᾶ Ἀρσένιε, πῶς τοσαύτην παίδευσιν Ῥωμαϊκὴν καὶ Ἑλληνικὴν ἐπιστάμενος, τοῦτον τὸν ἀγροῖκον περὶ τῶν σῶν λογισμῶν ἐρωτᾷς; Ὁ δὲ εἶπε πρὸς αὐτόν· τὴν μὲν Ῥωμαϊκὴν καὶ Ἑλληνικὴν ἐπίσταμαι παίδευσιν· τὸν δὲ ἀλφάβητον τοῦ ἀγροίκου τούτου οὔπω μεμάθηκα (trans. Ward 1975, 10).

an indispensable interpreter.[2] Beyond literary sources, we can recall the case of the anchorite Apa John, who was unable to "sign" in Greek the letter he wrote [Fig. 15].

However, this image of the Coptic-speaking monk incapable of speaking or reading Greek also conveys certain literary *topoi*, of which we need to be aware if we are to avoid being trapped by hagiographic sources dwelling on the culture and language of their heroes. In the name of the axiom "The person whose mind is sound has no need of letters," stated in the *Life of Antony*,[3] an anti-intellectualist movement ran throughout literature about the monks and presented the ideal of monastic purity as being contrary to the imperatives of Greek culture.[4] Yet we should not deprive literary evidence of all significance under the pretext that it may be ideological. While Pachomius, for example, is often presented as being incapable of communicating with Greek-speakers,[5] it is not only in the name of an ideal. He did attempt to learn Greek, as we discover in one of his *Lives*,[6] and the Pachomian corpus is clearly not devoid of inconsistencies surrounding the saint's monolingualism.[7] Nonetheless, most importantly of all, Pachomius effectively attempted to alleviate the problem of the majority of the monks' monolingualism by providing his communities with interpreters, of whom Theodore of Alexandria was the best representative.[8] They were essential for internal communication with foreign or non-Greek-speaking monks, for welcoming visitors, and for relations with the external world. The Pachomian corpus even contains evidence indicating that Pachomius may

[2] Cf. chapter 3, n. 51. See also the case of Ammon (cf. chapter 2, n. 18) or of Hilaria (Drescher 1947, text p. 6, 17–20, trans. p. 75: "And the words which Apa Pambo used to say to her, Apa Martyrion would say them for her in Greek. For this reason, also, the young girl learned the Egyptian tongue").

[3] § 73: Ὧι τοίνυν ὁ νοῦς ὑγιαίνει, τούτῳ οὐκ ἀναγκαῖα τὰ γράμματα.

[4] Wipszycka 1994, 40–41 (= Wipszycka 1996, 330–31); *P.Brux.Bawit*, 135; Papaconstantinou 2014, 19–20; Camplani 2015, 132–33. On the relationship between monasticism and written culture, cf. Vecoli 2017.

[5] Cf. chapter 2, n. 50 and more generally Papaconstantinou 2014.

[6] *Vita Prima*, 95 ed. Halkin 1982, 46: ἐσπούδασέ τε μαθεῖν ἑλληνιστὶ χάριτι Θεοῦ καίπερ Αἰγύπτιος ὤν, ὥστε συλλαλεῖν Θεοδώρῳ καὶ παραμυθίας μεταδιδόναι "And with God's grace he made every effort to learn Greek, although he was an Egyptian, so as to talk with Theodore and offer him encouragement."

[7] Papaconstantinou 2014, 19.

[8] Ammon, *De sanctis Pachomio et Theodoro epistula* 5, 6, 7, 22, 28, 29 (ed. Halkin 1982, 101, 102, 109, 112).

have valued multilingualism, as it allowed for fluid internal and external relations that did not require mediation.[9]

Even though it contains a certain historical reality, the figure of the exclusively Coptic-speaking monk has nonetheless fed two clichés that modern research has attempted to debunk. In the name of an opposition between Greek-speaking urban elites versus Egyptian-speaking peasants, Egyptian monasticism was seen as being an essentially rural phenomenon. While the majority of monks were indeed of rural origin, monasteries recruited within all social classes and attracted people from diverse backgrounds (for whom Greek served as the *lingua franca*[10]). The urban, educated, and Greek-speaking dimension of Egyptian monasticism must therefore not be underestimated, given that monasteries, which were not always located in the farthest corners of the countryside or in the middle of deserts, but also in the areas surrounding cities, had an economy that was closely connected to that of cities.[11]

The other cliché builds on the predominantly anti-Chalcedonian nature of monasteries. Let us recall that the Council of Chalcedon in 451 condemned the monophysite arguments defended by Dioscorus, Bishop of Alexandria, and led to a split between the official Church (Chalcedonian, the only one recognized by Byzantium) and the monophysite Church of Egypt (the anti-Chalcedonian Church), which developed its own parallel hierarchy in Egypt during the sixth century. In older scholarship, this fact legitimized a binary opposition, according to which Chalcedonians were predominantly Greek-speaking, as opposed to anti-Chalcedonians (to which our monks often belonged), who were above all Coptic-speaking. However, this opposition, which attempts to correlate theological opposition with ethno-linguistic division, is not based on any solid documentary foundations, as Ewa Wipszycka clearly demonstrated in 1992.[12]

As we can see, the problem of the relationship between monasticism and Coptic, which nonetheless seems to be clearly confirmed by papyri from the fourth century, is a minefield that we dare not enter, so numerous are its dead ends, pitfalls, and obstacles, starting with the documenta-

---

[9] Papaconstantinou 2014, 20–21.

[10] Papaconstantinou 2014, 17–18. For Latin-speaking monks, cf. Fournet 2009c, 428–29.

[11] Wipszycka 1994.

[12] Wipszycka 1992b, 119–25.

tion itself. Scholars do not have a clear idea of what path to take, caught as they are between literary sources, which are to be mistrusted due to their ideological assumptions or aesthetic intentions, and documentary sources, which are closer to reality, but desperately partial, thus preventing even the most rudimentary statistical attempts and condemning us to impressions.[13] Here, I would like to circumvent this methodological barrier by showing the role played by monasticism (and, through it, by the Church, as we will see) in the emergence of an "official" Coptic that moved beyond the boundaries of private epistolary communication, and in the development of the idea that this language could and should play a role in public life alongside Greek. To do so, I will present three documentary dossiers that will allow me to clarify the major impetus that monasticism exerted with regard to this phenomenon, and the various mechanisms that it followed. The first dossier is completely unedited, and the others are still poorly known.

A Graeco-Coptic Codex from the Louvre: Monasticism and Taxation

My first "piece of supporting evidence" is a codex of eight wooden tablets that the Louvre Museum acquired in 1992, when the wife of the archaeologist Raymond Weill (1874–1950) bequeathed his collection to it [Fig. 28].[14]

Wooden codices were used during Late Antiquity either as school notebooks, or as a medium for accounts, or for documents. Our codex is an example of the second type of use. The fourteen tablet faces contain around twenty-six receipts, some of which are related to taxation, written by different people. All of them concern a single taxpayer, a man named Jacob son of Ptōs or Tōs (depending on the receipts), who is the "master of a mill" (*mulonarchēs*) and who sometimes appears with his associates. These receipts are not written in the same language: twenty are in Greek,

---

[13] See the partial studies of Torallas Tovar 2010, 36–42 (referring to Torallas Tovar 2003) or Papaconstantinou 2014.

[14] This codex (Louvre E 24454) was briefly presented by Boud'hors 1998: the difference between the number of tablets that she gives on p. 3 and the number that I am giving here is due to the fact that two half-tablets were joined by mistake. The publication of this codex has been undertaken by Anne Boud'hors and myself, and is forthcoming.

Fig. 28. The Weill codex: a collection of receipts in Greek and Coptic from the sixth century. (Photograph courtesy of the Musée du Louvre, dist. RMN-Grand Palais / Christian Larrieu.)

as we expect; more interestingly, six are in Coptic. Here is an example in each language:

II RECTO [FIG. 29]

⳨ ὀν[ό(ματος) Ἰακὼβ ̣]α̣ς̣ο̣υ̣ δέδ̣ωκε[ς κα]ὶ̣ ἐπληρώθης ὑπὲρ τοῦ δημοσίου τοῦ ὑπὸ σὲ καρπ̣(οῦ) τετάρτης̣ [ἰ]νδικ(τίωνος). Ζαχαρίας̣ οἰκωνόμως Τριφίου στοιχεῖ μοι ὑποχὴ̣ ὡς πρόκ(ειται). Μεσωρη εἰκα<σ-> τρίτη̣{ς}

To the account of Jacob [. . .]: you have given and been fully paid (*sic* for "you have fully paid") for the public taxes concerning the crops you are responsible for of the fourth indiction < . . . >. I, Zacharias, steward of Triphion, am satisfied with the receipt as stated. Mesore twenty-third (= August 16).

IV VERSO

⳨ ⲁⲛⲟⲕ ⲇⲟ̣ⲣⲟⲑⲉⲟⲥ
ⲡⲣⲏⲧ ⲉⲓⲥϩⲁï ⲛ̇ ïⲁⲕⲱⲃ
ϫⲉ ⲁïϫ̣ï [ⲁ]ⲩ̣ⲱ ⲁïⲙⲟⲩϩ ⲛ̇-
ⲧⲟⲟⲧⲕ̄ ϩⲁⲡⲉⲕⲙⲉⲣ(ⲟⲥ) ⲛ̇ⲇⲏ-
ⲙⲟⲥⲓ(ⲟⲛ) ⲙ̀ⲡⲓⲁϩ ⲡⲁϫⲱ ϩ̣ⲁ-
ⲡⲕⲁⲣⲡⲟⲥ ⲛ̄ⲇⲉⲥⲥⲉⲣⲉⲥ-
ⲕⲁⲓⲇⲉⲕⲁⲧⲏⲥ ⲓⲛⲇ(ⲓⲕⲧⲓⲱⲛⲟⲥ).
ⲁⲛⲟⲕ
ⲇⲁⲩⲉⲓⲇ ⲡⲁⲛⲁⲅ(ⲛⲱⲥⲧⲏⲥ) ⲛ̇ ⲁⲧⲣⲓ-
ⲡⲉ ⲁïⲥϩⲁï ϯⲁⲡⲟⲭ(ⲏ). ϯⲟ ⲙ̄-
ⲙⲁⲣⲧⲩⲣ(ⲟⲥ). + Φαμενωθ
κε ἰνδ(ικτίωνος) ιδ.
+ Ἐγρ(άφη) δι᾽ ἐμ(οῦ) Δαυεὶδ
ἀπὸ Τριφίου.

I, Dorotheus, the *rēt*,[15] write to Jacob that I have received and have been fully paid for your part of the public taxes concerning the field of Padjō for the crops of the fourteenth indiction < . . . >.
I, David, the lector of Atripe, have written this receipt. I am witness (to it).
(*in Greek*) Phamenoth 25 (= March 11) of the 14th indiction.
Written by me, David from Triphion.

The absence of amounts on these receipts may seem to indicate that they are the writing exercises of an apprentice scribe, given that such a large number of them are on wooden codices, the most commonly used medium for learning. However, it turns out that the receipt sent by Zacharias should be compared to an ostracon belonging to the Ashmolean collection, of unknown provenance, edited in 1988 by John C. Shelton, who dated it to the sixth century. The comparison with the text of our tablet allows me to suggest an improved edition of this receipt:

O.ASHM.SHELT. 35 [FIG. 30]

⳨ ὀνό(ματος) Ζαχαρίας
κερ̣(αμέως?)
κ̣αὶ κοινων̣(ῶν)
ἀπὸ Τρϊφ( ). δεδωκας καὶ
ἐπληρωθης ὑπὲρ δημ(οσίων)
καρπ̣ῶν ἑνδεκάτης
ἰνδικτί(ωνος) τουτέστιν κρι-
θο̂ν ἀρτάβας τρῖς, γί(νονται)
κρ̣ι̣θ̣(ῶν) (ἀρτ.) γ. Ζαχαρίας
οἰκ(ονόμος)
ἔ̣γραψ(α) καὶ Τριφ( ) στοχεῖ μοι
υποχὴ ὡς πρόκ(ειται)
Μεσωρὴ ι̣. π̣ρ( ).

REVISED TEXT

ὀνό(ματος) Ζαχαρίας
κεφ̣(αλαιωτοῦ?)
κ̣αὶ κοινων̣(ῶν)
ἀπὸ Τριφ(ίου) δεδωκες καὶ
ἐπληρωθης ὑπὲρ δημ(οσίων)
καρ{ ̣}π̣ο̂ν ἑνδεκάτης
ἰνδικτί(ωνος) τουτέστιν κρι-
θο̂ν ἀρτάβας τρῖς, γί(νονται)
κρ̣ι̣θ̣(ῶν) (ἀρτάβαι) γ. Ζαχαρίας
οἰκ(ονόμος)
Πρατ καὶ Τριφ(ίου) στοχεῖ μοι
ὑποχὴ ὡς πρόκ(ειται)
Μεσωρὴ ι̣ ⳨.

[15] This may be a title (Crum, *CD*, 303b).

Fig. 29. One of the tablets of the Weill codex: a tax receipt issued by the steward Zacharias. (Photograph courtesy of the Musée du Louvre, dist. RMN-Grand Palais / Jean-Luc Fournet.)

To the account of Zacharias, foreman (?), and his associates from Triphion, you have given and been fully paid (*sic* for "you have fully paid") for the public taxes concerning the crops of the eleventh indiction, that is, three artabae of barley, total: 3 art. barley. I, Zacharias, steward of Prat and Triphion, am satisfied with the receipt as stated. Mesore 10 [= August 3].

Fig. 30. A tax receipt issued by the steward Zacharias (*O.Ashm.Shelt.* 35 [Panopolite, sixth century]). (Photograph courtesy of the Ashmolean Museum of Art and Archaeology.)

The receipt originates from the same place (Triphion) and is written by the same steward, Zacharias (here, we learn that he is the steward not only of Triphion but also of Prat); we recognize his writing and find the same spelling and syntactical errors. It belongs to a small collection of receipts on ostraca of unknown provenance dated by the editor to the sixth century.[16] Therefore, there is no doubt that the receipts of our codex are genuine and that they are originals rather than copies, written directly by the people issuing them. However, who are these people? To what milieu(s) do they belong?

[16] *O.Ashm.Shelt.* 35, 36, 39, 40, 41, 198, 227.

It is the job title accompanying their name (when it is given) that may put us on the right track. One of these is a *boēthos* (lat. *adjutor*), "assistant," a vague term that can denote all sorts of agents, who normally worked for a public administration, but also in a private context.[17] Perhaps more specific is the dual title of the issuer who appears most often in our receipts, a man named Basilios, who is said to be an *ergodiōktēs* and *riparius*. The first, meaning "foreman,"[18] is found above all in the archives of the large estate of the Apions;[19] the second refers to an agent in charge of security, working both for the government and at large estates.[20] This ambiguity is clearly due to the semipublic status of large estates, which took on a portion of the responsibilities of the state, as Jean Gascou has clearly shown.[21]

Less ambiguous is Zacharias's title of *oikonomos*, which he shares with the issuer of another receipt, John. The term, which could also denote the steward of a large estate, had a very specific meaning at the time of our codex: it was only used for the stewards of religious establishments, churches, or monasteries. David's title, namely *anagnōstēs*, "reader," is oriented toward the same milieus. The two titles are specified by an identical determination: οἰκονόμος Τριφίου "steward of Triphion" and ⲡⲁⲛⲁⲅ(ⲛⲱⲥⲧⲏⲥ) ⲛ̇ ⲁⲧⲣⲓⲡⲉ "reader of Atripe," *Triph(e)ion* being the Greek version of Atripe, a toponym dating back to the Egyptian *Ḥwt Rpyt*, "the House of Triphis." As its name indicates, this originally consisted of the sanctuary of the lion goddess Triphis (Eg. Repyt),[22] who was worshiped on the left bank of the Nile near Sohag, across the river from Panopolis. There are a few traces of this sanctuary in the papyri. One of these even tells us that the *palation*, where the Emperor Diocletian stayed during his visit in 298 following his defeat of the rebellion of Domitius Domitianus, was built within it.[23] By metonymy, the sanctuary gave its name to the village and its cemetery, which is well known for the numerous mummy labels that mention it.[24]

---

[17] *WB* IV, col. 371: "Oft nicht ersichtlich, ob die Bedeutung privater Hilfsarbeiter oder Hilfsbeamter vorliegt."

[18] This translation is due to Hardy 1931, 110.

[19] *P.Oxy.* LVII 3914, 5n.

[20] Torallas Tovar 2001 and 2012.

[21] Gascou 1985.

[22] Gauthier 1903.

[23] *P.Panop.Beatty* 1, 259. Cf. the other evidence of the sanctuary in Calderini, *Diz.*, *s. n.* Τριφεῖον.

[24] Cf. Chauveau 2002.

Moreover, it was near this village that a monastery was founded in 350, which became famous with its third abbot, Shenoute [Fig. 24], who directed it from 385 to 465 and expanded it (reusing blocks from the sanctuary of Triphis). Today it is known as the White Monastery (Ar. *dayr al-Abyaḍ*) or the Monastery of Anba Shenoute (Ar. *dayr Anbā Šinūdah*) [Fig. 31].[25] Were Zacharias and David members of its staff? To make things worse, traces of another monastery have been found partially located on the site of the Triphis sanctuary, which is currently being excavated by the University of Tübingen and the Yale Monastic Archaeology Project South.[26] It is believed to be a nunnery belonging to the Shenoutean Federation, along with the White Monastery and its neighbor, the Red Monastery (both of which were male monasteries) [Fig. 32].[27] This institution, built on the very site of the pagan *Triphion*, appears prima facie to be the natural candidate for the identification of the Triphion to which Zacharias and David belonged. However, let us not jump to conclusions: the so-called "mountain of Triphion/Atripe"[28] also gave its name to the entirety of the surrounding desert area, which extends the range of possibilities to the three monasteries located within it. We note that Zacharias is presented in *O.Ashm.Shelt.* 35 as the "steward of Prat and of Triphion": these could be the names of two of these monasteries—with that of Prat being a *hapax* up to this day.[29]

---

[25] Timm, II, 601–34; Coquin and Martin 1991; Wipszycka 2009, 161–67. Cf. also Amélineau 1893, 69–70 and 529; Flinders Petrie 1908, 14–15.

[26] See egyptology.yale.edu/expeditions/current-expeditions/yale-monastic-archaeology-project-south-sohag/atripe.

[27] Cf. egyptology.yale.edu/expeditions/current-expeditions/yale-monastic-archaeology-project-south-sohag/shenoutes-monastic. On the Red Monastery, cf. recently Bolman 2016 (and in particular the contribution of Emmel and Layton 2016). On the entirety of the territory of the Federation, cf. chapter 4, n. 30.

[28] Cf. the martyr of Panine and Panēu (fourth century) according to an Arabic version (*ğabal Adriba*, see Timm, II, 601); *Apophthegmata Patrum (collectio alphabetica)*, Pœmen 90 (ὄρος τῆς Ἀθλίβεως, see Timm, II, 602). In papyri contemporary to our codex, we find this expression to locate the White Monastery: *P.Cair.Masp.* III 67312, 38–40 (Antinoopolis, 567): τοῦ] εὐαγοῦ̣[ς μον]α̣στηρίου καλουμένου Ἄπα Σεν[ού]θ̣[ου], κ̣[ει]μ̣έ̣[νου] ἐ̣[ν τῷ ὄρει Τρι]φίο̣υ τοῦ Πανοπολίτου νομοῦ "The holy Monastery named Apa Senouthēs, located in the mountain of Triphion in the Panopolite nome"; *P.Ross. Georg.* III 48, 1 (Aphrodite, sixth century): τοῦ ἁγίου μοναστη]ρίου Ἄπα Σενούθ[ου] ἀρχιμ[ανδρ(ίτου) ὄ]ρο[υς Τρι]φί̣[ο]υ [? τοῦ Πανοπολ(ίτου) νομοῦ "of the Monastery of the archimandrite Apa Senouthēs of the mountain of Triphion in the Panopolite nome."

[29] At the time of our codex, documents continue to bear witness to the existence of the village of Triphion/Atripe: *P.CrumST* 436 (Panopolite, 619 or 634 [*CSBE*^{2}, 269:

Fig. 31. The White Monastery. (Photograph courtesy of Barbara Emmel.)

In any event, some of the receipts in our codex were issued by monks, while others were issued by laymen working for one of the monasteries or within an area dependent on this monastery. The fact that monks could be allowed to issue tax receipts just as a tax official would have done could be explained by the fact that they collected taxes on behalf of the admin-

634?]), loan contract established between Rhoubēn, monk of Smin, and another monk Pesnte, ⲡⲣⲙⲁⲧⲣⲓⲡⲉ "inhabitant of Atripe" (we cannot give the same translation as Timm, II, 609: "Pseynte <im Kloster> von Atripe" [see his n. 52]: ⲡⲣⲙ- introduces an *origo* and not his belonging to a religious institution); we cannot come to any conclusions from *CPR* IV 19, 16 (Panopolis, eighth century), which is too fragmentary. We could also venture the hypothesis that Zacharias was the steward of the Shenoutian Federation, which was in charge of the properties that it appears to have had within the territory of this village. However, it would be more difficult to explain it in the same way as the title of David, "lector of Atripe" (ⲡⲁⲛⲁⲅ(ⲛⲱⲥⲧⲏⲥ) ⲛ̇ ⲁⲧⲣⲓⲡⲉ).

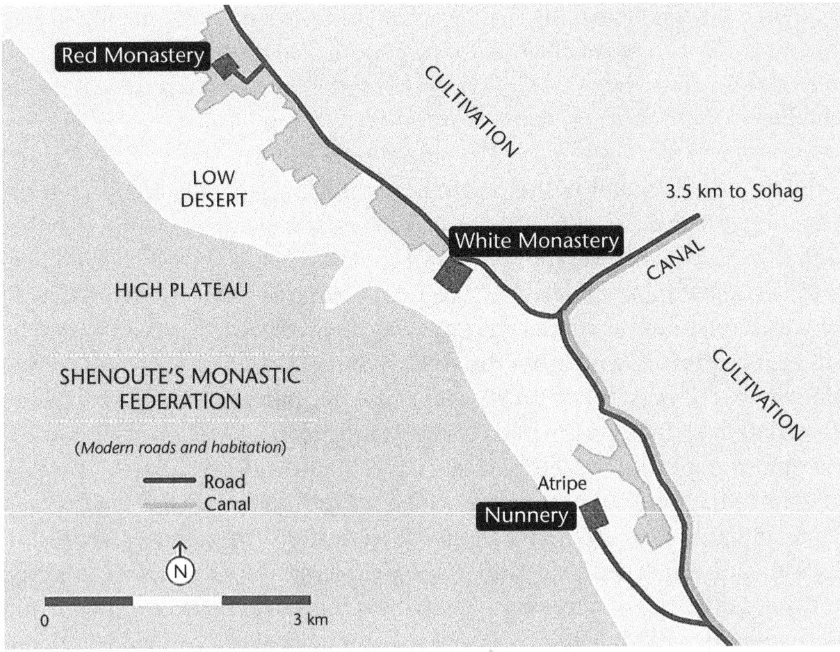

Fig. 32. Shenoute's Monastic Federation. (© Yale Monastic Archaeology Project South [Sohag].)

istration in territories that were economically dependent on the Monastic Federation or within their sphere of influence. We may also wonder whether these receipts were issued by monks for properties *belonging* to the Federation, according to a system similar to that of large estates in which taxes resembled a form of rent.[30] In that case, the Federation would have managed the collection of taxes internally, transferring the amounts collected to the tax authorities.

What interests us here is that Coptic was used concurrently with Greek. This may be due to the linguistic profile of certain issuers. But David concludes his receipt with a few Greek words, which seems to indicate that he was Hellenophone. And in any case, especially if the monks were working for the tax authority, it was still necessary for this language to be

[30] Cf. Gascou 1985, 12–19 (= Gascou 2008, 134–41). This would explain why we also find lease receipts among the receipts. The territory of the monastery is described by Shenoute (*Canons* 3, ed. Layton 2014, 118–19, rule 77): "Our territory is from the valley north of the village of Atripe as far north as the valley south of the building of our venerable father Apa Pshoi (= Red Monastery), where he originally lived in the desert" (trans. Emmel and Layton 2016, 14).

accepted for this type of use—a fact that seems to be clearly demonstrated by our dossier for a relatively ancient period. The most ancient Coptic tax receipt known to date was *CPR* IV 9 (Hermopolite), dated by its editor, on the basis of the writing, from "around 600."[31] A man named Papostolos, a scribe from a village in the Hermopolite nome, represented by Pamin, acknowledged receipt of the payment of public taxes (*dēmosion*) from the *clarissimus* Apa Basil, son of Anastasios. Pamin was not even able to write, and it was a deacon, Sarapiōn, who wrote the receipt. We are dealing here with a rural administration that was poorly educated and spoke no Greek, in which religious personnel were once again involved.[32] There may well be other receipts in Coptic from the sixth century; however, as these types of documents never contain an absolute date but rather an indiction, we are forced to date them on the basis of the writing alone, and Coptic documentary paleography is a discipline that currently still leaves much to be desired.

Our codex therefore offers early evidence that Coptic was used in a taxation context under the impetus of a monastic institution. The latter's responsibility for a portion of the collection process explains why Coptic was accepted for this use by the community—which was moreover confronted with and accustomed to bilingualism, as the dossier of our miller, consisting of documents in both Coptic and Greek, demonstrates. The formulary of Coptic receipts remained heavily dependent on Greek receipts, although with a few adaptations.[33] We are still far from the highly autonomous formularies of Coptic tax receipts from the Theban region in the early eighth century.

The following two dossiers, sharing the same provenance, will show more precisely the role of monasticism in the rise of Coptic and in its creation of a language that could compete with Greek in nonprivate usage.

The Wills of the Monastery of St. Phoebammon: Greek Documents in Coptic Dress?

The first of these two dossiers is a collection of texts that was largely unknown up until now and which, as the result of the discovery of an unedited text, has recently been the subject of a remarkable (re)edition.[34] It is

[31] Till 1947, 531: "etwas aus dem 7. Jahrhundert."

[32] Cf. chapter 4, pp. 145–46.

[33] The formula ⲁϊϫⲓ̈ [ⲁ]ⲩ̣ⲱ ⲁϊⲙⲟⲩϩ "I have received and have been fully paid" copies the Greek ἐδεξάμην καὶ ἐπληρώθην, but we find the prescript with the verb ⲉⲓⲥϩⲁϊ typical of Coptic epistolary documents.

[34] Garel 2015. A printed version of this dissertation (entitled *Héritage et transmission dans le monachisme égyptien. Les testaments des supérieurs du* topos *de Saint-Phoibammon à Thèbes* [Bibliothèque d'études coptes 27], Le Caire) is currently being published

Fig. 33. The Monastery of St. Phoebammon during the excavations of Deir el-Bahari by the Egypt Exploration Society from 1893 to 1905. (Photograph courtesy of the Egypt Exploration Society.)

composed of the wills of the four abbots of the Monastery of St. Phoebammon occupying the second and third terraces of the Temple of Hatshepsut at Deir el-Bahari on the western bank of Thebes [Fig. 33]:

P.Mon.Phoib.Test. 1:[35] The will of Abraham (end of the 610s) in Greek;
P.Mon.Phoib.Test. 2:[36] The will of Victor (4/12/634) in Coptic;
P.Mon.Phoib.Test. 3:[37] The will of Peter (660 or 675) in Coptic;
P.Mon.Phoib.Test. 4:[38] The will of Jacob (ca. 695) in Coptic.

Here I will discuss only the first two, which are prior to the Arab Conquest. They reflect the shift that took place during the first decades of the seventh century, resulting in a preference for Coptic rather than Greek, according to

at the Institut Français d'Archéologie Orientale (Cairo). On monastic wills, see Garel and Nowak 2017; and Giorda 2017.

35 = *P.Lond.* I 77 (p. 231), reed. Garel 2015, II, 5–56.

36 = *P.KRU* 77 + P.Sorb. inv. 2680, ed. Garel 2015, II, 57–108. The Greek portion is known as *SB* I 4319.

37 = P.Lyon without inv. (*deperdita*), ed. Garel 2015, II, 109–42.

38 = *P.KRU* 65, reed. Garel 2015, II, 143–79.

the same trend that I have already noted for other types of legal documents. Above all, they allow us to understand more fully the testators' motivations for employing Coptic rather than Greek, which at the time was the language typically used for wills. Let us take a closer look at these wills.

The first one was drawn up by Abraham, a figure of Theban Christianity who is well known from an abundant archive, to which I will return in the third dossier. During his time as a monk at the monastery named after Saint Phoebammon, situated in a remote desert location between Medinet Habu and Hermonthis, Abraham was appointed to the episcopal see of Hermonthis by Bishop Damian (578–605) around 595, and in any event before 601.[39] He remained there until his death, which may have been in 621.[40] Preferring monastic life, he refused to move to the city of the diocese, Hermonthis, but at the insistence of Damian, agreed to move closer by transferring the Monastery of St. Phoebammon to a location ceded to it by the village of Djeme at the former Temple of Hatshepsut.[41] As it appears, it was nevertheless in Hermonthis that he drew up his will and, even though he knew only Coptic, he ordered it to be written in Greek through the services of a notary (*nomikos*).

Abraham appointed his close collaborator Victor, who was also a monk and cleric (holding the rank of priest), as his heir and the abbot of the monastery.[42] Around fifteen years later, Victor however drafted a very different will from that of his predecessor [Fig. 34]: he ordered it no longer to be drawn up in the city but rather at the monastery itself, no longer in Greek but in Coptic, and no longer by a notary but instead by a scribe (*grammateus*) from the village of Djeme. In doing so, he inaugurated a tradition: starting with Victor, the wills of the monastery's abbots were all in Coptic.

The question that interests me here is how to interpret the shift from Greek to Coptic between the two wills. Is it idiosyncratic or, on the contrary, does it reflect an evolution? A first explanation might consist in attributing the language used to the personality of the testator:[43] Abraham was a bishop, and despite his lack of familiarity with Greek, he may have believed that this position forced him to use Greek, the language of the Church and therefore of its dignitaries. In that case, the symbolic value of

---

[39] Cf. Krause 1956, I, 21–22. I am also taking a portion of the results from the doctoral research of Renata Dekker (Dekker 2018).

[40] Date of the last evidence of Abraham as per *SB Kopt.* II 906 according to Dekker 2018, 90.

[41] I am following the scenario suggested by Krause 1985 (reused in Krause 1991).

[42] Regarding this figure, cf. Garel 2015, I, 87–97.

[43] This is the position of Garel 2015, I, 71.

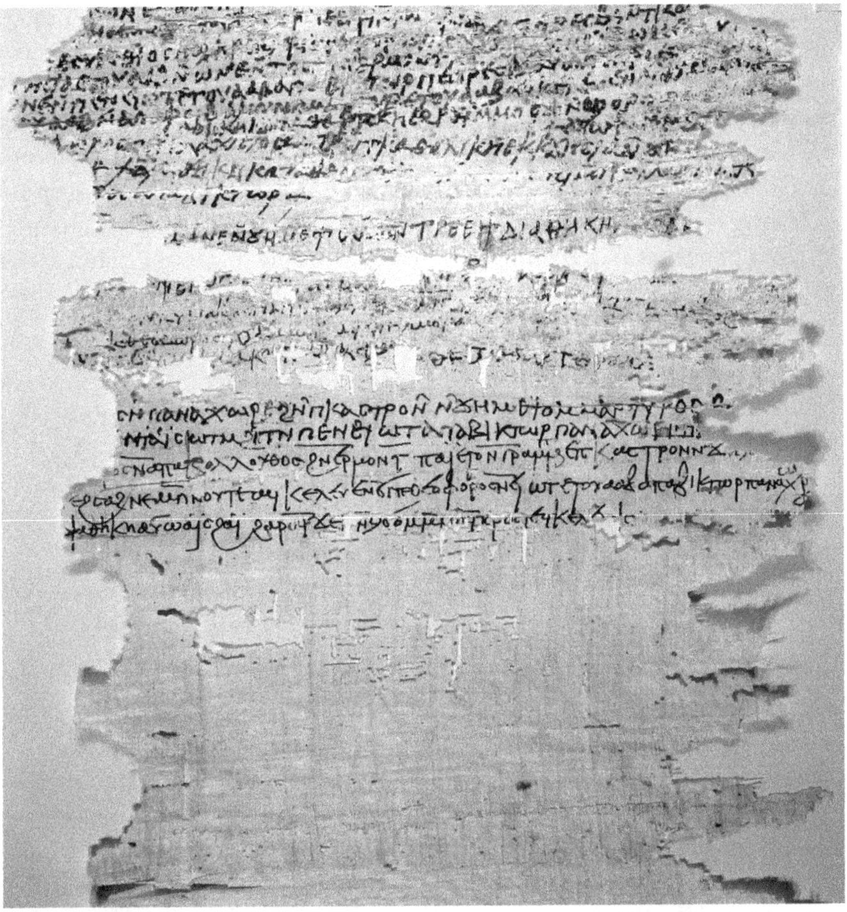

Fig. 34. End of Victor's will in Coptic with the subscriptions of the witnesses (P.Sorb. inv. 2680 = *P.Mon.Phoib.Test.* 2 [Monastery of St. Phoebammon, 634]). (Photograph courtesy of Adam Bülow-Jacobsen and the Institut de Papyrologie, Sorbonne Université.)

Greek would justify his choice, despite the complications that it implied for a non-Greek-speaker. As for Victor, he was not a bishop, and given that he was above all a monk, he was not subject to such an obligation. Nothing stopped him from using his everyday language, that of the milieu to which he belonged: the Monastery of St. Phoebammon and the village of Djeme in which it was located.

Really nothing? It was still necessary that the use of the language should be legally authorized. Yet Abraham's will confirms that it was imperative to use Greek for drawing up wills: "I have dictated my will in the language of the Egyptians but I have ordered it to be written in Greek *according to that which is prescribed by the imperial laws properly and piously established*."[44] In chapter 1, I mentioned the specific linguistic constraints that burdened the genre of wills. Why was the obligation of Greek, emphasized and respected at the end of the 610s, no longer in force some fifteen years later, as the fact that Victor's will is written in Coptic shows? We cannot yet doubt that the latter was legal; otherwise what would have been Victor's purpose in having it drawn up, given that wills were commonly disputed? In fact, it so happens that this was the case here, according to a letter found at the neighboring Monastery of Epiphanius:

> ***P.Mon.Epiph.* 257**[45]
>
> We ask your goodness to be kind enough to act for the sake of God and to request the *lashane* (= village headman) Elisaios to summon x son of Panachōre and John son of Eudoxia [. . .], to go in and cause Jacob to produce the will of our father, the priest Apa Victor, that they may learn whether it be that which he drew up, while yet he was in his body, and which they subscribed in their own handwriting; and that they may declare the truth onto us and our heart be at ease.

In Esther Garel's highly appealing interpretation, this letter may have been addressed by two monks sent away by the deceased Victor, to another monk, who could have been the abbot of the Monastery of Epiphanius. The latter monk would have had to ask the *lashane*, that is, the civil authority in Djeme, to make Jacob produce Victor's will (Jacob was the successor of Peter as the head of St. Phoebammon) and to gather witnesses for authenticating it.[46] The fact that the administrative authorities were called upon to initiate a process to open and authenticate the will—in the presence of witnesses, as was customary—shows that this will was treated like any other one and that it was granted legal value irrespective of the question of language.

---

[44] *P.Mon.Phoib.Test.* 1, 13–15: τὸ ἔσχατον̣ [βο]υ̣λημάτιον ἐπαγόρευσα μὲν τῇ τῶν Αἰγυπτίων φωνῇ, Ἑλληνικοῖς δὲ καὶ ῥήμασιν ἐπέταξα γραφῆναι κατὰ τὲ θειωδῶς ὑπὸ τῶν καλῶς καὶ εὐσεβῶς κειμένων νόμων διηγορευμένα.

[45] L. 2–10 (in the re-edition of Garel 2015, I, 67–68): (. . .) ⲧ̅ⲛ̅ⲡⲁⲣⲁⲕⲁⲗⲉⲓ ⲇⲉ ⲛ̄ⲧⲉⲧ̅ⲛ̅ⲁⲅⲁⲡⲏ | [ϫⲉ ⲉⲧⲉⲧⲛ]ⲁⲣ̄ ⲡⲛⲁ ⲛ̄ⲧⲉⲧ̅ⲛ̅ⲁⲁⲥ ⲉⲧⲃⲉ ⲡⲛⲟⲩⲧⲉ ⲛ̄ⲧⲉⲧ̅ⲛ̅|[ⲃⲱⲕ ⲛⲧⲉⲧⲛ]ⲡⲁⲣⲁⲕⲁⲗⲉⲓ ⲙ̄ⲡⲗⲁϣⲁⲛⲉ ⲉⲗⲓⲥⲁⲓⲟⲥ | [- - -]ⲛ̣ⲡⲁⲛⲁⲭⲱⲣⲉ ⲙ̅ⲛ̅ ⲓ̈ⲱϩⲁⲛⲛⲏⲥ ⲛ̄ⲉⲩⲇⲟⲝⲓⲁ | [- - -] ⲛ̅ϥ̅ⲃⲱⲕ ⲉϩⲟⲩⲛ ⲛ̅ϥ̅ⲧⲣⲉⲓ̈ⲁⲕⲱⲃ ⲛ̄ ⲧⲇⲓⲁⲑⲏⲕⲏ | [ⲙⲡⲉⲛⲉⲓⲱ]ⲧ? ⲡⲡⲣⲉⲥⲃ(ⲩⲧⲉⲣⲟⲥ) ⲁⲡⲁ ⲃ[ⲓⲕⲧ]ⲱⲣ ⲉⲃⲟⲗ ⲛ̄ⲥ̣ⲉ̣ⲉⲓⲙⲉ ϫⲉ | [ⲧⲁⲓ̈ ⲛⲧⲁϥ]ⲥ̅ⲙ̅ⲛ̅ⲧ̅ⲥ̅ ⲧⲉ ⲉⲧⲓ ⲉϥ̅ϩ̅ⲙ̅ ⲡⲥⲱⲙⲁ ⲉⲁⲩϩⲩⲡⲟⲅⲣⲁⲫⲉ | [ⲙⲙⲟⲥ ϩⲛ ⲧⲉ]ⲩ̣ϭⲓϫ ⲛ̄ⲥⲉⲧⲁⲩⲟ ⲧⲙⲉ ⲛⲁⲛ ⲛ̄ⲧⲉⲡⲉⲛϩⲏⲧ ⲕⲱ ⲉⲃⲟⲗ | [ⲙⲙⲟⲛ (. . .).

[46] Garel 2015, I, 69. I am using Crum's translation, which I have amended.

The use of Coptic in full legality some fifteen years after a time in which Greek was still considered compulsory seems clearly to demonstrate an evolution that goes beyond the question of the testators' status.

Rather than imagining a law removing the obligation of drawing up wills in Greek—we have no evidence of one—I am inclined to think that the ten years of Sasanian domination (619–29) softened the linguistic constraints weighing on the writing of wills as well as other documents, as we saw in chapter 3. Despite not significantly changing the institutional environment of the Egyptians, which the Persians barely touched, the ten-year break with the Byzantine regime must have symbolically undermined the obligation to use Greek exclusively in the legal domain by dissociating law and language from one another. The imperial laws imposing Greek, which Abraham's will expressly mentions (indicating that these laws were still respected on the eve of the Sasanian Conquest), no longer had such an imperious nature and therefore effectiveness in 634.

The legal-linguistic context had changed, as had the function of the will; this is another reason that accounts for the shift from Greek to Coptic illustrated by our dossier. When we compare Abraham's and Victor's wills, we are struck by an essential difference. Victor introduces narrative elements (which we also find in the last two wills), which justify the choice of his successors and motivates the writing of his will, going so far as directly addressing his heirs (he names three of them) in a long, highly elaborate passage:[47]

> so that you may be of one single opinion in complete submission, obeying one another with humility [. . .] and so that none of you three act against the collective will of a common agreement (. . .), so that you respect the teachings and rules according to the canon of our holy fathers [. . .] who have passed away before us; so that you take care of the brothers that live with you according to the will of God, as we have done at all times since the beginning; and so that they may also obey you in all that you order them for the management of the holy *topos* (= monastery) (. . .).[48]

[47] *P.Mon.Phoib.Test.* 2, 93–114.

[48] L. 99–108 : ϫⲉⲕⲁⲥ ⲉⲧ̣ⲉ̣ⲧ̣ⲛⲛⲁϣⲱⲡⲉ | [ϩ]ⲛ̅ ϯⲅⲛⲱⲙⲏ ⲛ̅ⲟⲩⲱ̣ⲧ̣ⲉ̣ ϩⲛ̅ ϩⲩⲡⲟⲧⲁⲅⲏ ⲛⲓⲙ ⲉⲧⲉⲧⲛ̅ⲥⲱⲧⲙ ⲛ̅ⲥⲁ ⲛⲉⲧⲛ̅ⲉⲣⲏⲩ ϩⲛ̅ ⲑⲃⲓⲟ | [± 4]ⲁ̣ ⲁⲩⲱ ϫⲉ ⲉⲛⲉⲗⲁⲩⲉ ⲛ̅ϩⲏⲧⲏⲩⲧⲛ̅ ⲛⲡϣⲟⲙⲛ`ⲧ´ ⲣ̅ ⲟⲩϩⲱⲃ ⲡⲁⲣⲁ ⲡⲉⲧⲛ̅ⲟⲩⲱϣ` ϩⲓ ⲟⲩⲥⲟⲡ | [ϩⲛ] ⲧ̣ⲓ̣ϩⲟⲙⲟⲛⲟⲓⲁ ⲛ̅ⲟⲩⲱⲧⲉ (. . .) ϫⲉⲕ̣[ⲁⲥ] ⲉ̣ⲧ̣ⲉ̣ⲧ̣ⲛ̣̅||[ⲁⲙⲁ]ϩⲧⲉ ⲛ̅ⲛⲉⲥⲃⲟⲟⲩⲉ ⲙⲛ̅ ⲛⲉⲛⲧⲟⲗⲏ̣ ⲡⲣⲟⲥ ⲡⲕⲁⲛⲟ̣ⲛ ⲛ̅ⲛⲉ̣ⲛ̣ⲉⲓⲟ̣ⲧⲉ̣

In other words, in addition to a legal function consisting of the establishment of heirs, Victor's will takes on a spiritual function: truly a parting speech, it institutes the course of his successors and ensures the cohesion of the community. Transcending the strict limits of a private law document, it transmits a message with a collective destination and a spiritual and edifying purpose.[49]

Clearly, this function required communication in a language that the community understood. Accordingly, the will could be fully operative only in Coptic. We can easily understand why the abbots of monasteries instituted the custom of drawing up wills in this language as soon as the legal conditions permitted it.

Yet, despite everything, it would be a mistake to consider that the shift from Greek to Coptic took place clearly and definitively simply through the substitution of one for the other. The process was, in fact, less schematic, consisting of overlapping and hybridization. Therefore, despite its language and its legal irregularities with respect to Roman law,[50] Victor's will bears witness to a very large degree of dependency on Greek: it takes a legal name directly borrowed from Greek;[51] it starts with Christian invocations and regnal dating expressed in Greek;[52] it is riddled with

---

ⲉⲧⲟⲩ̣ⲁ̣ⲁ̣ⲃ̣ ⲛ̣ⲁ̣ⲓ̈ . [.] . | [ⲛⲧⲁ]ⲩ̣ⲡⲁⲣⲁⲅⲉ ϩⲁ ⲧⲉⲛϩⲏ vacat ⲁ̣ⲩ̣ⲱ̅ ⲛⲧⲉⲧⲛ̅ϭⲱϣⲧ ⲛ̅ⲥⲁ ⲛⲉⲥⲛⲏⲩ ⲉⲧⲟⲩⲏ̣ϩ ⲛⲉ̣ⲙ̣ⲏ[ⲧ]ⲛ̅ ⲡⲣⲟⲥ̣| [ⲡⲟⲩ]ϣ̣ϣ ⲙ̅[ⲡ]ⲛⲟⲩⲧⲉ ⲕⲁⲧⲁ ⲑⲉ ⲉⲧⲛⲉⲓⲣⲉ `ⲙⲙⲟⲥ´ ⲛ̅ⲟⲩⲟⲉⲓϣ ⲛⲓⲙ ϫⲓⲛ̅ ⲛϣⲟⲣ̅ⲡ̅ ⲛ̅ⲧ̣ⲟ̣ⲟ̣ⲩ̣ ϩⲱⲟⲩ ⲟ̅ⲛ̅| [ⲛⲥⲉⲥ]ⲱ̅ⲧ̅ⲙ̣̅ ⲛⲥⲱ̅ⲧ̅ⲛ̅ ϩ̅ⲛ̅ ϩⲱⲃ ⲛⲓⲙ ⲉⲧⲉⲧⲛ̅ⲛⲁ̣ⲕⲉⲗⲉⲩⲉ ⲙⲙⲟϥ̣ ⲛⲁ̣[ⲩ] ⲉ̣ⲧⲇⲓⲟⲓⲕⲏⲥⲓⲥ̣ ⲛ̅|[ⲡⲧⲟⲡⲟ]ⲥ̣ ⲉ̣ⲧ̣ⲟ̣ⲩ̣ⲁⲁⲃ.

49 Garel 2015, I, 69–75.

50 See Garel and Nowak 2017.

51 ⲇⲓⲁⲑⲏⲕⲏ (διαθήκη) or ⲃⲟⲩⲗⲉⲩⲙⲁ (βούλευμα).

52 L. 1–10: ☩ Ἐν ὀνόματι τῆς ἁγίας καὶ ζωοποιοῦ καὶ ὁμοουσίου Τριάδος] | [πατρὸς καὶ υἱοῦ καὶ ἁγίου πνεύματος, βασιλείας τοῦ θειοτάτου] | [καὶ γαληνοτάτου καὶ θεοστεφοῦς ἡμῶν δεσπότου Φλ(αυίου)] | [Ἡρακλείου τοῦ αἰωνίου Αὐγούστου καὶ αὐτοκράτορος καὶ] | [μεγίστου] εὐεργέτου ἔτους εἰκουσ[τοῦ πέμπτου καὶ ὑπατείας τοῦ] | [αὐτοῦ] εὐσεβεστάτου ἡμῶν δε[σπ(ότου) καὶ] ἔτους εἰκουστοῦ τετάρτο[υ] | καὶ Φλ(αυίου) Ἡρακλείου Νεοῦ Κωνσταντίνου τοῦ θεοστẹ[φοῦς] | [αὐ]τοῦ \υἱοῦ/ ἔτους εἰκουστοῦ τρίτου, Χοιακ [η], ἰνδικ(τί)ο(νος) ηׅ//, ἐν τῷ [ἁγίῳ] | [τό]πῳ τοῦ ἀθλοφόρου μάρτυρος ἀββᾶ Φοιβάμωνọς τοῦ ὄρου[ς] Μẹμ̣νọ[νίων] | [νο]μοῦ Ἑρμώνθεως, ἐπὶ Ἰωάννου Δαυεὶδ τ(ο)ῦ τιμιωτ(άτου) πρωτοκωμ[ήτου] "In the name of the holy, life-giving, and consubstantial Trinity, Father, Son, and Holy Spirit, in the reign of our most divine and most serene master, crowned by God, Flavius Heraclius the eternal Augustus and emperor, the greatest benefactor, the twenty-fifth year, and in the consulship of the same most pious master, the twenty-fourth year, and of his son, Flavius Heraclius Novus Constantinus, crowned by

Greek loanwords (we find 300 in 174 lines of Coptic) and even Greek phrases used in their original form,[53] to the extent that, despite the difference in language, some of the expressions are almost identical to those in Abraham's will;[54] when Greek words for technical vocabulary are not used,[55] translation loanwords are employed (that is, Coptic words that are granted a specifically Greek meaning that they do not otherwise convey in Coptic),[56] which are sometimes accompanied by the Greek word that they are intended to express;[57] and lastly, its wording may be affected by Greek

---

God, the twenty-third year, 8th of Choiak of the 8th indiction, in the holy *topos* (= monastery) of the victorious martyr Abba Phoebammon of the mountain of the Memnonia, in the Hermonthite nome, under John son of David, the most honorable village headman."

[53] L. 129: ⲟⲩⲕ ⲉⲝⲉⲥⲧⲓ (οὐκ ἔξεστι); l. 141–42: ⲉⲡⲓ ⲧⲱ ⲡⲣⲱⲧⲟⲛ | [ⲙ]ⲉⲛ (ἐπὶ τῷ + πρῶτον μέν).

[54] Cf. the following note.

[55] One example among so many others: *P.Mon.Phoib.Test.* 1, 7–9, δίχα παντὸς δόλου καὶ φόβου καὶ βίας καὶ ἀπάτης καὶ | ἀνάγκης τινὸς καὶ πάσης νομίμου παραγραφῆς καὶ συναρπαγῆς καὶ μηχανῆς παντοίας | ἄνευ οἱασδήποτε διχονοίας τε καὶ κακονοίας "with no ruse, nor fear, nor violence, nor trickery, or constraints of any kind, with no legal exception or subterfuge, nor artifice of any kind, with no disputes nor bad intentions of any kind," to be compared to *P.Mon.Phoib.Test.* 2, 35–36, ϫ̣[ⲓ] ⲛ̣ϭⲟⲛⲥ ⲕⲏ ⲛⲁϊ ⲉϩⲣⲁϊ ⲟⲩⲇⲉ ⲁⲡⲁⲧⲏ ϩⲓ ⲁⲛⲁⲅⲕⲏ ⲟⲩⲇⲉ ⲥⲩⲛϩⲁⲣⲡⲁⲅⲏ | [ϩⲓ ⲡⲉⲣⲓⲅⲣⲁ]ⲫ̣[ⲏ] ⲉ̣ⲙⲛ̣ [ⲟⲩ]ⲁ̣ⲛ̣ⲁⲅⲕ̣[ⲏ] [ⲛ]ⲟ̣ⲩ̣ⲱⲧⲉ ⲕⲏ ⲛⲁϊ ⲉϩⲣⲁϊ "without having been subject to violence, trickery or constraints, with no subterfuge nor fraud, with no constraints being exercised upon me." We note that it is the most concrete concept, βία "violence," that was the only one translated into Coptic, with the others purely and simply being taken from Greek.

[56] Cf. Garel 2015, I, 166–67. I note, among others, the verb ⲁⲙⲁϩⲧⲉ (lit. "to seize") translating the legal concept of κρατεῖν, which has the meaning of "to seize," but which in the legal context means "to possess" in the Latin legal sense of "to have the *possessio* of a thing," as opposed to the verb ⲣ ϫⲟⲉⲓⲥ (lit. "to become the master of"), which conveys κυριεύειν in the sense of "to have the *dominium* over a thing."

[57] L. 123–25, where ⲣ ϫⲟⲉⲓⲥ is accompanied by the Greek rendering κυριεύεσθαι (see the preceding note): ⲛⲧ̣ⲉⲧⲛ̣ⲣ̣ | [ϫⲟⲉⲓⲥ] ⲉⲣⲟⲟⲩ ϩⲛ ⲙⲛⲧϫⲟⲉⲓⲥ ⲛⲓⲙ ⲡⲣⲟⲥ ⲑⲉ ⲛⲧⲁϊϩⲟⲣ̣ⲓ̣ⲍⲉ ⲙⲙⲟⲟⲥ ⲛⲏⲧⲛ ⲛⲧⲡⲉ | [ⲛⲧⲉ]ⲧ̣[ⲛ] ⲕⲩⲣⲓⲉⲩⲉⲥⲑⲁⲓ ⲙⲙⲟⲟⲩ "you will be the owners of it in full ownership, as I have decided for you above, and you will be the owners of it." Note that these translation loanwords are not specific to Victor, but are a common feature in Coptic legal documents (see Richter 2008b, 181 for ⲁⲙⲁϩⲧⲉ and 358 for ⲣ ϫⲟⲉⲓⲥ).

syntax.[58] In short, it would not be an exaggeration to say that in many respects, Victor's will is "a Greek document in Coptic dress."[59]

Yet upon closer examination and despite being written in Greek, Abraham's will is not exempt from any suspicion either, and under no circumstances can it be considered to be a model of a Greek will. It contains a certain number of anomalies compared to other Byzantine Greek wills. The most obvious of these are the bilateral contract clauses that are here used in a documentary genre in which they should not appear. For example, we find the formula guaranteeing that the testator has not been subjected to violence and trickery (which is typical of contracts but unexpected in a will),[60] the security and penalty clause,[61] or an oath by the emperor.[62] Other syntactic particularities further make it an atypical document. This leads Esther Garel to state that "in a certain way, Abraham's will is closer to Coptic wills."[63] In other words, to reverse the above-mentioned phrase, it can be considered a "Coptic document in Greek dress!"

Are these anomalies due to the fact that the will was dictated by a person who was not a legal specialist, and moreover in Coptic, as we

---

[58] L. 26–27: ⲙⲏⲡⲟⲧ[ⲉ] | [ϩⲛ ⲟⲩϣⲟⲡ] ⲛ̄ϣⲟ̄ⲡ̄ ⲁⲩⲱ ⲡⲁⲣⲁ ⲧⲁⲡⲣⲟⲥⲇⲟⲕⲓⲁ ⲛ̄ⲧⲁϫⲱⲕ ⲉⲃⲟⲗ "may I not die suddenly and unexpectedly." Garel 2015, I, 169, correctly remarked that the final position of the verb is abnormal and that it must be a copy of the equivalent Greek expression that is found in *P.Mon.Phoib.Test.* 1, 4: [μ]ὴ ἐξαίφνης καὶ παρὰ προσδοκίαν τὸν τῇδε μεταλλάξω βίον "it is to be feared that I may depart from this life suddenly and unexpectedly."

[59] MacCoull 1995, 343, seems to borrow this expression from a study by Bagnall (*Through a Papyrus Darkly*, a working title that was changed to *Reading Papyri, Writing History* in the final publication), but I could not find it in the published version. The expression was used once again by MacCoull 2007a, 75 (this time without quotation marks) and by Cromwell 2010, 221n3.

[60] See chapter 4, n. 55.

[61] L. 41–57. The penalty clause was already found in late Byzantine wills (*P.Cair. Masp.* II 67151, 216–19), but here it takes on a new scope; in *P.Mon.Phoib.Test.* 2, 143–45, it was combined with a spiritual penalty: ⲙⲛ̄ⲛ̣ⲥ̣ⲱ̣ⲥ̣ ⲛ̄ⲥⲉϩⲏ̣ⲉ ⲉⲣⲟ̄ϥ̄ ϩⲓ ⲡⲃⲏⲙ̣ⲁ̣ | [ⲙⲡ]ⲁ̣ⲅⲁⲑⲟⲥ ⲙⲙⲉ ⲡⲛⲟⲩ̣ⲧⲉ ⲛ̄ⲡ̄ⲧ̄ⲏ̄ⲣ̄ϥ̄ ⲉⲩⲕⲣⲓⲛⲉ ⲙ̄ⲙⲟϥ ⲁⲩⲱ ⲉⲩⲕⲟ̣ⲗ̣ⲁ̣ⲍⲉ̣ ⲙ̣ⲙ̣ⲟ̣ϥ̣ | [ϩⲁ ⳿ϩⲩ]ⲡⲟⲑⲉⲥⲓⲥ ϫⲉ ⲁ̣ϥ̣ⲟⲩⲱϣ ⲉⲡⲁⲣⲁ\ⲃⲁ/ ⲛ̄ⲡⲁⲛⲁϣ ⲙⲛ̄ ⲡⲣⲟⲥⲧⲓⲙⲟⲛ "next, he will be summoned before the court of the true God who is all goodness to be judged and punished for these facts, because he will have wanted to violate the oath and the penalty."

[62] L. 80–81: σὺν | θείῳ ὅρκῳ "with an imperial oath" (see also the religious oath l. 63–64: ἐπωμοσάμην | πρὸς τῆς ἁγίας καὶ ὁμοουσίου τριάδος καὶ τοῦ περιβεβλημμένου μοι σχήματος κτλ. "I swear on the holy and consubstantial Trinity and on the habit that I am wearing, etc.").

[63] Garel 2015, I, 52.

have seen? Yet the notary, as a professional who would be literate in both languages, should have eliminated them. Concluding that we are dealing with a second-rate professional—which he certainly was—does not constitute an explanation that is fully satisfactory, given that some of the noted irregularities are found again amplified in later Coptic acts and are therefore not the idiosyncrasies of a pen pusher with little education in inheritance law. It is more legitimate to ask whether these might not pertain to the phenomenon of the growing autonomy of the Coptic documentary practice, which I discussed earlier.[64] Before moving on to the language, this process took place at the level of content and of the formulary through an increasingly apparent indifference to the Greek model and through the development of wording that constantly departed from the restrictive framework of the Greek notarial tradition for this type of document. It was during the second stage that it became institutionalized through the use of the Coptic language and the creation of a school of Coptic-speaking practitioners (not to call them notaries).

For the moment, wills have allowed us to account for this phenomenon in the restricted milieus of monastic communities. However, its scope went beyond the walls of monasteries, spreading throughout society, within the circles of both clerics and laypeople. This is what we are going to see with the third dossier, in which some of the protagonists are the same people with whom we have just become acquainted.

The Legal Documents of Abraham, Bishop of Hermonthis: The Decisive Role of the Theban Bishops

In addition to his will, Abraham left behind a large number of texts related to his episcopal position. These texts were (re)edited by M. Krause in 1956 in a remarkable and still unpublished thesis,[65] which explains why this dossier has not yet attracted the attention that it deserves.[66] This collection, which I call *O.Abraham*, is composed of 114 Coptic ostraca

---

[64] Cf. chapter 2, pp. 40–41, and 3, p. 79.

[65] Krause 1956. Other texts belonging to this collection have been spotted since then (in particular in the Columbia collection); however, in the absence of a systematic study of this dossier, I will limit myself here to the series edited by Krause. Nick Venable is finishing a PhD at Chicago on the Abraham archive.

[66] Nonetheless, along with that of Pisenthios of Coptos, it is the subject of Dekker 2018. The following pages are based on Fournet 2018b.

preserving documents (copies or originals[67]) revolving around the person of Abraham, in which he is either the recipient (52 texts) or the writer (58 texts), or in which he is mentioned (4 texts). Even though the place of discovery of these texts is unknown, it is likely that it was the Monastery of St. Phoebammon.

Typology of the Texts

The great interest of this collection for our current concern has to do with the nature of the texts comprising it: almost half of them are legal documents (51, alongside 63 letters). Datable from around 595 (the ascension of Abraham to the episcopacy) to 621 (the presumed date of his death), these texts constitute to date the oldest and most plentiful dossier of non-epistolary Coptic documents that are unquestionably datable and that benefit from the contextual information provided by their protagonist. This is also the first time that a Graeco-Coptic papyrological collection offers a ratio between the number of letters (63) and non-epistolary documents (51) that is so favorable to the latter.

What are the types of legal documents contained in it? We can classify them into seven categories:

(a) Declarations of engagement (26 texts): these are documents through which one or multiple individuals committed to take on a position (deaconate or priesthood) according to the rules that it involved,[68] to fulfill the obligations related to this position,[69] to provide a service for the bishop or for the monastery in question,[70] to submit to

[67] Certain documents present various hands in the subscriptions (for example, *O.Abraham* 15), a fact that leads to the idea that they are originals, while others are definitely copies. We can regret the fact that differences of hands are not signaled the majority of the time in the edition ("Trotzdem ist eine Kollationierung aller Texte noch unbedingt erforderlich" [Krause 1956, I, 7]): the latter, for practical reasons, remains dependent on editions by Crum, who did not judge it necessary to indicate them.

[68] *O.Abraham* 2–5, 8–9.

[69] For example, *O.Abraham* 26: Hello commits to a certain number of tasks concerning a church (sleeping there—himself or his father—taking care of the lamp in the morning, holding the religious service); 81: the priest John commits to not leave the diocese again; 85: Mēnas acknowledges that if he does not learn the Scriptures by heart before the end of Thōt (= September) and does not recite them, he will be expelled from the clergy.

[70] *O.Abraham* 88: Jacob declares that if his father Pesynthios swears in the name of God, he will come to tell Abraham of this fact; 103: the priest Mōusēs declares that he is ready to provide something to the monastery [of Phoebammon] (the nature of which is unclear).

the judgement of the bishop,[71] or to serve a sentence.[72] For example, *O.Abraham* 2 (= *O.Crum* 30):

> I, Papas, deacon, son of Abraham, write to our holy father, bishop Apa Abraham: after I applied to you, you ordained me as a deacon to the monastery (*topos*) of Saint-Apa-Victor. Now, I am ready to observe the commandments, canons, and skills, to learn by heart the gospel according to John within 2 months, to come and recite it to you and to retain it, fasting during the 40 days and watching in my bedroom (i.e., my cell) during the 40 days. And (I am ready) to watch in my bedroom on the appointed days of communion and not to go elsewhere without permission. I, Papas, deacon, agree.[73]

The engagement may take on the form of a self-surety in which the declarant acts as the guarantor that he will fulfill his obligations, or it may be combined with the surety of a third party.[74]

(b) Sureties (11 texts[75]): this category of texts constitutes the counterpart or the complement to the previous one. It consists of documents by means of which one or multiple individuals act as guarantors for the fact that a third party will properly comply with his obligations,[76]

---

[71] *O.Abraham* 63–65 (these texts may also be classified in the category of *dialyseis*), 67.

[72] *O.Abraham* 80: after having been excluded from the celebration of the Eucharist by Abraham for disobedience, the priest Athanasios asks the latter to allow him to participate in it once again. To do so, Abraham required him to learn by heart a portion of the Scriptures before a certain date, and the priest acts as a guarantor before Abraham for the fulfillment of this obligation.

[73] ⳨ ⲁⲛⲟⲕ ⲡⲁⲡⲁ ⲡ[ⲇⲓⲁⲕ(ⲟⲛⲟⲥ) | ⲡϣⲏⲣⲉ ⲛⲁⲃⲣⲁϩⲁⲙ | ⲉϥⲥϩⲁï ⲛ̄ⲡⲉⲛïⲱⲧ ⲉⲧ[ⲟⲩ]||ⲁⲁⲃ ⲁⲡⲁ ⲁⲃⲣⲁϩⲁⲙ ⲡⲉⲡⲓⲥ|ⲕⲟⲡⲟⲥ ϫⲉ ⲉïⲡⲉïⲇ̣ⲏ̣ ⲁïⲡⲁⲗ[ⲁ]||ⲅⲁⲗⲉï ⲛ̄ⲙⲟⲕ ⲁⲕϫⲉ[ⲣⲟⲇ]ⲟⲛⲉï ⲛ̄|ⲙ̄ⲙⲟï ⲛ̄ⲇⲓⲁⲕ(ⲟⲛⲟⲥ) ⲉⲡⲧⲟⲡⲟⲥ ⲛ̄ⲫⲁ|ⲅⲓⲟⲥ ⲁⲡⲁ ⲃⲓⲕⲧⲱⲣ ϯⲛⲟⲩ ϯⲟ̄ ⲛ|ϩⲁ̣ⲓⲧⲓⲙⲟⲥ ⲉⲧⲣⲁϩⲁⲣⲉϩ ⲉⲛⲉⲛ|ⲧⲟⲗⲏ ⲙⲛ̄ ⲛ̄ⲕⲁⲛⲱⲛ | ⲙⲛ̄ ⲛ̄ⲉⲡⲓⲥⲧⲏⲙⲏ | v° [ⲁⲩ]ⲱ ⲛ̄ⲧⲁϫⲉï ⲡⲉⲩⲁⲛ||[ⲅⲅ]ⲉⲗⲓⲟⲛ ⲛ̄ⲅⲁⲧⲁ ïⲱϩⲁⲛ|ⲛⲏⲥ ⲛ̄ⲁⲡⲟⲥⲧⲏⲑⲟⲥ ⲛⲥⲛⲁⲩ | ⲛ̄ⲉⲃⲟⲧ ⲛ̄ⲧⲁⲉⲓ ⲉϩⲟⲩⲛ ⲛ̄ⲧⲁ̣|ⲧ̣ⲁ̣ⲩⲟⲟϥ̣ ⲉⲧⲟⲟⲧⲕ̄ ⲛ̄ⲧⲁⲁⲙⲁϩ|ⲧⲉ ⲛ̄ⲙⲟϥ ⲛ̄ⲧⲁⲣ ϩⲙⲉ ⲛ̄ϩⲟⲟⲩ | ⲉⲓⲛⲏⲥⲧⲉⲩⲉ ⲛⲧⲁⲣ ϩⲙⲉ ⲛ|ϩⲟⲟⲩ ⲉïⲣⲟⲉⲓⲥ ⲉⲡⲁⲙⲁ ⲛ̄ⲛⲕⲟ|ⲧⲕ ⲁⲩⲱ ⲛ̄ϩⲟⲟⲩ ⲛⲥⲉⲛⲁⲅⲉ ⲉ̣ⲧ|ⲧⲏϣ ⲉⲧⲣⲁϩⲁⲣⲉϩ ⲉ̄ⲣⲟⲟⲩ | ⲉⲡⲁⲙⲁ ⲛ̄ⲛ̄ⲕⲟⲧⲕ̄ ⲁⲩⲱ ⲛ̄ⲛⲉï|ⲃⲱⲕ ⲉⲙⲁ ⲉϫⲛ̄ ϣⲓⲛⲉ. | ⲁⲛⲟⲕ ⲡⲁⲡⲁⲥ ⲡⲇⲓⲁⲕ(ⲟⲛⲟⲥ) ϯⲥⲧ<ⲟⲓ>|ⲭⲉ̣ⲓ̣.

[74] *O.Abraham* 6, 7, 10, 11. Cf. also *O.Abraham* 83–84, which I have categorized below in sureties.

[75] Without counting "self-sureties" (cf. chapter 4, n. 91) and sureties included in declarations of engagement that I have classified in the category regarding the latter.

[76] *O.Abraham* 12–16.

will not commit a certain reprehensible act,[77] or will appear at his "proceedings."[78] For example, *O.Abraham* 61 (= *O.Crum* 86):

I, Jacob, son of Paham, am writing to my father the Bishop. I am acting as a guarantor before you for John for that he will appear at the proceedings against Hatre, the brother of his father, regarding the room that is in the *stoa* (?), for which they are involved in legal proceedings. And the ruling that is pronounced, whether it is in favor of John or whether it is in favor of Hatre, regardless of the results, I am ready to comply with it. I, Jacob, agree.

(*Addition*) If I do not do so, I am ready to pay one *solidus* as a penalty, to appear and to submit myself to judgement. I, Apa Jacob, agree.[79]

(c) Appointments by Abraham of clerics or monks at the head of churches or monasteries (7 texts).[80] Here is one sample (*O.Abraham* 20):

First of all, I greet your sonship. Behold, I appoint you at the head of Apa Biktor. Now be kind enough to pay attention to the carelessness that (may occur) within this place and to prevent them (= clerics or monks) from being careless, but to teach them to go in the fear of God. And whoever disobeys you among the clergy or the laity will be excluded from the Eucharistic celebration until he comes to me. Therefore, take care to teach them (to do so). All their care rests on you. If you find carelessness in this place and neglect it, their guilt will fall on you in the court of God.

Deliver (this document) to my son, the deacon Apa Dios, from Bishop Abraham.[81]

---

[77] *O.Abraham* 83 (slander), 84 (slander), 86 (to behave foolishly), 87 (bad action).

[78] *O.Abraham* 61, 62.

[79] [+] ⲁⲛ[ⲟⲕ ⲓⲁⲕⲱⲃ] ⲡϣⲏⲣⲉ ⲛ[ⲡⲁ]‖ϩⲁⲙ ⲉⲓ̈ⲥϩⲁⲓ ⲙⲡⲛⲉ̣[ⲓⲱⲧ] | ⲡⲉⲡⲓⲥⲕ(ⲟⲡⲟⲥ) ⲉⲓϣⲧⲱⲣⲉ ⲉ|ⲧⲟⲧⲕ ⲛⲓⲱϩⲁⲛⲛⲏⲥ ⲉⲧⲣⲉ|ϥⲃⲱⲕ ⲉⲡϩⲁⲡ ⲙⲛ ϩⲁⲧⲣⲉ | ⲡⲥⲟⲛ ⲙⲡⲉϥ<ⲉⲓ>ⲱⲧ ϩⲁ ⲡⲥⲉⲙ|ⲡⲟⲥⲓⲟⲛ ⲉⲧⲛϩⲟⲩⲛ ⲧⲉⲥⲧⲟⲩ|ⲁ̣ϩ ⲉⲧⲟⲩⲇⲓⲕⲁⲍⲉ ⲉϫⲱϥ | ⲁ̣ⲩⲱ ⲡⲉⲧⲛⲏⲩ ⲉⲃⲟⲗ ϩⲉ |ⲡ̣ϩⲁⲡ ⲕⲁⲛ ⲁϥⲣ ⲡⲁ ⲓⲱ̣ϩⲁ|ⲛⲛⲏⲥ ⲕⲁⲛ ⲁϥⲣ ⲡⲁ ϩⲁⲧⲣⲉ | ⲡⲉⲧⲛⲏⲩ ⲉⲃⲟⲗ ⲧⲏⲣϥ ϯ|ⲱ ⲛϩⲉ̣[ⲧⲉⲙⲟⲥ ⲉ-]ⲧⲣⲁⲉⲓⲣⲉ | ⲕⲁⲧⲁⲣⲟϥ. ⲁⲛⲟⲕ ⲓ̈ⲁⲕⲱⲃ | ϯⲥ{ⲧⲩ}ⲧⲟⲓⲭⲉⲓ. ⳨ ⲉⲓ̣ⲧⲙⲉⲓⲣ̣ⲉ ⲧⲉⲱ ⲛϩⲉ|ⲧⲉⲙⲟⲥ [ⲉϯ ⲛⲟ]ⲩ ϩ̣ⲟ̣ⲗⲟ̣ⲕ̣(ⲟⲧⲧⲓⲛⲟⲥ) | ⲛ̄ⲕⲁⲧⲁ[ⲇⲓⲕⲏ ⲛⲧ]ⲁⲉⲓ ⲉϩ̣|[ⲟⲩⲛ ⲛⲧⲁϩ]ⲱⲛ ⲉⲡϩ̣ⲁ̣[ⲡ]‖ [ⲁⲛⲟⲕ] ⲁⲡⲁ ⲓⲁⲕⲱⲃ [ϯⲥⲧⲟⲓⲭⲉ].

[80] *O.Abraham* 19–25.

[81] ⳨ ϣⲟⲣⲡ ⲙⲉⲛ ϯϣⲓⲛⲉ ⲉⲧⲉⲕⲙⲛⲧϣⲏ|ⲣⲉ ⲉⲓⲥ ϩⲏⲧⲉ ϯⲟⲩⲱϩⲉ ⲙⲙⲟⲕ ⲉϫⲛ ⲡⲁ[ⲡⲁ] | ⲃⲓⲕⲧⲱⲣ ϯⲛⲟⲩ ⲁⲣⲓ ⲡⲛⲁ ⲛⲅϯ ϩⲧⲏ[ⲕ] | ⲉⲛⲕⲁⲧⲁⲫⲣⲟⲛⲏⲥⲓⲥ ⲉⲧⲛϩⲟⲩⲛ ⲙⲡ[ⲙⲁ] | ⲉⲧⲙⲙⲁⲩ

(d) Submission of witness statements in matters that Abraham must resolve (3 texts).[82]
(e) Dispute resolutions (1 or 2 texts).[83]
(f) Payment of salary (1 text).[84]
(g) Request for ordination accompanied by a surety (1 text).[85]

The Transposition Process

These documents consist of legal texts that are to some extent comparable with Greek documents that are contemporary to them. Moreover, they all have Greek names[86] and most often imitate Greek formulas by retaining their main word.[87] They also contain numerous technical words borrowed from contemporary Greek documents.[88]

ⲛⲅⲕⲱⲗⲩ ⲙⲙⲟⲟⲩ ⲉⲧⲙ[ⲁ]‖ⲁⲩ ⲁⲗⲗⲁ ⲛⲅϯ ⲥⲃⲱ ⲛⲁⲩ ⲛⲧⲟϥ ⲉ[ⲧ]‖ⲣⲉⲩⲙⲟⲟϣⲉ ϩⲛ ⲑⲟⲧⲉ ⲙⲡⲛⲟⲩ|ⲧⲉ ⲡⲉⲧⲛⲁⲣ ⲁⲧⲥⲱⲧⲙ ⲇⲉ ⲛ|ⲥⲱⲕ ϩⲛ ⲛⲕⲗⲏⲣⲓⲕⲟⲥ | ⲏ ⲛⲗⲁⲓⲕⲟⲥ ⲛⲟϫϥ | ϩⲓⲃⲟⲗ ⲙⲡϣⲁ | [ϣ]ⲁⲛⲧϥ[ⲉⲓ] | [ⲛⲁⲓ] ⲡⲗⲏⲛ ⲁⲣⲓ ⲁⲡⲁⲧⲟⲟⲧⲕ ⲉϯ‖[ⲥⲃ]ⲱ ⲛⲁⲩ ⲁⲩⲱ ⲉⲓⲥ ⲡⲟⲩⲣⲟⲟⲩϣ ⲧⲏⲣϥ | [ϩⲓ]ϫⲱⲕ ⲉⲕϣⲁⲛⲛⲁⲩ ⲉⲕⲁⲧⲁⲫⲣⲟⲛ‖[ⲏ]ⲥⲓⲥ ⲛϩⲟⲩⲛ ⲙⲡⲙⲁ ⲉⲧⲙⲙⲁⲩ ⲛⲅⲟⲃ‖[ϣ]ⲕ ⲉⲡⲉⲩⲕⲣⲓⲙⲁ ⲛⲁϣⲱⲡⲉ ϩⲓϫⲱⲕ | ϩⲓ ⲡⲃⲏⲙⲁ ⲙⲡⲛⲟⲩⲧⲉ. ⲧⲁⲁⲥ ⲙ|ⲡⲁϣⲏⲣⲉ ⲁⲡⲁ ⲇⲓⲟⲥ ⲡⲇⲓⲁⲕ(ⲟⲛⲟⲥ) | ϩⲓⲧⲛ ⲁⲃⲣⲁϩⲁⲙ | ⲡⲉⲡⲓⲥⲕ(ⲟⲡⲟⲥ).

[82] *O.Abraham* 49, 50, 68.

[83] *O.Abraham* 48: a priest (?) writes to the opposing party, the priest Plēin, recognizing that they went to see Abraham, who found an arrangement; an identical document must have been written by the other party. *O.Abraham* 66 (called σύμφωνον "arrangement") is related to this type: the deacon Ezekias, after Abraham expelled Ebōn(e)ch from said church, acknowledges that he will no longer contact the bishop regarding the matter and will put an end to his disagreement with him. The engagement of *O.Abraham* 63–65 can also be likened to these *dialyseis*: these are types of anticipated or prospective *dialyseis* in which the declarant acknowledges that he will submit to the ruling that will be pronounced.

[84] *O.Abraham* 92.

[85] *O.Abraham* 1, in which the priest John, the *sakho* David, and the lector Simeōn ask Abraham to ordain the priest Isaac by acting as surety for his proper fulfilment of priest duties.

[86] Ὁμολογία "declaration" (*O.Abraham* 50, 80, 88, 89); ἀσφάλεια "guarantee" (*O.Abraham* 7); ἐγγύη "surety" (*O.Abraham* 14); σύμφωνον "arrangement" (*O.Abraham* 66).

[87] For example, the key verbs of the body of the document: ϯⲟ ⲛ̄ϩⲉⲧⲟⲓⲙⲟⲥ, ϯϩⲟⲙⲟⲗⲟⲅⲉⲓ "I am ready to," ⲟⲩⲕ ⲉⲝⲉⲥⲧⲓ ⲛⲁⲓ ⲉ- "I am not allowed to," ϯⲥⲧⲟⲓⲭⲉⲓ "I agree," ϯⲟ ⲙⲙⲁⲣⲧ(ⲩⲣⲟⲥ) "I bear witness," ⲁϥⲡⲁⲣⲁⲕⲁⲗⲉⲓ ⲙ̄ⲙⲟⲓ̈ ⲁⲓ̈ⲥϩⲁⲓ̈ ϩⲁⲣⲟϥ, ⲙⲙⲡⲣⲁⲩⲁⲓⲧⲓ/ⲁϥⲁⲓⲧⲓ ⲙⲙⲟⲓ̈ ⲁⲓⲥϩⲁⲓ "I wrote (for him) at his request."

[88] ⲁⲙⲫⲓⲃⲁⲗⲗⲉ "to be in dispute" (*O.Abraham* 48); ⲡⲣⲟⲑⲉⲥⲙⲓⲁ "legal delay" (*O.Abraham* 67); ⲕⲁⲧⲁⲇⲓⲕⲏ (*O.Abraham* 61, 62, 65) or ⲉⲡⲓⲧⲓⲙⲓⲁ (*O.Abraham* 87) "fine," systematically used with one exception in which the Coptic word was preferred ⲟⲥⲉ (*O.Abraham* 63), etc.

This diplomatic, which borrows a great deal from contemporary Greek documents, is nonetheless more than just a translation. The form of our documents is the result of a double transposition process, which is not only linguistic (from Greek to Coptic), but which is, above all, also typological, insofar as it adapts documentary types that had been designed for radically different situations to the requirements of the Church—a subject that I have addressed elsewhere and that I will not dwell on here.[89] However, this double typological and linguistic *translatio* does not go without certain modifications, which can sometimes follow from errors or a poor grasp of the legal vocabulary and processes. Thus, if we compare our documents with the Greek ones that are likely to have influenced them, the first thing we notice is a significant simplification of the formulary, which leads to the drastic shortening of these acts: they are between seven and forty-one short lines (the average is around fifteen to twenty-five lines), which is a very small number of lines compared to the equivalent documents in Greek. Moreover, they also contain false loanwords, namely formulas that do not correspond to Greek practice despite their Greek origin.[90] More seriously, we also note incorrect legal usages, such as self-surety,[91] or certain diplomatic anomalies: the absence of the subscription of the declarant in one declaration of undertaking;[92] or, in a surety, the fact that the persons who are acting as surety for two deacons are also committing themselves to abide by the laws of the Church, turning this surety into a crypto-engagement.[93]

[89] Fournet 2018b, 215–18.

[90] For example, ϯϩομολογει εϯϩομολογια (*O.Abraham* 88); ϯϭⲛⲁⲩⲛⲉⲩⲉ ϩⲁ "I am acting as a guarantor at my risk and peril for" (*O.Abraham* 11); ειχρεωcτε "I oblige/bind myself to" resulting in "I commit to, I shall" (*O.Abraham* 7)—the Greek χρεωστεῖν belongs to the lexicon of the law of obligations (debts), but it does not appear in the context of an engagement for a job position, as is the case here.

[91] *O.Abraham* 8, 18, 63, 80 with the formula ϯ ϣ(π)τωρε ετρⲁ- lit. "I act as surety that I shall . . ." which led Krause to consider documents where this expression was present as "self-sureties" (*Selbstbürgschaft*). I admit that I do not understand what this could legally mean; I would also be tempted to see them as being declarations of an undertaking given that ϣ(π)τωρε can have the nontechnical meaning of "to undertake" (Crum, *CD*, 425a).

[92] *O.Abraham* 6.

[93] *O.Abraham* 11: Theodore, Apa Victor (founder of the monastery), Paul (father of one of the deacons), Christopher, and [- - -], after having requested Bishop Abraham to ordain the deacons John and Achilleus, act as guarantors that the latter will correctly fulfill their duties and that they themselves will respect the laws of the church.

In short, while they bear witness to their debt toward Greek practice, the texts from the dossier of Abraham nonetheless show discrepancies and diplomatic-legal irregularities in the processes of recovering and adapting Greek models. How could it have been otherwise, considering that they were not produced by professional notaries but rather by monks or clerics attempting to transpose a variety of Greek texts designed for civil society into Coptic, and above all, into the clerical domain? Moreover, in doing so, these "transposers" sometimes seem to improvise and to feel their way around, which explains why there are some anomalies.

The Problem of Legal Value

Nonetheless, what is more essential for us is the problem of the validity of these documents, which are among the oldest in Coptic. In an article first published in 1992, Ewa Wipszycka denies them all legal value. Her argument deserves to be cited at length:

> From a legal point of view, the guarantees and declarations in question do not make any sense. Contrary to the documents that served as their model, they could not create obligations or provide a basis for potential action before a court. They did not give the bishop any supplementary rights with regards to his clerics in addition to those that he already possessed (. . .). From a legal point of view, the liability of the guarantors was null. What could be demanded of the man who acted as a guarantor for a deacon, if this deacon, for example, did not learn the Scriptures by heart? The only thing that the guarantor could do was to denounce the guilty party.
>
> It is clear that the documents presented to the bishop only make sense at the moral and social levels. We are dealing with a society that believes in the power of documents formulated according to rules established by the state and with which everyone is familiar through the notarial profession. The candidate for an ecclesiastical position feels more bound by his own declarations if he makes them in writing and not just orally.
>
> There is another aspect to the problem. By requesting not only declarations but also written guarantees, the bishop likely wanted to create, for his clerics, a system of pressures within local communities. By asking important locals to act as their guarantors, the future deacons that had to be ordained by the bishop Abraham were making a commitment to them: their

> potential transgressions would have involved these influential figures; it was not just a matter between the bishop and the cleric that was at issue. The anger of a dignitary could be more terrible and therefore more effective than the reprimanding words of the bishop.[94]

I certainly share Wipszycka's opinion on the socio-ethical dimension of our documents and the network of responsibilities that they forge in society. We can even ask, as Steinwenter has previously done,[95] whether clerics' sureties were genuine ones or whether, on the contrary, they did not mask testimonials of good moral character, since we know through numerous canonical sources that three testimonials were required for a deacon and five for a priest.[96] What could further support this idea is that, unlike

[94] Wipszycka 1992a, 78:

> Dal punto di vista giuridico, le garanzie e le dichiarazioni in questione non hanno senso. Contrariamente ai documenti che servivano ad esse come modello, esse non potevano creare delle obbligazioni, fornire una base a una eventuale azione davanti a un tribunale. Per mezzo di esse il vescovo non acquistava, nei confronti dei suoi chierici, nessun diritto in più, oltre a quelli che già possedeva (. . .). La responsabilità dei garanti era, dal punto di vista giuridico, nulla. Che cosa si poteva esigere da uno che avesse prestato garanzie per un diacono, se questo diacono, per esempio, non imparava il Vangelo a memoria ? L'unica cosa che il garante poteva fare, era andare a denunciare il colpevole.
>
> È chiaro che i documenti presentati al vescovo hanno un senso solo sul piano morale e sociale. Abbiamo a che fare con una società che crede nel potere del documento formulato secondo le regole stabilite dallo Stato e che tutti conoscono attraverso la prassi notarile. Il candidato a una dignità ecclesiastica si sente più legato dalle proprie dichiarazioni se le fa per iscritto, e non solo oralmente.
>
> La cosa ha anche un altro aspetto. Chiedendo non solo dichiarazioni, ma anche garanzie scritte, il vescovo voleva verosimilmente creare, per i suoi chierici, un sistema du pressioni all'interno delle comunità locali. I futuri diaconi che dovevano essere ordinati dal vescovo Abraham, chiedendo ai notabili locali di prestare garanzia, si impegnavano davanti a questi: le loro eventuali trasgressioni avrebbero coinvolto questi personaggi influenti, non sarebbero state soltanto delle facende tra il vescovo e il dato chierico. L'ira di un notabile poteva essere più temibile, e dunque più efficace, che parole dure del vescovo.

[95] Steinwenter 1931, 31.

[96] *Canons of Pseudo-Basilius*, 47 (ed. Riedel 1900, 261); *Didascaliae Apostolorum, Canonum ecclesiasticorum, Traditionis apostolicae versiones latinae*, chap. 65 (ed.

their secular equivalents, our sureties never mention that the guarantor should pay a fine in the event that the ordained cleric should fail to fulfill his obligations.[97] The only exception is *O.Abraham* 16, in which Psate acts as the guarantor for his two sons and agrees, in the event of failure on their part, to leave the monastery: however, this is not really a surety backing recently ordained clerics, but rather one backing clerics who have defaulted and whom the bishop is pardoning in exchange for a guarantee, and we are dealing with a disciplinary-type sanction due to the very fact that the guarantor is a cleric.[98] What happened, however, in secular milieus?

While the absence of a penalty clause is upsetting and indeed does cast doubt on the legal nature of the clerics' sureties—I will return to this—let us note that documents relating to justice give a radically different impression. As the majority of them were engagements for the acceptance of a future sentence or for sureties guaranteeing the appearance before the court of the litigating parties, they almost always make provision for a monetary fine to which is added, if appropriate, a disciplinary sanction [Table 2].

The mention of the magistrate (*archōn*) to whom the fine is paid in *O.Abraham* 64 is of the utmost interest, especially if it should be inferred from the other documents as suggested by Krause.[99] It shows that the legal activities of the bishop were seconded by the civil administration, which could execute certain penalties if necessary. Therefore, we are dealing with a context that extends beyond the purely ecclesiastical circle and that involves state authorities. This somewhat undermines Wipszycka's argument.

It could be argued that these texts do not concern the judicial activities of the bishop, but rather that they are guarantees that he sought to obtain on behalf of his clerics who were involved in proceedings with nonreligious individuals before a civil court, that of the *archōn*. In fact, our seven texts do not explicitly state that the judgments in question are those of the bishop. However, this objection disappears in view of the remainder

Tidner, 107)—regarding these sources, cf. Wipszycka 1992a, 73n13. Cf. also Krause 1956, II, 43.

97 At best, they allude to a vague punishment with the formula пєчкрімⲁ ⲛⲁϣⲱⲡⲉ ϩⲓϫⲱⲓ "his κρῖμα (lit. judgment) will be upon us," variously understood by scholars: Krause 1956 translates as "sein/ihre Urteil wird auf mich/uns kommen"; Crum, *O.Crum*, 11, translates кріⲙⲁ as "responsibility"; Förster 2002, *s. v.* κρῖμα 1, follows Krause ("Urteil, Beschluss"). I understand: "the responsibility of his fault will fall on us."

98 See also *O.Abraham* 80–86, 89, which establish disciplinary sanctions for clerics who engage themselves or act as surety under various circumstances.

99 Krause 1956, II, 245.

TABLE 2

	Operation	Fine
O.Abraham 61	*cautio iudicio sisti* and *cautio iudicatum solui*	1 *solidus*[1]
O.Abraham 62	*cautio iudicio sisti* and *cautio iudicatum solui*	1 *solidus*
O.Abraham 63	engagement for submitting to a ruling	doubling of the disputed amount[2]
O.Abraham 64	engagement for submitting to a ruling	6 *solidi* to be paid to the *archōn*
O.Abraham 65	engagement for submitting to a ruling	1 *solidus* + exclusion from the celebration of the Eucharist
O.Abraham 66	*dialysis*	1 ounce of gold
O.Abraham 67	engagement for resolving a dispute	1 *solidus* and 5 *likna* of copper

[1] A gold monetary unit. One *solidus* corresponds to the bread supply of a family (two parents and two children) for about four months.

[2] Moreover, ⲙⲛ ⲥⲧⲁⲩⲣⲟⲥ ⲛⲧⲟⲟⲧ ϩⲙ ⲙⲁ ⲛⲓⲙ ⲉ̣ⲛⲁⲃⲱⲕ ⲉⲣⲟ̄ϥ: Krause 1956, II, 241, translates as "(. . .) ist kein Kreuz in meiner Hand an jedem Ort, zu dem ich gehen werde" and recognizes (245) that the expression is unclear (it may refer to exclusion from the Eucharist or the clergy). We see the same predicament in Crum (*O.Crum*, 20).

of the dossier: in it, we clearly see that Abraham, who was solicited by the parties,[100] settled their disputes and pronounced sentences. Moreover, in two texts (*O.Abraham* 63, 65), certain fines are combined with disciplinary sanctions such as exclusion from the celebration of the Eucharist, which clearly shows that the bishop was the protagonist of these judicial hearings and that the parties in question are clerics, contrary to the other texts in which the monetary fine alone indicates that we are dealing with secular individuals.[101] We therefore have to conclude that Abraham ruled on disputes at adversarial hearings of opposing parties, who were not only clerics but also laymen, and that the execution of certain penalties could be carried out by the civil authorities.

[100] For example, *O.Abraham* 51–54, 58, 78.

[101] John and Hatre (*O.Abraham* 61 and 62) and Mēna (*O.Abraham* 64) have indeed no ecclesiastical title.

Such a conclusion goes somewhat against the view that, regarding the long-debated question of the episcopal jurisdiction (*episcopalis audientia*), does not recognize the bishop as having real judicial authority beyond the ecclesiastical circle, instead preferring to attribute an arbitrating power to him.[102] Our texts demonstrate the contrary, at least for the very end of the sixth century and the beginning of the seventh, and are supported in this by the Justinian legislation, which not only recognized the bishop's judicial authority in matters of a civil nature between clerics and monks (and in matters of a criminal nature when they touched upon ecclesiastical interests), as well as requiring them to turn to the bishop to resolve their disputes,[103] but also encouraged laymen involved in a dispute with a cleric to refer to the bishop before all others, providing for the proceedings and possible appeals:[104] for example, if the two parties agreed with the bishop's ruling, the state acknowledged the decision; otherwise, the parties had to report to the civil court within ten days and would be judged by it. The minutes of the sentence would then be sent to the bishop. The state even requested that the bishop oversee its action, in particular by ensuring that a cleric did not undergo a violent summons or execution, or by referring to the emperor if the penalty was not applied.[105] Inversely, the state could intervene in the event of an abusive excommunication.[106]

All of these laws bear witness to a large degree of integration and complementarity between civil justice and ecclesiastical justice, and oblige us to conclude that in terms of justice, there was cooperation between the Church and the state, in spite of some inevitable tensions to which *O.Abraham* testifies.[107] This cooperation confirms the legal value of certain documents in our dossier: therefore, if a cleric or a layman involved

[102] On the *episcopalis audientia*, see in general (to limit myself to recent publications): Harris 1999, 191–211; Frakes 2001, 195–229 (prior bibliography, 196n4); Huck 2008. In papyri: Bell 1924; Steinwenter 1929; Lammeyer 1933, 193–202.

[103] Justinian, *Novellae*, LXXXIII (539) for clerics; LXXIX (539) for monks.

[104] Justinian, *Novellae*, CXXIII (546), c. 2 for a cleric; and LXXIX (539), c. 1 for a monk.

[105] Justinian, *Novellae*, CXXIII (546), c. 27.

[106] Justinian, *Novellae*, CXXIII (546), c. 11.

[107] In *O.Abraham* 78, Abraham intervened before the *lashane* on behalf of an individual (unnamed) that the latter had imprisoned. He prohibited the celebration of the Eucharist until this man was returned to his previous situation (?). This reflection made by Abraham in *O.Abraham* 100 is also informative: "If I were a magistrate (ⲁⲣⲭⲱⲛ) writing you to meet you, you would have come rapidly."

in proceedings before the bishop did not appear despite having made an engagement to him, he could be found to be guilty.

Did the Church take on a role complementary to that of the state because of the moral aura of its bishops and their increasingly entrenched social position? Or, was it compensating for the increasing inadequacies of civil jurisdictions, especially during the first decades of the seventh century? Alternatively, I would argue, as I demonstrated in chapter 3, that by offering less constraining and less costly justice in a language accessible to the majority, it played a role comparable to that of the *defensor* and could attract a large number of litigating parties, which significantly relieved civil courts.

Can we extend these conclusions regarding the validity of the judicial documents to the other documents in our dossier, and in particular to the engagements of recently ordained clerics and the sureties made on their behalf, to which Wipszycka denies all legal value? To begin, one could argue that this is a false problem. Why indeed should one be concerned about the legal value of texts regulating the activities of clerics inasmuch that they can only be understood in a context in which the bishop was the keystone of the ecclesiastical hierarchy? It is he who had the complete authority to ordain new clerics, to settle their disagreements, or to impose or lift a disciplinary sanction. Not acknowledging the legal constraint implied by an engagement to a bishop would simply mean exiting the system.

This explanation, however, does not suffice. If the cooperation between the state and the Church gives a certain number of rights to the bishop, it also imposes responsibilities on him. In fact, imperial legislation strictly demarcated the ordaining of bishops and that of clerics, not only subject to ecclesiastical canons.[108] For example, according to *Novellae* CXXIII (546), c. 14, if following his ordination, a cleric is convicted for not fulfilling the necessary conditions, the bishop is held responsible and can be stripped of his dignity and his possessions. This shines new light on the declarations of engagement and sureties found in our dossier, which may have had the function not only of creating "a system of pressures within local communities," to reuse the words of Wipszycka, but also—and perhaps especially—of clearing the name of the bishop before the state in the event of a problem.

[108] Justinian, *Novellae*, CXXIII (546), c. 2, 12–18.

Why in Coptic?

All of the non-epistolary documents of Abraham's dossier, in compliance not only with canonical law but also imperial legislation, are therefore genuine legal documents endowed with full legal value, involving the bishop, as well as nonreligious individuals and clerics, in a network of responsibilities under the oversight of both the state and the Church. And yet, Abraham chose not to write them in Greek. Why is that? The most natural response would be to conclude that he proceeded as he did due to necessity, since he did not know Greek, as indicated by his will, in which he states that he has dictated it in Egyptian and requested that someone subscribe in Greek on his behalf.[109] Nonetheless, it was not the bishop himself who drew up the numerous declarations that he made his flock sign: he had a secretariat and could easily find a Greek-speaker who would have written these documents at his request. If he did not do this, it is because he did not wish to do so or did not see the need for it.

It is true that the documents in question have a limited scope: they do not establish sensitive transactions involving the law of obligations such as real estate sales or other property transfers that could have resulted in appeals before a civil court.[110] The majority of these engagements or declarations, which are often more morally oriented than they are truly legal, concern the bishop (respect of obligations tied to an ecclesiastical position, to a settlement made by the bishop, etc.). This self-referential frame, despite the oversight of the state under certain circumstances, gave leeway to the bishop and allowed him to take into account the language effectively spoken and written by the persons involved in these documents. Why impose the binding framework of Greek diplomatics when the large majority of the clerics, monks, or laymen having recourse to these documents were not Greek-speaking, any more than was the keystone of the system, the bishop? Nonetheless, Greek models were still used, albeit transposed into Coptic.

In a certain way, this form of linguistic independence indicates the rise to power of the Church as a coauthority of the state. Above all, it marks the

---

[109] *P.Mon.Phoib.Test.* 1, 81–82: Ἰωσὴφ Ἰωάννου ἐλάχ(ιστος) πρεσβύτερ(ος) ἁγίας ἐκκλησίας Ἑρμώνθ(εως) κελευσθείσης μοι ἔγραψα ὑπὲρ αὐτοῦ γράμματα μὴ ἐπισταμένου. Justinian, *Novellae*, CXXIII, c. 1, requires these bishops to know how to read and write (γράμματα εἰδέναι), but he does not specify in what language. Nonetheless, we could think that Justinian intended Greek, the official language.

[110] We have seen (chapter 3, pp. 80–82) that the same goes for the majority of the other legal documents from the years 550–642.

constantly growing role played by clerics and monks in written documentary culture—a phenomenon that is still little known and would need to be systematically investigated. Starting in the sixth century, papyri attest to the development of the figure of the notary-cleric (deacon or priest).[111] This process even reaches as far as the administration, as an unedited papyrus from Copenhagen dating from 622 demonstrates. It consists of a transfer of taxation where a man named Christologos, "archdeacon and tabellion of the administration of the annona of Hermopolis," appears.[112] This "clericification" of the notarial profession was only the first stage of the phenomenon that interests us. The second stage was the shift toward Coptic, with the multiplication of clerics acting as notaries without *stricto sensu* being such, responding to a demand that real bilingual notaries were not yet numerically capable of fulfilling.

While it is above all visible in documents subsequent to the Arab Conquest,[113] the weight of the Church in the development of a Coptic language practice has more ancient roots, as shown in the archive of Abraham. In this process, monasticism indeed played a major role, through Damian, Bishop of Alexandria's (578–605) policy of recruiting bishops from southern monastic milieus, which were more profoundly Coptic-speaking, such as Abraham and his contemporary Pisenthios, Bishop of Coptos (from ca. 600 to 632). Part of the latter's archive illustrates the same phenomenon, and he, like Abraham, appears to have at least

---

[111] Already during the fifth century with the priest Phōsphorios (*Byz.Not.*, 94, Syene, 493). See later the priest Theōnas (*Byz.Not.*, 56, Heracleopolis, 538); the deacon Theophilus (*Byz.Not.*, 93, Syene, 578–82); the deacon Anastasius (*Byz.Not.*, 78, Oxyrhynchos, 579–95; cf. *P.Oxy.* XVI 1989, 27 [590]: Ἀναστ̣ά̣σιος ἐλέῳ Θεοῦ διάκονο̣ς̣ (καὶ) συμβολαιογράφ(ος)); the deacon Phōcas (*Byz.Not.*, 74, Hermopolite, sixth to seventh century); the deacon Cyril (*Byz.Not.*, 33, Edfu, 618–19); the deacon Kosmas (*Byz.Not.*, 43, no. 10.10.1, Arsinoite, seventh century; cf. *SPP* III^2 115, 9: Κοσμᾶ σὺν Θ(εῷ) διακόνου συμβολ(αιογράφου)); the deacon Mēnas (*Byz.Not.*, 45, no. 12.10.1–2, Arsinoite, seventh century); the deacon Severus (*Byz.Not.*, 71, Hermopolite, seventh century); the deacon Theodorus (*Byz.Not.*, 96, Arsinoite or Heracleopolite, seventh century). Here, I am not mentioning those who are definitely subsequent to the Arab Conquest.

[112] L. 22: Χριστόλογος σὺν Θ̣ε̣ῷ̣ ἀρχιδιάκ(ονος) κ(αὶ) ταβελλί(ων) τῆς χ(ει)ρ(ογραφείας) Ἑρμ(οῦ) πόλ(εως). Regarding what must be understood by *cheirographeia*, cf. *P.Sorb.* II 69, 37–38. The sense of "administrative office" derived through the metonymy of that of "registry" seems to me to be favored by the present papyrus.

[113] See the examples from the Arsinoite nome given by Kovaric 2014, 491.

partially exercised his ministry at a monastery.[114] These bishops, chosen by the archbishop in view of their moral qualities that converted them, in the eyes of the population, into sorts of *holy men* capable of serving as intermediaries with the administration—with which the Church had increasingly consubstantial ties in any event—contributed to deploying the practices originating from monastic communities on a larger scale. Their episcopal positions granted them the status necessary to impose their natural language in written domains in which Greek remained exclusive. They contributed to the creation of a stock of documentary types that could be infinitely reproduced, as well as to the development of an array of legal formulae and expressions borrowed from Greek, and which were, from then on, integrated into a Coptic "documentality." Alongside attempts made as early as the sixth century in secular society, they thus contributed to paving the way of, and "de-complexifying," Coptic by continuously providing it with more of the prestige over which Greek held a monopoly.[115]

Therefore, they foreshadow what would take place a few decades later when, with the Arab Conquest, the link between Egypt and Byzantium was definitively broken, and Coptic no longer encountered any obstacles to its autonomy in the legal domain. After having started by "nibbling away at" the world of written culture in the domain of Christian manuscripts, and later, in that of private epistolary communication, from that point on, Coptic was able to impose itself in the (local) administrative and legal

[114] In any event, this is what we learn from his Coptic biography (Amélineau 1887, 133–34). However, other episodes of his life show us that he was active at Coptos. Cf. Fournet 2000a, 210. The archive of Pisenthios is currently being (re)published by a team directed by J. van der Vliet (cf. van der Vliet 2002 and Dekker 2011). On the bishops and monks, cf. Giorda 2009. For the role of Abraham and Pisenthios in the rise of Coptic, cf. Camplani 2015, 149. See also Wipszycka 1992b, 110, for other Coptic-speaking bishops from the end of the sixth and beginning of the seventh century known by literary sources: John of Parallos (cf. Müller 1991); Constantine of Lycopolis/Siout (cf. Coquin 1991); John of Hermopolis/Shmoun (cf. Orlandi 1991); and Rufus of Hypselē/Shōtep (cf. Sheridan 1998). Certain bishops from the same period nonetheless continued to give priority to Greek, such as the Senouthios bishop of Apollinopolis Minor and the one bishop of Antinoopolis (Benaissa 2008); however, we do not know from which milieus they originated.

[115] The role of monasteries in this process was due not only to the fact that, at the very beginning of the seventh century, monks were successfully recruited as bishops, but also that, like churches in urban milieus, monasteries became places that could be used as storage spaces for archives at a time when state archives no longer existed. However, this is a problem that remains to be explored.

domain. However, the new regime did not give it all the freedom from which it could have benefited, and continued to promote Greek before playing the card of the all-Arabic. Coptic would carry on being heavily dependent on Greek tradition, not finding its formal and formulary independence until around 800–850. However, it did not much benefit from this: curbed by Arabization, the legal use of Coptic then entered into a period of recession (the last Coptic legal documents are from the eleventh century[116]) and—dare I say—degeneration, with the impoverishment of its vocabulary and the increasingly substantial influence of the Arabic formulary and vocabulary.[117]

Therefore, it was only a bit more than at the midpoint of its history (that is, from 642 until 1063) that Coptic finally became a language capable of infiltrating all of the domains of written culture (literature, private letters, legal and administrative acts). Until that time, it had to compromise with the other language, Greek, which limited its written usage to certain "niches." By saying that, I would not want to give the impression that I subscribe to an antagonistic view of the coexistence of the two languages. If Coptic had to compete with Greek, this was certainly not because there was a hostile relationship between the two languages, but rather by virtue of a dynamic internal to Coptic, which, as the result of sociocultural and institutional transformations during Late Antiquity, led it to gain ground. To take up again words of J. van der Vliet, "I am inclined to see Greek and Coptic within the cultural constellation of late-antique Egypt as Siamese twins rather than as markers of conflicting or national identities. As soon as the shared culture of late-antique Egypt started to lose its hold, under the Abbasids, from 750 onwards, both halves of the twin couple started to wither and decline."[118] I hope that I have somewhat clarified this twofold dynamic through the prism of written culture of a legal and administrative nature.

---

[116] They belong to the archive of Teshlot (1022–63): cf. Richter 2000.

[117] Richter 2010 (esp. 43); and van der Vliet 2013 (esp. 201–5).

[118] Van der Vliet 2013, 194–95.

APPENDIX I

Coptic Endorsements in Greek Legal Texts

For these Coptic endorsements, cf. chapter 1, pp. 21–22.

Translation is given only for the Coptic portions.

Archive of Taurinos

• *BGU* IV 1094 (Hermopolis, 525), statement (*ekmartyrion*) of Dōrotheos, *defensor* of Hermopolis concerning the violation of a demarcation in the village of Sigkerē.[1]

19 ⲡⲏⲥⲫⲣⲁⲕⲓⲥⲙⲁⲙ̄ⲡⲉⲕ-
20 ⲧⲓⲕⲟⲥⲍⲁⲛ . ⲱⲙⲥⲏⲛ . .
21 ⲣⲉⲍⲡ [.]ⲅ̣[

Read :

19 ⲡⲏⲥⲫⲣⲁⲕϊⲥⲙⲁ ⲙ̄ⲡⲉⲕ-
20 ⲧⲓⲕⲟⲥ ϩⲁ ⲛⲣ̣ⲱⲙⲥⲏⲛ̣ϭⲓ-
21 ⲣ̣ⲉϩⲧ̣

"The *defensor*'s (ἔκδικος) statement (ἐκσφράγισμα) concerning the inhabitants of Sēnk^{y}ireht."

19 ⲡⲏⲥⲫⲣⲁⲕϊⲥⲙⲁ: the scribe made a mistake (MacCoull 1995, 351 [= *BL* X 19] thinks that the mistake is due to Schubart, which is not the case). Read ⲡⲉⲕⲥⲫⲣⲁⲅⲓⲥⲙⲁ (despite the ed.).

20–21 ⲥⲏⲛ̣ϭⲓⲣ̣ⲉϩⲧ̣ is a new attestation of the Coptic form of the toponym Σιγκερη (that appears on the recto). Cf., in documents, *P.Lond.Copt.* I 1067, 1 (ⲧⲥⲓⲛϭⲉⲣⲉϩⲧ) and *CPR* IV

[1] This text belongs to the Taurinos archive according to Gascou 1983, 234.

25, 2 (ⲧⲥⲉⲛϭⲓⲣⲉϩⲧ). On this village, cf. Drew-Bear 1979, 254–56.

• *BGU* XIX 2783 (= *SB* XIV 11377) (Hermopolis, 523), tax receipt.

6 ⲧⲁⲡⲟⲭⲏ ⲙⲫⲓⲣⲙⲏ̣ ϩⲁ ⲧⲉⲡⲣⲱⲧⲉ ⲟⲩ{ϩ}-
7 ϩⲟⲗⲟⲕⲟⲧⲓⲛ

"Receipt (ἀποχή) of Firmē for the first (πρώτη) <indiction>: one *solidus* (ὁλοκόττινος)."

It should be noted that the ϩ have the shape of a S. This could be indicative of a low literacy level.[2]

6 ⲧⲁⲡⲟⲭⲏ ⲙⲫⲓⲣⲙⲏ̣ : ⲧⲁ ⲁⲡⲟⲭⲏ ⲙⲫⲓⲣⲙ[ ] ed.
ⲧⲉⲡⲣⲱⲧⲉ : cf. below *BGU* XVII 2683, 22 (with the same ending and the absence of ἰνδικτίων).

Two other texts that hypothetically belong to this archive:

• *BGU* XVII 2683 = *SB* XIV 11373 (Hermopolis, 523?), lease contract [Fig. 9].

"Gehört zum Dossier der Aurelia Kyra alias Eustorgia" (ed.).

21 μί(σθωσις) Θεοδώρου Κολλο[ύ(θου)] ἀπὸ Ἑ̣ρ(μουπόλεως)

and an unedited Coptic text (written upside down):

22 ⲧⲉⲕⲧⲏⲥⲓⲥ ϩ̣ⲁ ⲕ̣ⲁⲣⲡⲟ̣ⲥ ⲡⲉⲙ̣ⲧⲉ ⲫⲓⲡ̣ⲏ̣ⲥ ϣ̣ⲙⲟ̣ⲩ̣<ⲛ>
23 ϩⲟⲗⲟⲕⲟⲧⲓⲛ ⲡⲁⲣⲁ ϫⲟⲩⲧⲁϥⲧⲉ ϭ̣ⲁⲣⲁⲧⲉ ⲕⲟⲗⲑⲉ
24 ⲑⲱⲛⲉ ϣⲙⲟⲩ<ⲛ> ϩⲟⲗⲟⲕⲟⲧⲓⲛ ⲡⲁⲣⲁ ⲧⲓⲉ ⲡⲟⲩⲁ ⲕⲟⲩϩⲓϫ

"The payment (ἔκτεισις) for the crops of the fifth (πέμπτη) <indiction> [. . .] eight *solidi* (ὁλοκόττινος) minus (παρά) twenty-four carats (κεράτιον). Kolthe <of> Thōne: eight *solidi* minus (παρά) five each [. . .]."

There is no connection between the endorsement and the text written on the recto.

22 ⲡⲉⲙ̣ⲧⲉ cf., above, *BGU* XIX 2783, 6n.
ⲫⲓⲡ̣ⲏ̣: or ⲫⲓⲧ̣ⲓ̣ⲛ̣. A very incorrect form of ἰνδ(ικτίωνος) would be highly unlikely.
ϣ̣ⲙⲟ̣ⲩ̣<ⲛ>: reading proposed by Alain Delattre *per litteras* (as in l. 24). As in l. 24, the *shai* is written awkwardly.

[2] The same form is attested in *P.Lond.* VI 1922.

• *BGU* XII 2187 (Hermopolis, 520), lease contract.

7 μί(σθωσις) Παμο̣υ̣ν̣[ίου . . . .]
vacat
8 ⲧϥⲕ̣ⲧⲏ̣ⲥ̣[
9 ⲧⲓⲱϩⲉⲛ[

Read:

8 ⲧⲙⲓⲥⲧϣ̣`ⲥ̣´ⲉ̣[ⲓⲥ ? - - -]
9 ⲧⲓⲱϩⲉ ⲛ[- - -]

"The lease [. . .] fields of [. . .]."

Archive of the Monastery of Apa Sabinos (Also Called "Of the Northern Rock of Antinoopolis")

• *P.Prag.* I 46 (Antinoopolite, 522), sale of containers for future delivery.

32 ⲡⲉⲅⲣⲁⲙⲁⲧⲓⲟⲛ ⲙ̄ⲡⲕⲁⲧϣⲟϣⲟⲩ

"The acknowledgment of debt ((γραμμάτιον) of the manufacturer of containers."

Archive of the Monastery of Apa Apollō (Bawīt)

Cf. M. R. M. Hasitzka, *Korr.Tych.* VI, n° 118 (= *BL* X 252) about *P.Athen.Xyl.*

• *P.Athen.Xyl.* 5 (Bawīt, 539), loan.

15 ☧ χ(ει)ρ(όγραφον) Μαθίας Παμουνίου μετ' ἐγγ[υητοῦ - - -]
16 ⲡⲙⲟⲉⲓⲣ ⲙⲁⲑⲓⲁⲥ ⲡϣⲉ ⲛⲡ[ⲁⲙⲟⲩⲛⲉ ⲁⲩⲱ ⲁⲃⲣⲁϩⲁⲙ]
17 ⲡϣⲉ ⲛⲧ[ⲁ]ⲛⲓⲏⲗ ⲛⲟⲩϩⲟⲗⲟⲕⲟ[ⲧⲧⲓⲛⲟⲥ - - -]

"Pmoeir: Mathias son of Pamoune and Abraham son of Daniēl for one *solidus* (ὁλοκόττινος) [. . .]."

16 ⲡⲙⲟⲉⲓⲣ: Coptic equivalent of Greek toponym Μοῖραι (now *Mair*), known so far by the form ⲙⲟⲉⲓⲣ (cf. Drew-Bear 1979, 348).
ⲁⲩⲱ ⲁⲃⲣⲁϩⲁⲙ]: my restoration according to l. 5 and to *SB* XXII 15322 (cf. below).

• *P.Athen.Xyl.* 6 (Bawīt, sixth cent.), loan.

17 ἀπὸ κώμης Δημητρ(ίου) τοῦ Ἑρ(μοπολίτου νομοῦ).
18 *vac.* ⲓⲥⲁⲕ ⲡ[ϣⲉ ⲛ - - -]

"Isaac son of [. . .]."

Before l. 17 the first editor read χ(ει)ρ(όγραφον) οἴ(νου) μέτρων ρν παρὰ . . . but see *BL* X 251.

• *SB* XXII 15322 = *P.Athen.Xyl.* 8 + 13 (Bawīt, 535), loan.

11 ⲁⲃⲣⲁϩⲁⲙ ⲡϣⲉ ⲛⲡⲁⲡ[ⲛⲟⲩⲧⲉ ⲁⲩⲱ ⲙⲁⲕⲁⲣⲉ ⲡϣ]ⲉ ⲛⲃⲓⲕⲧⲱⲣ ⲉϥⲭⲣⲱⲥ<ⲧⲉ> ⲛ[- - - ⲡϣⲉ ⲛⲡⲁⲡ-]
12 ⲛⲟⲩⲧⲉ ⲡⲙⲁⲛϭⲁ[ⲙⲟⲩⲗ ⲛⲟⲩϩⲟⲗⲟⲕⲟⲧⲧⲓⲛⲟⲥ ⲡⲁⲣⲁ] ⲕ̣[ⲉⲣ(ⲁⲧⲓⲁ) ⲥⲟⲟⲩ]

"Abraham son of Papnoute and Makare son of Biktōr, who is in debt (χρεωστεῖν) to [. . .] son of Papnoute, the camel driver for one *solidus* minus (παρά) six carats (κεράτιον)."

11 ⲉϥⲭⲣⲱⲥ<ⲧⲉ> ⲛ[: ⲉϥⲭⲣⲱⲥ ⲛ[ed.
12 ⲛⲟⲩϩⲟⲗⲟⲕⲟⲧⲧⲓⲛⲟⲥ ⲡⲁⲣⲁ] ⲕ̣[ⲉⲣ(ⲁⲧⲓⲁ) ⲥⲟⲟⲩ]: ⲟⲩⲁ ϩⲟⲗⲟⲕⲟⲧⲧⲓⲛⲟⲥ ⲁ ⲡⲁⲣⲁ ⲕⲉⲣ(ⲁⲧⲓⲁ) ϛ - - -] ed.

• *P.Athen.Xyl.* 12 (Bawīt [cf. *P.Louvre Bawit*, p. 150], sixth cent.), loan.

16 [- - - τ]όκ(ου) . . . . κερκερ( ) γί(νεται) χρ(υσοῦ) νό(μισμα) π(αρὰ) κερ(άτια) ϛ τόκ(ου)
vacat
17 [ⲁⲛⲟⲩⲡ ⲡϣⲉ ⲛⲇⲁⲩⲉⲓⲇ] ϥⲭⲣⲱⲥⲧⲉ ⲛⲡⲁⲡⲁ ⲁⲛⲇⲣⲉⲁⲥ

"Anoup son of David, who is in debt (χρεωστεῖν) to Apa Andreas."

17 [ⲁⲛⲟⲩⲡ ⲡϣⲉ ⲛⲇⲁⲩⲉⲓⲇ]: my restoration according to l. 6. ⲁⲛⲇⲣⲉⲁⲥ: see Delattre 2004, 385, n. 1 (ⲁⲛⲇⲣⲉⲁ ed.).

• *P.Athen.Xyl.* 17 (Bawīt, 548/549), loan.

17 ⲧⲉϭⲣⲟⲙⲡⲉ ⲧϣⲉ ⲛ[- - -]
vacat (and then, upside down:)
18 [- - -]ου γί(νεται) χρ(υσοῦ) νο(μισμάτια) α π(αρὰ) κερ(άτια) ϛ

"Tek^{y}rompe daughter of [. . .]."

17 ⲧⲉϭⲣⲟⲙⲡⲉ : M.R.M. Hasitzka's reading (= *BL* X 252) (ⲧϩⲣⲟ<ⲟ>ⲙⲡⲉ ed.).

Apparently there is no connection between the endorsement and the recto: the declaring party is Αὐρήλιος Φοιβάμμων Χόιτος (and Αὐρήλιος

Βασιλείδης Σερήνου); but the beginning of the text is lost: Tek^{y}rompe could be the wife of the declaring party.

• *P.Athen.Xyl.* 18 (Bawīt, sixth cent. [*P.LouvreBaouît*, p. 15: 487/488 ed.]), loan.

10 [χ(ει)ρ(όγραφον) Αὐρηλίου] Βίκτωρ[ος Ὀλυμπίου]
11 ⲃⲓⲕⲧⲱⲣ ⲡϣⲉ ⲛⲟⲗⲩⲙⲡⲓⲟⲥ [ⲉϥⲭⲣⲱⲥⲧⲉ ⲛ̄ - - -]

"Biktōr son of Olympios, who is in debt (χρεωστεῖν) to [. . .]."

APPENDIX 2

Five Samples of Fourth-Century Coptic Letters

Sentences typed in bold are in Greek. Underlined words are Greek loanwords.

1. *P.Kellis* VII 84 (Kellis, House 3)

Κυρ̣[ί]ῳ μου̣ ἀδ̣ε̣λ̣φῶι Ψάϊτ̣ι
Θεόγγ̣ωστ[ο]ς ἀδελφὸς χαίρει̣ν.
ϯϣⲓⲛⲉ ⲁ̣ⲣⲁⲕ ⲧⲟⲛⲟⲩ ⲙⲛ̅ ⲛⲓⲗ̣ⲁⲩ̣
ⲉ ⲁⲩⲥⲁⲡ <u>ⲕⲁⲧⲁ</u> ⲛⲟⲩⲣ̣ⲉⲛ ⲛ̅ⲛⲁϭ
ⲙⲛ̅ ⲛ̅ⲕⲟⲩⲓ̈ ϯ ⲣ̅ϣⲡⲏⲣⲉ ⲧⲟⲛ̣ⲟ̣ⲩ̣
ϫⲉ ⲙ̅ⲡⲉⲧⲛ̅ⲧⲁⲓ̈ⲁⲓ̈ ⲁⲥϩⲉⲓ̈ ⲛⲏⲓ̣̈
<u>ⲟⲩⲧⲉ</u> ⲛ̅ⲧⲛ ϩⲱⲙ’ <u>ⲟⲩⲧⲉ̣</u> ⲛ̅ⲧⲛ̅
ϩⲱⲣ <u>ⲙⲁⲗⲓⲥⲧⲁ</u> ⲉⲧⲃⲉ ⲧⲥϩⲓⲙ̣ⲉ̣
ⲉⲧϣⲱⲛⲉ ϫⲉ ⲉⲥ̣ⲟ ⲛ̅ⲉ̣ϣ̣
ⲛ̅ϩⲉ ϫⲉ <u>ⲁⲣⲁ</u> ⲛⲁ̣ⲥϯ ⲁⲡⲟⲩϫⲉ̣ⲓ̣̈
ⲧⲉ ϫ̣[ⲛ] ⲙ̣ⲡⲉ· ⲁⲓ̈ϣⲛ̅ ϩⲱⲙ
ⲁ̣ⲛ̣ ⲡ̣[ⲉ] ⲡ̣ⲁϫⲉϥ ϫⲉ ⲙⲛ̅ ⲛⲁϭ
ⲛ̅ϣⲱⲛⲉ ⲙ̅ⲙⲁⲥ· <u>ϩⲟⲙⲱⲥ</u>
ϯϥⲓ ⲣⲁⲩϣ ϫⲉ ⲙ̅ⲡ̣ⲉⲧ̣ⲛ̅ⲥϩⲉⲓ ⲛ̣ⲏ̣
ⲓ· ϯ̣̅ⲛⲟⲩ ⲉϣⲱⲡⲉ ⲛⲁⲙⲏⲉ ⲉ
ⲙⲛ̅ ϩⲟⲩⲟ ϣⲱⲛⲉ ⲙ̅ⲙⲁⲥ ⲉ
ⲣⲉ ⲡⲛ̅ϣⲏⲣⲉ ⲁⲛⲇⲣⲉⲁⲥ ⲥⲣⲁϥⲧ
ⲛ̣̅ⲛⲓϩⲟⲟⲩ ⲉⲟⲩⲛ̅ ϣϭⲁⲙ ⲁⲧⲣⲉϥ̣
ⲉⲓ ϩ̣ⲱ̣ϥ̣ ϥⲣ̅ ϥⲧⲟⲩ ϩⲣⲉⲩ ϩⲁ
ⲧⲏ̣ⲛ̣ ⲛ̣̅ⲛⲓⲙⲁ <u>ⲏ̅</u> ⲛ̅ⲧⲁⲕ <u>ⲫⲩ</u>
<u>ⲥⲉ̣ⲓ</u> `ⲛ̅ⲓ̣ⲉ´ ⲙⲁ̣ⲣⲉ `ⲡ´ⲟⲩⲉ ⲙ̅ⲙⲱⲧⲛ̅ ϯ
ϩ̣ⲁ̣ⲓ̈ ⲙ̅ⲙ̣ⲁϥ ⲉϣⲱⲡⲉ ⲉⲙⲛ
ⲟⲩϣⲱⲛⲉ ⲙ̅ⲙⲁ̣ⲥ̣ ⲉⲛϣⲁ
ⲣ̣ ⲡ̣ϩⲟⲟⲩ ⲥ̣ⲛ̣ⲟ ϩⲱ̣ⲉ̣ ⲁϥ . . [.] .

ⲕⲉ̣ ⲧⲛ̄ⲛⲁϭ̣ⲛ[ⲧ]ⲛ̣ ⲙⲛ̄ ⲛⲉⲛ̣
ⲉⲣ̣ⲏ̣ⲩ̣ ⲧ̣ⲁⲣ̣ⲛ̄ϫⲓ ϩⲏⲧ ⲁ̣ⲛⲉⲛⲉⲣⲏⲩ
ϩ̣ⲓ̣ ⲡ̣ⲙⲁ̈ⲓ̈ⲧ ⲙ̄ⲙⲁⲛ ϯⲟⲩⲱϣ̣
ⲉⲓ̣ . ⲉⲧ̣ ϩⲛ̄ ⲡⲓϯⲟⲩ ⲛ̄ϩⲟⲟⲩ·
ⲉϣⲱⲡⲉ ⲇⲉ ⲉⲥϣⲱⲛⲉ ⲛⲁ
ⲙ̣ⲏⲉ *vac.* ⲧⲟⲛⲟ̣ⲩ̣ ⲉⲓⲉ
ϩⲱⲃ ⲛⲏⲓ̈ ⲧⲁⲭⲩ̣ ⲧⲁⲛⲟ ϫⲉ
ⲛ̄ϯⲛⲁ̣ϭⲛ̄ ⲣⲱⲙⲉ ⲧⲁⲉⲓ
ⲁϩⲏⲓ̈· ⲁ ⲡⲥⲁⲛ ϩⲱϥ̣ ⲁⲛ
ⲕⲩ̣ⲣⲟⲥ ⲥⲱⲧ̣ ⲁϩⲟⲩ̣ⲛ̣ ⲁⲡ
ϣⲱⲛⲉ ⲡϥ̄ⲙⲁⲓⲧ ⲡ̣ⲉ̣ ⲉⲙ
ⲡ̣ⲉ̣ϥ̣ⲕⲃⲟ· ϩⲱⲃ̣ ⲛⲏⲓ̈
vac.
ⲛ̄ⲟⲩⲱ ⲛⲓⲙ· ⲛ̄ⲧⲛ̄ ⲡⲉⲧⲛⲁ
ⲛ̄ ϯⲉⲡⲓⲥⲧⲟⲗⲏ ⲛⲏⲧ̣ⲛ̄ **Ἐρ-**
ρῶσθαί σε εὔχο-
μαι πολλοῖς χρό-
οις κύριε ἀδελφέ.

Verso

Κυρίωι μọυ ἀδẹλφῶι Ψάΐτι X **Θεό̣γνωστο̣ς ἀδελφός**

"**To my master (and) brother Psais; (from) brother Theognostos,—greetings.** I greet you warmly and the children, each one by their name, the large (5) and the small.

I am very astonished that you (pl.) did not honor me (enough) to write to me, either by way of Hom or by Hor;—especially about the woman who is ill, how she is? (10) Whether she was tending towards health or not? I have again asked Hom: He says that there is no great sickness for her. Nevertheless, I am concerned that you did not write to (15) me.

Now, truly, if there is no exceptional sickness for her: Is our son Andreas unoccupied these days? Is it possible for him to come (and) spend four days with (20) us here; or you, naturally? So, let one of you take the trouble; if there is no sickness for her. If we spend the two days . . . (25) we will be reunited with one another, so that we take heart (from) one another on the path! Otherwise, I want . . . in five days. However, if she is truly very ill, (30) then send to me quickly and I will see whether I can find someone and come up. Also, brother Kyros himself has relapsed into (35) sickness. It is his path as he did not keep cool.

Send me any news by way of the one who will bring you (pl.) this letter. **I pray for your health** (40) **for many years, master brother.**"

Verso

"To my master brother Psais. (From) brother Theognostos" (trans. edition).

2. *P.Kellis* VII 107 (Kellis, House 3)

Τῷ̣ τιμιωτάτῳ̣ υἱῷ̣
[μο]υ̣ Ἀνδρεαντι [?]
Δορόθεος χαίρειν.
ϩⲁⲑⲏ ⲛ̣̄ϩ̣ⲱ̣ⲃ̣ ⲛ̣ⲓ̣ⲙ̣ ϯϣⲓ
ⲛⲉ ⲁⲧ̣ⲉⲕ̣ⲙ̄ⲛⲧϣⲏⲣⲉ
ⲉⲧⲁⲓⲁⲓⲧ ⲛ̄ⲧⲟⲧ ⲧ̣ⲟⲛⲟⲩ
ⲡ̣ⲉⲧⲣ̄ⲁ̣ⲛⲏⲓ̈ ϩⲱ̣ⲧ
ϩⲛ̄ ⲧⲁ[ⲯⲩ]ⲭⲏ ⲉⲓ̈ϣⲁ
ⲟⲩⲱϣ[ⲉ] ⲙⲉⲛ ⲉⲧⲁⲟⲩⲟ
ⲁⲣⲁⲕ ⲛ̄ⲛⲉⲧϩⲛ ⲡⲁϩⲏⲧ
ϯⲛⲁϣ[ϭⲛ̄] ⲑ̣ⲉ̣ ⲉⲛ̣ ϩ̣ⲛ ⲡ
ⲥϩⲉⲓ̈ ⲁⲛ̣ⲁ̣ⲕ̣ [ⲉⲧ]ϫ̣ⲱ ⲙ̄ⲙⲁⲥ
ϫⲉ ⲕⲣ̄ⲁⲓⲥⲑ̣ⲁ̣ⲛⲉ ⲁⲣⲁⲩ
ⲁⲗⲗⲁ ⲉⲡⲓⲇⲏ ⲁ̣ⲩ̣ⲱⲧⲣⲉ
ⲡϩⲱⲃ ⲉⲧⲛ̄ⲧⲛ̄ⲙⲏ̣ⲧ̣ⲉ
ϯⲛⲟⲩ ϭ̣ⲉ̣ ϯⲧ̣ⲉⲟⲩⲟ ⲡⲥⲉ
ϫⲉ ϩⲛ̄ ⲟⲩⲥ̣ⲩ̣ⲛ̣ⲧ̣ⲟ̣ⲙ̣ⲓ̣ⲁ̣
ⲡ̣ϩ̣[ⲱⲃ ⲁⲛ] ⲉⲧⲁⲕⲥϩⲉⲓ
ⲛⲏⲓ [ⲉⲧ]ⲃ̣ⲏ̣ⲧ̄ϥ ⲙⲛ̄
ϣϭ̣ⲁ̣[ⲙ . . .] ⲛ̣̄ⲗⲁⲩⲉ
ⲉ̣ⲓ̣ⲙⲏⲧⲓ ⲁ̣ⲧⲛ̄ⲟⲩ̣ⲉ̣ⲓ̣ⲉ̣
ϫⲉ ⲡⲥⲉϫⲉ̣ ⲡⲉ ⲙ̄ⲡ
ⲥⲙ̣ⲁ̣ⲧ̣ ⲙ̄ⲙⲉⲧⲉ ϫⲉ
ϩⲁⲓ̈ⲟ̣ⲩⲱ ⲉⲓ̈ⲣ̄ ⲁⲛ̣ⲁ̣ϣ
ϩⲛ̄ ⲟ̣ⲩ̣ⲛ̣ⲁ̣ϭ ⲛ̄ⲱⲣ̣ⲕ
ⲉⲧ̣ⲁ̣ϭ̣ⲛ̣ ⲕ̣ⲉϩⲱⲃ ⲉϣⲱ
ⲡⲉ ϯ̣ϯ̣[. .] . . ⲱ̣ⲗ̣ϫ ⲥ
ϣⲟⲡ̣ ϯⲛ̣ . . ⲟ ⲉⲧⲟⲧ ⲁ̣ⲣ̣ⲁϥ
ⲥⲧ̣ⲁ̣ⲙ̣ⲉ̣ ⲁ̣ⲧ̣ⲉ̣ⲟⲩⲟ ⲧⲙⲏ
ⲉ ⲁ[ⲣ]ⲁⲕ ⲡ̣[ⲁ]ϣⲏⲣⲉ
ⲉ̣ⲛ[ⲁ]ⲛⲟⲩ[ϥ] **Ἐ̣ρρῶσθαί**
σε̣ ε̣ὔχομαι
πολ̣λ̣οῖς χρόνοις.

"To my most honored son Andreas; (from) Dorotheos,—greetings.

Before everything: I greet (5) your sonship, greatly honoured by me; the one who also pleases me in my soul. Indeed, though I should love to tell (10) you the things in my heart, I will not be able to [find] the way in the letter. I am saying that you perceive them; but, since (15) the matter between us has been fixed, therefore I am now recounting the affair in brief. [Again], the matter about which you wrote to me: There is no (20) possibility [to do] anything, except to go away; in that the affair is only of such a kind that I have already pledged (25) with a great oath to resist (?) another matter. If . . . occurs . . . to him, it is appropriate to tell the truth (30) to you, my good child.

I pray for your health for many years" (trans. ed.).

3. *P.Neph.* 15 (=*SBKopt.* II 899) [Fig. 6] (Archive of the Hathor Monastery)

ⲁⲡⲁ ⲡⲁⲡⲛⲟⲩⲧⲉ ⲡⲉⲧⲥϩⲁⲉ[ⲓ ⲛ̄ⲛⲉⲫⲉⲣⲱⲥ ⲡ]ⲡⲣⲉⲥⲃⲩⲧⲉⲣⲟⲥ ⲉⲙⲛ̄ ⲡⲁⲓ̈ⲏⲟⲩ
ⲇⲓⲁⲕⲟⲛ ⲙ̄ⲙⲉⲣⲁⲧⲉ ⲛ̄ⲧⲉϯⲟⲉ[±9]ⲧⲉ ⲙ̄ⲙⲁⲉⲓⲥⲟⲛ ⲛⲙ̄ⲙⲁⲉⲓϣⲉⲙⲙⲱ
ⲁⲗⲏⲑⲱⲥ ⲛ̄ⲅⲁⲣ ⲁⲡⲉⲧⲛ̄ⲕⲩϩ ⲧ̣ [±8]̣ ⲁⲡⲉⲧⲛ̄ⲥⲧⲓⲛⲟⲩϥⲉ {ⲧ}ⲧⲉⲃⲥ ⲟⲩⲙⲏ`ϣⲉ´
ⲥⲡⲟⲩⲇⲁⲥⲉ̣ ⲟ̣ⲩⲛ ⲛ[ⲁ]ⲙⲉⲣⲁ[ⲧ]ⲉ [±10]ⲉⲛⲏⲉⲓ ⲉⲣⲏⲥ ⲉⲡⲙⲉϣⲱⲟⲩⲧ
ⲡⲉⲃϣϣⲟⲧ ⲛ̄ⲧⲛ̄ ⲡⲓⲛⲟⲩⲧⲉ [±10] ⲙ̄ⲡⲉⲙⲁⲟⲩ ⟦**ἀσπάζομε τοὺ̣ς̣** . . . . .⟧

Verso

ⲧⲓϣⲓⲛⲉ ⲉⲡⲁⲛⲏϥ ⲇⲓⲁⲕⲟⲛ ⲉⲙ̣[ⲛ̄ ±8]ⲉⲙⲛ̄ ⲛⲉⲥⲛⲏⲩ ⲧⲏⲣⲟⲩ
ⲕⲁⲧⲁ ⲛⲉⲩⲣⲁⲛ ⲛ̄ⲧⲟⲕ [±9] ⲡⲁⲓ̈ⲏⲟⲩ ⲧⲓⲥⲟⲟⲩⲟⲩⲛ ⲛ̄ⲧⲉⲕ
ⲥⲡⲟⲩⲧⲏ ⲙ̄ⲡⲉⲣⲁⲙⲉⲗⲏ ⲁ̣[ⲗⲗⲁ ⲛ̄ⲧⲟⲕ ⲁⲙ]ⲟⲩ ⲉⲡⲙⲉϣⲱⲟⲩⲧ

(hand[2]) Αὐρη[λ]̣[1] (hand[1]) **Ἀπ<ό>δ(ος)[2] Νεφερῶτ(ι) πρ(εσβυτέρῳ).**

"It is Apa Papnoute who writes to the priest Nepheros and to the deacon Paieou, the dear ones of five [. . .] who love the brothers and strangers. For truly your zeal has [. . .], your fragrance has spurred a quantity (of persons). So hurry, my dear, [. . .] south to Pmeschoout. (5) His pillow is with Pinoute [. . .] the tomb. ~~**I greet the**~~ . . ."

---

[1] The editor reads Ἄπα [Παπνοῦτ]ε̣ and considers it as part of the address. In fact, the script is very different: it is probably a later addition or the remains of an earlier text that has nothing to do with the letter itself. I omit it in the translation.

[2] The editor did not see that the first omicron was omitted.

Verso

"I greet Panef, the deacon, and [. . .] and all the brothers according to their names. Concerning you [. . .] Paieou, I know your zeal. Do not be careless, but come yourself to Pmeschoout.

Deliver (this letter) to the priest Nepheros."

4. *SBKopt.* IV 1695 (Archive of Apa John)

ⲁⲡⲁ ⲡⲁⲯⲏⲟⲩⲉⲓ ⲡⲁⲛ̣[ⲁⲭⲱⲣⲓ̈ⲧⲏⲥ]
ⲡⲉⲧⲥⲁϩⲉⲓ̈ ⲛⲁⲡⲁ ⲓ̈ⲱ̣[ϩⲁⲛⲛⲏⲥ ⲡⲁⲛⲁ-]
ⲭⲱⲣⲓ̈ⲧⲏⲥ ϩⲙ̅ⲙⲏⲉ [ϩⲛ̅ ⲡϫⲟⲉⲓⲥ ⲭⲁⲓ-]
ⲣⲉⲓⲛ̅. ϩⲁ ⲑⲏ ⲛ̅ϩⲱ`{ϥ}´ⲃ ⲛ̣[ⲓⲙ ϯϣⲓⲛⲉ ⲉⲣⲟⲕ]
ⲙ̅ⲛ ⲛⲉⲥⲛⲏⲟⲩ’ ⲧⲏⲣⲟⲩ’ ⲉ[ⲧ]ⲛ̣ⲙ̣ⲉ̣[ⲕ ⲕⲁⲧⲁ]
ⲡⲟⲩ’ ⲣⲁⲛ’ ⲁⲩⲱ ϯϣⲓⲛ[ⲉ] . . [. . . . . . .]
ϩⲏⲧⲕ ⲕⲁⲧⲁ ⲑⲉ ⲛ̅ⲧⲁ̣ⲕ̣ⲛ̣ . [. . . . . .]
ⲛⲁⲕ’ ⲁϯ ⲧⲟⲧϥ ⲛ̅<ⲟⲩ>ⲟⲛ ⲛⲓⲙ ⲉⲧ[. . . . . .]
ⲧⲙⲉ`ⲛ̣ⲛⲧ´ϩⲏⲕⲉ ⲁⲩⲱ ⲛⲧ`ⲑⲉ´ⲉϩⲉ ϩⲁ̣ϩ ⲛ . [. . . .]
ⲙⲟⲩ’ ⲁ̣ⲣⲟⲕ ⲛ̅`ⲉ´ⲧⲉ ⲥⲉⲥⲟⲟⲩⲛ . [. . . . .]
ϯⲛⲟⲩ ϭⲉ ϯⲡⲓⲥⲧⲉⲩⲉ ⲛ̅`ⲟⲩ´ⲱ̅ . [. . . . . .]
ϩⲏⲧⲕ̅ ⲛⲁⲥⲟⲩⲱ̅ⲛ̅ⲟ̅ⲩ ϫⲉ· ⲉ[. . . . . . .]
ⲡⲛⲟⲩⲧⲉ ⲉⲧⲱ̅ⲛ̅ϩ̅ ⲧⲁϥⲉⲓ̈[. . . . . . .]
ⲉⲧⲃⲉ ⲧⲉⲯⲓⲭⲏ· ⲧⲁⲣ̣ⲣ̣ⲑ̣[ⲉ . . . .]
ⲙⲱ̅ⲕ̅ϩ ⲛ̅ϩⲏⲧ ⲉⲧ[. . . . .]
ϯⲛⲟⲩ ϭⲉ’ ⲉⲣⲱⲁ’ ⲡⲥⲟⲛ [.]ⲙ . [. . . . . .]
ⲙⲛ ϯⲉⲡⲓⲥⲧⲟⲗⲏ· ⲁⲣⲓ ⲡ̅ⲛ̅ⲁ̅[. . . . . .]
ⲁⲛ ⲉⲥⲁϩⲉⲓ̈ ⲛⲁⲕ· ⲉⲧⲃⲉ ⲗⲁⲟⲩ [. . . . . .]
ⲉⲕⲟⲩ{ϩ}ⲱ̅ⲛ̅ϩ ⲛ̅ⲧⲉⲕ’ⲧⲙⲧ̅ⲛ̅ⲟⲩⲧ[ⲉ . . . . .]
ⲁϩⲟⲩ ⲉ<ⲟⲩ>ⲟⲛ ⲛⲓⲙ’ ⲉⲧⲛ̅ⲛⲏⲩ ⲟ̣ⲩ[. . . . .]
ϫ̣ⲉ· ϥϩⲁⲙⲁⲗⲟ`{ϭⲓ̈}´ⲅⲓ̈ ⲅⲁ̣ⲣ̣ ⲛⲁ̣ⲓ̅ ϫ[. . . . .]
ⲕⲉⲥⲟⲡ ϥ`ⲁ´ϯ {ϩ}ⲙ̅ⲧⲟⲛ ⲛ̅ⲧⲁⲯ[ⲓⲭⲏ . . . .]
ⲥⲁϩⲉⲓ ⲛ̅ⲁⲕ ⲡⲙⲉⲣⲓⲧ ⲛ̅[. . . . .]
ϫⲉⲕⲁⲥ ⲉⲕⲉⲁⲣ ⲁⲡⲁ[ⲧⲟⲧⲕ . . . . .]
ⲡⲓⲕⲉⲥⲟ̅ⲡ̅ ⲛ̅ⲛ̅ϩ̅ⲟ`ⲟ̣´ⲉ ⲛ̅ . [. . . . . ⲣⲱ-]
ⲙⲉ· ⲉⲧⲙⲱϣⲉ ⲛ̅ⲛ . [. . . . .]
ⲧⲁⲥⲓ̈ⲁ ⲁⲩⲱ ⲛ̅ⲛⲁϭ̣ ⲛ̅ⲥⲟⲛ̣ [. . . . .]
ⲁⲩ{ⲟⲩ}ⲑⲗⲓ̈ⲃⲉ ϩⲙ̅ ⲡ̣ⲓⲛⲁ[ⲃⲉ . . . .]
ⲉⲧⲡ ⲉ̅ⲣⲁϥ ⲡ̣ⲉ̣ⲧ̣ⲓ̣[. . . . .]
ⲁⲁϥ `ⲛⲁϥ´ ⲁⲩⲱ ⲁ̣ⲛ̣ⲧ̣ . [. . . . .]
ⲉⲡϩⲱⲃ ϫⲉ . ⲃ̣[. . . . .]

Left Margin

ϩ̅ⲓⲡⲱⲙⲓ̈ⲛⲉ̣ ϫ̣ⲉⲕⲁⲥ ⲉϥⲉϭⲓ ⲑⲉ ⲛ̅ⲃⲱⲕ ⲉⲡⲉϥ`ⲏⲉⲓ´ ⲙⲉⲛ̅ⲥⲉ ⲡⲛⲟⲩⲧⲉ ⲉⲃⲟⲗ
ⲛ̅ⲧⲟ`ⲧ̣ⲕ̣´

Verso

ⲡⲉⲧⲛⲁϯ ⲧⲟⲉ ⲛⲏϥ ⲉⲡⲗⲏⲣⲟ`ⲩ´ ⲛ̄ⲛ̣-
ⲡⲉϥ̣ϩ̣ⲱ̣ⲃ̣ ⲉⲡⲓⲇⲉ ⲙⲉⲛ ϣϭⲟⲙ ϩⲙ-
ⲙⲟⲟⲩ’ ⲉⲥⲙⲉⲙⲉ ⲛ̣̄ⲧⲁⲕ ϭⲉ ⲡⲉⲧ-
ϣⲱⲡⲉ ⲙⲉⲛⲥⲉ ⲡ̣ⲛⲟⲩⲧⲉ ⲉⲃⲟⲗ ⲛ̣-
ⲛ̣̄ⲃⲟϩⲩⲉⲑⲓⲥ ⲛ̣̄<ⲟⲩ>ⲟⲛ ⲛⲓⲙ ⲉϫⲏⲩⲟⲩ ⲛ̄ⲛ-
ϭⲟⲛⲥ ⲁⲩⲱ ⲕⲁⲧⲁ ⲑⲉ ⲉⲧⲥⲁϩⲉⲓ ⲛ̄ⲛⲓ̈-
ⲥⲁⲏ̣̄ⲁⲥ ϫⲉ ⲁⲩⲥⲟⲩⲱⲛⲧ ⲛ̄ⲛϭⲓ ⲛ-
ⲛ̄ⲉⲧⲉ ⲥⲉⲥⲟ̣ⲟⲩⲛ̣ ⲉⲙ̄ϩⲙⲁϥ ⲁⲛ̄
ϯⲛⲟⲩ ϭⲉ ϩⲙ̄ⲡⲣ ⲕⲁ̣ϥ ⲛ̄ⲛ̄ⲥⲱⲕ ⲉⲓⲁ̄-
ⲣ· ⲁⲕⲍⲓⲟⲩ ⲛⲉ̣ⲥ̣ ⲛ̣̄ⲙⲟⲕ ϫⲉ ⲥⲉⲣ ⲁ .
[. . . . . . .] ⲉⲧⲃⲉ ⲧ̣ⲟ̣ⲗ̣[. . . . . . .]
[. . . . . . .]. ⲓ̣ⲟ̣ⲏ̣ⲛ̣[
- -

“Apa Papseouei the [anchorite] writes to Apa [Iohannes the] true anchorite: [In the Lord(?), -] greetings! Before everything: [I greet you] and (5) all the brothers [who are with you by] their name. And I seek [from(?) . . .] you, just as you [. . .] to you to help everyone who [. . .] poverty; and as surely many [. . .] . . . (10) to you,—they who do not(?) know [. . .] Indeed, now, I believe [. . .] in you will know them; in that [. . .] the living God is he who has come(?) [. . .] on account of the soul, and will be like(?) . . . (15) grief that [. . .] Indeed, now, if the brother [. . .] with this letter, be so good [. . .] who writes to you about some [. . .] you display your godliness [. . .] (20) to anyone who comes. A(?) [. . .] that: for he agrees with me(?) that(?) . . . another time he can give rest to my soul [. . .] write to you, the loved one, [. . .] so that if you can do your utmost [. . .] (25) this other time [. . .] man (?) who walks [. . .] . . . , and the great brothers [. . .] they were distressed (?) by this sin (?) [. . .] . . . to him [. . .] (30) do it for him, and [. . .] to the work, in that [. . .] wait(?), so that he can find a way to go to his house. Apart from God, you(?) (verso) are the one who will give him a way to complete his work; since they are not able. (35) It is known. Indeed, you are the one who can be, apart from God, of assistance to anyone who is oppressed(?). And just as what is written by Isaiah: ‘They have known me, namely (40) they who did not know him.’ Indeed, now, do not you neglect it, as I ask it from you; in that they make [. . .] on account of [. . .]” (trans. ed.).

5. *P.Nag Hamm.* C 4 (Nag Hammadi)

ⲇⲁ̣[ⲛⲓ]ⲏⲗ ⲡⲉⲧⲥϩⲁⲓ̈ ⲙⲡⲉϥⲙⲉⲣⲓⲧ ⲛⲛⲉⲓ̣ⲱ̣ⲧ̣ ⲁ̣ⲫ̣[ⲣ]ⲟ̣ϯ̣ⲥ̣ⲓ̣ [ϩⲙ]
ⲡϫⲟⲉ̣ⲓ̣ⲥ· ⲭⲁⲓⲣⲉ : ϩⲁⲑⲏ ⲛϩⲱⲃ ⲛⲓⲙ ϯϣⲓⲛⲉ ⲉⲣⲟⲕ [ⲙⲛ]

ⲛⲉⲥⲛⲏⲟⲩ· ⲧⲏⲣⲟⲩ· ⲉⲧϣⲟⲟⲡ· ϩⲁⲧⲏⲕ· ⲕⲁⲧⲁ ⲛⲉⲩⲣ[ⲁⲛ ⲟⲩⲁ]
ⲟⲩⲁ : ⲧⲉⲛⲟⲩ ϭⲉ : ⲡⲁϫⲟⲉⲓⲥ ⲛⲛⲉⲓⲱⲧ ⲕⲱ ⲛⲛⲁⲕ̣ ⲉ̣ⲃⲟⲗ̣ [ⲙ]
ⲡⲉⲕϩⲏⲧ· ⲧⲏⲣϥ· ⲁ̣ⲓ̈ⲥⲱⲧⲙ· ⲅⲁⲣ̣ ϫ̣ⲉ̣ ⲁⲕϣ̣ⲱ̣ⲛ̣ⲉ̣ ϩ̣[ⲛ ⲟⲩⲛⲟϭ]
ⲛϣⲱⲛ̣ⲉ· ⲁ ⲡ̣ⲁ̣ϩ̣ⲏ̣[ⲧ ⲙ]ⲕⲁ̣ϩ· ⲉ̣ⲙ̣[ⲁⲧⲉ . . . . . .] . [
. . . . [. . . . .] . . [.] . . [
[ϩ]ⲟ̣ⲙ̣ⲱ̣ⲥ̣ ⲇ̣ⲉ ⲁⲛⲟⲕ· ⲟⲩϭⲱⲃ ⲛⲧⲁⲗⲁⲓⲡⲱⲣⲟⲥ ⲛⲣ̣[ⲉϥⲣ] ⲛⲟ̣[ⲃⲉ]
ⲙⲡⲓⲙϣⲁ· ⲁⲧⲣⲉ ⲡⲛⲟⲩⲧⲉ : ⲕⲁⲁⲧ : ⲉ̣ⲧ̣ⲉⲓⲥⲙⲟⲧ̣ . . [
ⲛⲓⲙ : ⲡⲛⲟⲩⲧⲉ· ⲡⲉⲧⲥⲟⲟⲩⲛ· ⲡⲉⲧϩⲙ ⲫⲏⲧ· ⲛ̄ⲛⲟⲩ . . . . [
ϫⲉ ⲛⲧⲁⲣⲉⲓⲥⲱⲧⲙ ⲁ ⲡⲁϩⲏⲧ· ⲙⲕⲁϩ ⲉⲉⲓϣⲓ̣ⲛ̣ⲉ̣ ϭⲛ̣ [ⲡⲉⲕ]
ⲟⲩⲱ ⲉⲡⲓⲇ̣ⲏ̣ ⲛⲕⲟ̣ⲩⲉ̣ ⲉ̣ⲧⲙ̣ ⲡⲏⲓ ⲉⲧⲛⲉ̣ⲙⲙⲉ ⲇ̣ⲓⲁ̣[
ⲉ̣ⲩⲣ̣ ϣⲁⲩ· ⲕⲁ̣ⲗ̣ⲟⲥ· ⲧⲉⲛⲟⲩ ϭⲉ ⲉⲣ̣ⲉ ⲡ̣[ⲉ]ⲕ̣ⲟⲩⲱ· ⲛⲁⲗⲟ̣ ⲉ̣[
ⲙ̣ⲙ̣ⲟⲕ : ⲁϥⲧ̣ⲉ̣ⲕ̣ ⲡⲁϩⲏⲧ ⲉⲙⲁⲧⲉ [ⲉ]ⲡⲉⲧⲓ̣ϣ̣ⲓ̣ⲛ̣ⲉ ⲛ̣[ⲥⲱϥ]
ⲉ̣ⲉⲓⲟⲩⲱϣⲉ· ⲉϭ̣ⲛ· ⲡⲉⲕⲟⲩⲱ· ⲧⲉⲛⲟⲩ ϭ̣ⲉ ⲡⲁϫ̣ⲟⲉ̣ⲓ̣ⲥ̣ [ⲛⲛ]
ⲉⲓⲱⲧ ⲉⲡⲓⲇⲏ ⲉⲁ ⲡⲁϫⲟⲉⲓⲥ ⲛⲥⲟⲛ· ⲥⲟⲩⲣⲟⲩⲥ̣ ⲧⲁ[ⲙⲟⲓ]
ϫⲉ ⲁⲕⲧⲓ ⲁⲧϩ̣ⲏ̣· ⲁ ⲡⲁϩⲏⲧ ⲙⲙⲧⲟⲛ ⲉ̣ϥⲥⲏϩ ⲅ̣ⲁ̣ⲣ̣ ϫⲉ [ⲡⲉⲧⲉ]
ⲣⲉ ⲡϫⲟⲉⲓⲥ ⲙⲉ ⲙⲙⲟϥ ϣⲁϥⲡⲉⲇⲉⲩⲉ ⲙⲙⲟ[ϥ] ϣⲁϥ̣[ⲙⲁⲥ]
ⲧⲓⲕⲟⲩ̣· ⲛϣⲏⲣⲉ ⲛⲓⲙ ⲉⲧϥⲛⲁϣⲟⲟⲡⲟⲩⲓ ⲉⲣⲟϥ [ⲉ]ⲡⲓ̈ⲇⲏ [ⲡⲁ]
ⲙⲉⲣⲓⲧ· ⲁⲡⲛⲟⲩⲧⲉ ⲧⲟⲩⲛⲟⲥⲕ ⲅ̣ϫⲁⲕⲁⲙ̣ ϩⲙ ⲡ̣[. .]ⲛⲟ . [
ⲛⲟⲃⲉ : ⲉⲉⲓⲉ· ⲧⲱⲕ· ⲛϩⲏⲧ ⲛⲧⲁⲱϩⲉ· ⲉⲣⲁⲧ·[. .]ⲧ . [
ϯϩⲉⲗⲡⲓⲥ ⲉⲡⲛⲟⲩⲧⲉ ϫⲉ ⲥⲉⲛⲁⲧⲁⲧ ⲛⲙ̣ⲁ̣ⲕ̣· ⲁⲣ̣[ⲓ ϩ]ⲙ̣ⲟⲧ [ⲛⲅ]
ⲛⲉϫ ϣⲗⲏⲗ ⲛ̄ⲛⲧⲟⲕ ⲙⲛ̄ ⲛⲉⲕⲙⲁⲕ[ⲁⲣⲓⲟⲥ ⲛⲥⲟ]ⲛ̣ ⲉ̣[ⲧϣ]
ⲟⲟⲡ· ϩⲁⲧⲏⲕ· ⲧ̣ⲉⲛⲟⲩ ϭⲉ ⲛⲁⲙⲉⲣ̣[ⲁⲧⲉ
ϩⲛ ⲛⲉⲧⲛϣⲗⲏⲗ ⲛⲁϫⲓⲥⲟⲟⲩⲉ· ⲛⲁⲥ̣ . [. . .] . . [
ⲙ̣ⲁ̣ ⲛⲧⲁϫⲣⲟ ⲙⲛⲥⲁ ⲡⲛⲟⲩⲧⲉ̣ ϯⲧⲏ̣[ⲧ ⲛ]ϩⲏⲧ̣ [
ⲙ̣ⲙⲁ ϩⲙ ⲡⲕⲟⲥⲙⲟⲥ· ⲉⲛϣⲁⲉⲓ ϭⲉ ⲉⲕ[ⲛⲁ]ϣ̣ⲱⲡⲉ̣ [ϩ]
ⲙⲟⲧ ϯⲛⲁⲱⲛϩ ϫ[. . ϩⲙ] ⲡϫⲟⲉⲓⲥ̣

"It is Daniel who writes to his beloved father Aphrodisi(os), in the Lord, greetings. Before everything I greet you and all the brothers who are with you, each by name. Now then, my lord father, be relieved with (5) your whole heart. For I heard that you fell sick with a serious sickness, and my heart was much grieved . . . But nevertheless I am a wretched, sinful weakling; I was not worthy that God should set me in this role. [For] (10) who [am I ?] It is God who knows what is in the heart [of everyone]. For when I heard, my heart was grieved, while I sought to get news of you, since the others who are in the house with me continue (?) to be greatly benefited. Now, therefore, since news of you will . . . you, it cheered my heart greatly concerning what I was searching after, (15) desiring to get news of you. Now, therefore, my lord father, since my lord brother Sourous has told me that you have improved, my heart has been relieved. For it is written: 'Whom the Lord loves, he is wont to chastise; he scourges every son whom he will receive to himself.' Since, my (20) beloved, God has raised you up, you are cleansed by the sin[less blood]; then be of good cheer, and I shall stand [with you, for] I put my hope in God that I shall be set with you. Have the goodness to send up prayers, both you and your blessed brothers who are with you. Now, therefore, my beloved [brothers, remember me] (25) in your prayers; my [ascetic] lords, [you are our] strong refuge, after God. I am convinced [that if we are in any] place in the world, when we then come, you will become [a] blessing [for me], and I shall live. Be [strong] in the Lord" (trans. ed.).

APPENDIX 3

The First Legal Documents in Coptic before the Arab Conquest

I will stick to texts that have been *precisely* dated and that are prior to the Arab Conquest (641–42). I am adding a few texts without dates that can nevertheless be dated rather precisely (number followed by a *).[1] The numerous texts of the archive of Abraham, which are covered in chapter 4, pp. 133–45, are not included in this table. All the texts are in Sahidic.

The names are spelled according to the Greek/Coptic orthography (except for Dioscorus of Aphrodite, whose name has passed into common use with its Latin spelling):

TABLE 3A

	papyrus	provenance and date	genre and designation in the text	parties	writer	miscellaneous
1	P.Berol. inv. 11349 [unedited][1]	Aphrodite, **534/535** or **549/550** (13th ind.)	settlement (ὅρος)	• Dioscorus • Iōsēph son of Hermauō (currier)	? (Kallinikos son of Biktōr, the arbitrator, only signed the document in Greek).	private report. No protocol (beginning: ⲁⲛⲥ̣ⲱⲧⲙ̄ ⲉϥⲱⲃ ⲕⲧⲗ), no date. End: subscription of the arbitrator Greek (l. 51–52: ἐπειδέδωκα τοῦτ[ο]ν τὸν ὅρον) Archive of Dioscorus (trismegistos.org/archive/72)

[1] This list is somewhat different than that of Richter 2008b, 23–24.

	papyrus	provenance and date	genre and designation in the text	parties	writer	miscellaneous
2	*P.Lond.* V 1709[2]	Antinoopolis, **566/567**[3]	settlement (ⲙⲉⲥⲓⲧⲉⲓⲁ)	• Phoebammōn The Weak (? ⲡϭⲱ̣ⲃ) and his sister Biktorinē • Philadelphia, their half-sister	Dioscorus (arbitrator, writer)	private report. Beginning: ⲕⲁⲧⲁ ⲙⲉⲥⲓⲧⲉⲓⲁⲥ ⲧⲣⲟⲡⲟⲛ ⲁⲓ̈ⲥⲱⲧⲙ̄ ⲉⲑⲩⲡⲟⲑⲉⲥⲓⲥ ⲛ̄ⲫⲱⲃ ⲕⲧⲗ End lost Archive of Dioscorus (trismegistos.org /archive/72)
3	(a) *P.Cair. Masp.* III 67176 + P.Alex. inv. 689 + *BKU* III 503 + Corpus Christi College Ms. 541 [very partially edited][4] (b) *P.Cair. Masp.* III 67353 r° (duplicate) [unedited][6]	Aphrodite,[5] **28/10/569**	settlement (ⲙⲉⲥⲓⲧⲉⲓⲁ)	• Paulos son of Theophilos (priest and monk), Khrestēs son of Iōannēs and Leontios son of Apollō • Anoup son of Apollō, and Ioulios son of Sarapammōn	Dioscorus (arbitrator, writer of (a))	private report. Beginning: ⲕⲁⲧⲁ ⲙⲉⲥⲓⲧⲉⲓⲁ ⲧⲣⲟⲡⲟⲛ ⲁⲓ̈ⲥⲱⲧⲙ ⲉⲑⲩⲡⲟⲑⲉⲥⲓⲥ End: (1) epistolary-type address (ⲧⲁⲁⲥ ⲛ̄ⲛ̄ⲙⲁⲓ̈ⲛⲟⲩⲧⲉ ⲛ̄ⲛⲟϭⲛ̄ⲣⲱⲙⲉ ⲛ̄ⲡⲧⲟⲟⲩ ⲛ̄ⲫⲁⲣⲟⲟⲩ ⲙⲛ̄ ⲛⲁⲡϯⲙⲉ̣ ⲧⲏⲣϥ ϩⲓⲧⲛ̄ ⲇⲓⲟⲥⲕⲟⲣⲟⲥ ⲡⲓⲉⲗⲁⲭ(ⲓⲥⲧⲟⲥ) ⲡϣⲏⲣⲉ ⲛ̄ⲁⲡⲁ ⲁⲡⲟⲗⲗⲱ ⲛ̄ⲫⲁⲣⲟⲟⲩ "Deliver to the God-loving great men of the Monastery of Pharoou and to the inhabitants of the entire village on behalf of the very humble Dioscorus, son of Apa Apollōs of Pharoou"); (2) conclusion of an epistolary type (Ἡ ἁγία Τρι[ὰς καὶ] αἱ̣ εὐχαὶ ὑμῶν ἐμ[ὲ] διαφυλάττοι ἄπ[ωθε]ν παντὸς κακοῦ. Ἔρρω[σθε ἐν Κ(υρί)ῳ̣] "May the holy Trinity and your prayers protect me from all harm. Salute in the Lord."

(continued)

TABLE 3A Continued

	papyrus	provenance and date	genre and designation in the text	parties	writer	miscellaneous
						Indictional and regnal dating in Greek (only in (a)). Endorsement: summary of the document in Coptic (only in (b)) Archive of Dioscorus (trismegistos.org /archive/72)
4*	P.Lond. inv. 2849[7]	Aphrodite, **580–590**	land lease (ⲙⲓⲥⲑⲱⲥⲓⲥ)	• Kollouthos son of Apa Sia • [- - -]	Geōrgos, tabellion	*Tabellionenurkunde*: first notarized contract in Coptic Beginning: lost End: subscriptions (l. 14–23); notarial *completio* in Greek (l. 24) Calque of the Greek formulary (security, validity clauses, *stipulatio*) Archive of Dioscorus (trismegistos.org /archive/72)
5	*CPR* IV 90 (= *CPR* II 6)[8]	Hermopolite, **596**	sale of 23 pounds of wool for future delivery (ⲁⲥⲫⲁⲗⲉⲓⲁ)	• Phib son of the Hatre of the village of Pouanneshoos (gr. Ποαμποιμῆνις) • Apa Iōhannēs *diakonētēs* of Hermopolis	Iōsēp	Nonnotarized *cheirographon*[9] End: date in Greek (l. 7); subscriptions (l. 8–9); pseudo-*completio* of the writer in Greek (l. 10) Endorsement: summary of the document in Greek[10]

	papyrus	provenance and date	genre and designation in the text	parties	writer	miscellaneous
*	*P.KRU* 105[11]	Djeme, **ca. 600**	acknowledgment of ownership rights over the Monastery of St. Phoebammon	• the village of Djeme represented by its *lashane* Papnoute • the Monastery of St. Phoebammon represented by its elders(s)	Damianos, *grammateus* (who writes the document at the request of Papnoute)	Beginning: lost Penalty, validity clauses, *stipulatio* End: subscriptions of the declarant and witnesses (l. 24–44) as well as that of Damianos (in Greek) writing on behalf of Papnoute, who is illiterate (l. 45–47) Archive of the Monastery of St. Phoebammon
	CPR IV 23 = *SBKopt.* II 932[12]	Panopolite (Tin/This), **29/08/608**[13]	marriage contract (ⲁⲥⲫⲁⲗⲉⲓⲁ)	• Pahōm/ Pachymios son of Psatē (father of the bride) • Dioskoros son of Arsenios (son-in-law)	Paulos son of Megas (who writes this text at the request of the declarant and acts as a witness)	Nonnotarized *cheirographon* Beginning: invocation and regnal dating in Greek (l. 1–5 = *SB* I 5287) Sticks to the Greek formulary (ⲉⲓⲥⲟⲙⲟⲗⲟⲅⲉⲓ; penalty and validity clauses) End: absence of the subscription of the declarant; subscriptions of witnesses (l. 21–27) and that of Paulos, who also acts as a witness (l. 27–30) Archive of Pachymios (trismegistos.org /archive/36)
3*	*P.Lond.Copt.* I 446	Syene, **beginning of the seventh century (before 613?)**[14]	settlement (ⲙⲉⲥⲓⲧⲉⲓⲁ)	• Sourous (?) • [- - -]	?	Very damaged Archive of Patermouthis (trismegistos.org /archive/37)

(continued)

TABLE 3A Continued

	papyrus	provenance and date	genre and designation in the text	parties	writer	miscellaneous
9*	*P.CrumST* 96 = *SBKopt.* III 1395[15]	Syene, **beginning of the seventh century (before 613?)**[16]	debt settlement (1 *tremissis*) (†ⲗⲩⲥⲓⲥ = διάλυσις)	• Kako • Paeiōn	Petros, deacon (who writes this text at the request of the declarant and acts as a witness)	Nonnotarized, very rudimentary *cheirographon* Absence of date Penalty clause End: Subscription of the declarant in a hand other than his own (as he is illiterate) and of Petros, who also acts as a witness (l. 6–8) Archive of Patermouthis (trismegistos.org/archive/37)
10	*P.CrumST* 436[17]	Panopolite, **619** or **634** (8th ind.)[18]	acknowledgment of debt	• Rhoubēn son of Kōstantinos (monk) • Pes(y)nte of Atripe	?	Parchment Nonnotarized *cheirographon*? Beginning: regnal dating in Greek (l. 1–5) End: lost
11	*CPR* IV 48 (= *CPR* II 5)[19]	Hermopolite (Pousire), **8/11/625** (14th ind.)	sale of flax for future delivery (36 *solidi* of flax) (ⲁⲥⲫⲁⲗⲉⲓⲁ)	• 14 inhabitants of the village of Pousire • the Persian Perēs Kōsrōi	Apollō, the village scribe (who writes this text for the declarants)	Nonnotarized *cheirographon* Sticks to the Greek formulary (oath, in this case on the King of Kings; security clause) End: date (in Greek) (l. 23–24); subscriptions (the 14 declarants are illiterate and Apollō writes for them) (l. 24–29)
12	*P.CrumST* 48[20]	Apollonopolis/ Edfu, **625** (13th ind.)[21]	agreement concerning a former deed (ⲉⲅⲅⲣⲁⲫⲟⲛ)	• Dorōtheos son of Isak • Terēt son of Biktōr	Daniēl	Nonnotarized *cheirographon* End: date (in Greek) (l. 8); subscriptions (l. 8–10); *completio*

	papyrus	provenance and date	genre and designation in the text	parties	writer	miscellaneous
						of Daniēl (in Coptic sticking to the Greek formulary: ϩⲓⲧⲟⲟⲧ ⲇⲁⲛⲓⲏⲗ ⲁⲡⲓ̈ⲉⲅⲅⲣⲁⲫⲟⲛ ϣⲱⲡⲉ, l. 11) Links with **13** and *SB* I 5112 (618)
13	*P.CrumVC* 5 + Bodl. Ms. Gr. class. C 25 (p)[22]	Apollonopolis/ Edfu, **22/1/627**[23]	joint declaration about inheritance (κοινὴ ὁμολογία)	• Biktōr son of Daniēl • Hēraei daughter of Zakharia, his wife	Daniēl	Nonnotarized *cheirographon* Beginning: summary in Greek (l. 1, at the top); invocation in Greek (l. 3–4); date and place in Greek (l. 4) Security clause, *stipulatio* (l. 36–38) End: subscriptions; *completio* of Daniēl (in Coptic sticking to the Greek formulary: ϩⲓⲧⲟⲟⲧ̄ ⲇⲁⲛⲓⲏⲗ ⲁϯϩⲟⲙⲟ[ⲗⲟⲅⲓⲁ ϣ]ⲱ̣ⲡⲉ) Links with **12** and *SB* I 5112 (618)
14	*P.Mon. Phoib.Test.* 2 = *P.KRU* 77 + P.Sorb. inv. 2680[24]	Monastery of St. Phoebammon (Djeme), **4/12/634**	will (ⲇⲓⲁⲑⲏⲕⲏ)	Biktōr, the abbot of the Monastery of St. Phoebammon	[- - -], priest of Apa Kollouthos (Hermonthis) and scribe of the *kastron* of Djeme (who writes the text at the request of the testator, who is illiterate)	First will in Coptic: nonnotarized Beginning: invocation, regnal, and indictional dating, place in Greek (l. 1–10); indictional dating in Coptic (l. 11) End: subscriptions of the testator (written by the writer of the text) and of the witnesses (l. 150–82); *completio* (l. 182–85) Archive of the Monastery of St. Phoebammon

I am adding two texts whose dating is more approximate:

TABLE 3B

	papyrus	provenance and date	genre and designation in the text	parties	writer	miscellaneous
15*	*P.Mon. Apollo* 36	Monastery of Apa Apollō at Bawit, **VII?**[25]	sale of oil for future delivery (ГРАММАТІОН)	• Biktōr son of Mathias • Apa Enōkh, monk of Apa Apollō	Paulos son of Iōsēph	Nonnotarized *cheirographon* End: subscription of the declarant and a guarantor (l. 4–5) and that of a witness (l. 5–6) and Paulos (l. 6); date in Greek (l. 7); endorsement in Greek (v°)
16*	*P.Köln ägypt.* I 13 (+ *SB* XVIII 13633) = *FHN* III 339	Pathyris, **575–599**[26]	emancipation (?)	• Barakhia, King of the Blemmyes • Amnas alias Sophia	Agathōn, *grammateus*	Nonnotarized *cheirographon* End: subscriptions of the declarant in Coptic as well as in Greek as a witness (l. 8–10), of 8 witnesses in Greek (l. 10–12); date in Greek (l. 12); *completio* in Greek by Agathōn (l. 13–14).

Last of all, I am adding a collection of texts from the archive of Phoibammōn and Kollouthos,[2] the dating of some of which is still subject to discussion (either just before or just after the Arab Conquest):

TABLE 3C

	papyrus	provenance and date	genre and designation in the text	parties	writer	miscellaneous
17*	*P.Vat.Copt. Doresse* 1[27]	Aphrodite, **mid-seventh century**[28]	Sale of a portion of a carriage (1 1/6 *solidi*) (ПРАСІС)	• Daueit son of Khristophoros • Kollouthos son of Khristophoros[29]	Iakōb son of Geōrgios (who writes the document and acts as a witness)	Nonnotarized *cheirographon* Beginning: lost End: subscription, in Coptic, of the declarant and of the 3 witnesses

[2] Regarding these archives, cf. Fournet 2016.

	papyrus	provenance and date	genre and designation in the text	parties	writer	miscellaneous
						(l. 36–42) as well as, in Greek, of Iakōb, who also signs as a witness (l. 43) Endorsement in Greek Archive of Phoibammōn and Kollouthos (trismegistos.org /archive/193)
18*	*P.Vat.Copt. Doresse* 2 + 3[30]	Aphrodite, **625/626** or **640/641**[31]	Division of property (ⲙⲉⲣⲓⲥⲙⲟⲥ)	• Kōnstantinos son of Iōannēs • Iakōb son of Iōannēs, his brother, and his wife Thaumastē daughter of Paulos	[- - -]	*Information not available* Archive of Phoibammōn and Kollouthos (trismegistos.org /archive/193)
19*	*P.Vat.Copt. Doresse* 4[32]	Aphrodite, **first half of the seventh century**	Sale of a plot of land (ⲡⲣⲁⲥⲓⲥ)	• wife of Kollouthos? • [- - -]	[- - -]	*Information not available* Archive of Phoibammōn and Kollouthos (trismegistos.org /archive/193)
20*	*P.Vat.Copt. Doresse* 5[33]	Aphrodite, **625/626** or **655/656**[34]	Sale of a plot of land (ⲡⲣⲁⲥⲓⲥ)	• Kollouthos and Markos sons of Khristophoros (purchasers) • Taham daughter of Promaō and wife of Markos (seller)	Theodosios 2, tabellion[35]	Notarial contract Beginning: lost End: subscriptions of Taham (through the intermediary of a *hypographeus*) and 3 witnesses (l. 43–52); notarial *completio* in Greek (l. 53) Archive of Phoibammōn and Kollouthos (trismegistos.org /archive/193)

(*continued*)

TABLE 3C Continued

	papyrus	provenance and date	genre and designation in the text	parties	writer	miscellaneous
21*	*SB Kopt.* III 1369	Aphrodite, **646/647**[36]	exchange of Property (ⲁⲛⲧⲓⲕⲁⲧⲁⲗⲗⲁⲅⲏ)	• Thaumastē daughter of Paulos & her daughter Anastasia daughter of Iakōb • Kollouthos & Markos son of Khristophoros	Apa Rhasios, *sumbolaiographos*	Notarial contract Beginning lost End: subscriptions of the two parties and of 5 witnesses (l. 108–119); notarial *completio* in Greek (l. 120) Archive of Phoibammōn and Kollouthos (trismegistos.org /archive/193)

[1] Cf. Fournet 2010b, 130–32.

[2] Cf. Till 1954, 216–20 (with a translation).

[3] Cf. Fournet 2010b, 130.

[4] Cf. MacCoull 1997, 357–58, n° III.

[5] Although Dioscorus was still living in Antinoopolis, this settlement does appear to have been carried out in Aphrodite. In any case, it is regarding this village (cf. address). The edition should clarify this point.

[6] Cf. Fournet 2010b, 125–30.

[7] Ed. Förster, Fournet, and Richter 2012.

[8] Cf. MacCoull 1997, 358–61, n° IV

[9] Despite Bagnall and Worp, 2004, 248n7 ("the earliest Coptic legal document signed by a notary"); and Fournet 2010b, 133: cf. Kovaric 2014, 487n8.

[10] I suggest reading: ⳨ Ἀ̣σφ(άλεια) π(αρὰ) Φιβίου Ἀτρῆτος ἐρ̣ε̣ο̣ῦ̣ λι(τρῶν) κ̣γ ἀπὸ κώ̣μ̣(ης) Ποανπ(οιμήνεως) ϊδ ἰνδ(ικτίωνος) ☩.

[11] Reed. Garel 2015, II, 180–88 ("Annexe 2"). The dating of the text is disputed (see Garel 2015, I, 77–80).

[12] Cf. MacCoull 1997, 361–63, n° V.

[13] *CSBE*², 103.

[14] This document belongs to the last layer of the Patermouthis archive (574–613).

[15] Cf. Till 1964, 224 (trans.); Clackson 1995, n° 3; Porten 1996, 579–80, E. 3 (trans.).

[16] This document belongs to the last layer of the Patermouthis archive (574–613).

[17] Till 1964, 229 (trans.).

[18] Bagnall and Worp, *CSBE*², 269: 634? Cf. also Worp 1990, 142, who prefers 634 rather than 619 ("less likely").

[19] Cf. MacCoull 1997, 345–65, n° VI.

[20] Till 1954, 221; Till 1964, 220.

[21] This date is the most likely, taking into account the date of the following papyrus.

[22] Ed. Salomons and Sijpesteijn, 55–59, pl. 7–9. Cf. also Till 1954, 224–26 (trans.).

[23] Date given by Salomons & Sijpesteijn 1987 (cf. Gascou and Worp 1982, 94).

[24] Ed. Garel 2015, II, 57–108, n° 2.

[25] The editor dates this papyrus to the first half of the sixth century due to resemblance of the writing with *P.Athen. Xyl.* 5 v° (539). The second half of the sixth century or the beginning of the seventh century can be considered. Moreover, I would be tempted to place the writing of this document within the first decades of the seventh century, given that the protocol on the reverse side in my opinion appears to be a lot more stylized than those of the sixth century (cf. Diethart, Feissel, and Gascou 1994, 34): we no longer recognize the initial φ.

[26] Cf. F. Mitthof, *SPP* III^{2}, xxviii.

[27] Ed. Förster and Mitthof 2004.

[28] Bagnall and Worp 2004, 252, suggest 625/626 or 655/656.

[29] The text signals that it is a Khristophoros other than the father of the seller (l. 27).

[30] Currently being edited. L. 22–35 have been reproduced and edited by MacCoull 1997, 355–57 (with an incorrect ate).

[31] Bagnall and Worp 2004, 251–52, suggest 624/625 (in reality, 625/626 since the text dates to the fourteenth indic- on) or 655/656. However, *P.Vat.Copt.Doresse* 2 + 3 is earlier than *SBKopt.* III 1369: Thaumastē is presented in the rst as the wife of Iakōb, whereas she is called the widow of Iakōb and of Kōnstantinos in the second. If *SBKopt.* III 369 dates to 646/647, *P.Vat.Copt.Doresse* 2 + 3 cannot be from 655/656. We note that the writing does not allow us to ate the document from much later than the mid-seventh century. Therefore, possible dates would be 625/626 or, as sther Garel suggested to me, 640/641.

[32] Currently being edited.

[33] Ed. Förster 2012. L. 12–19 are reproduced and edited by MacCoull 1997, 352–55 (with an incorrect date).

[34] Bagnall and Worp 2004, 251–52. The editor retains the second date.

[35] The hand of the *completio* is not identical to that of *P.Mich.* XIII 663. Therefore, we are dealing with two different heodosios, unless the same notary adopted two different writing styles.

[36] Bagnall and Worp 2004, 252, suggest 647/648, but are mistaken by one year (the text speaks of the fifth indiction nd not the sixth). This error is corrected in Förster and Mitthof 2004, 224.

BIBLIOGRAPHY

Papyrological publications are abbreviated according to the *Checklist of Greek, Latin, Demotic and Coptic Papyri, Ostraca and Tablets* (http://papyri.info/docs/checklist). Otherwise:

AAES IV = Littmann, Enno. 1905. *Publications of an American Archaeological Expedition to Syria in 1899–1900*, vol. IV, *Semitic Inscriptions*. London.

ACO I–III = Schwartz, Eduard. 1914–20. *Acta Conciliorum Œcumenicorum*, vols. I–III. Berlin.

BL = Preisigke, Friedrich. 1922. *Berichtigungsliste der griechischen Papyrusurkunden aus Ägypten*, vol. I. Berlin-Leipzig; Friedrich Bilabel. 1929–33. Vol. II/1–2. Heidelberg; Martin David, Bernard A. van Groningen, and Emil Kiessling. Vol. III. Leiden; *iid.* 1964. Vol. IV. Leiden; Ernst Boswinkel, Bernard A. van Groningen, and Emil Kiessling. 1969. Vol. V. Leiden; Ernst Boswinkel, Pieter W. Pestman, and Hans-Albert Rupprecht. 1976. Vol. VI. Leiden; Ernst Boswinkel, Willy Clarysse, Pieter W. Pestman, and Hans-Albert Rupprecht. 1986. Vol. VII. Leiden; Pieter W. Pestman and Hans-Albert Rupprecht. 1992. Vol. VIII. Leiden; *iid.* 1995. Vol. IX. Leiden; *iid.* 1998. Vol. X. Leiden; Hans-Albert Rupprecht and Arthur M. F. W Verhoogt. 2002. Vol. XI. Leiden; Hans-Albert Rupprecht and Klaas A. Worp. 2009. Vol. XII. Leiden; Francisca A. J. Hoogendijk and Andrea Jördens. 2017. Vol. XIII. Leiden-Heidelberg.

Byz.Not. = Diethart, Johannes M., and Klaas A. Worp. 1986. *Notarunterschriften im byzantinischen Ägypten* (MPER XVI). Vienna.

Calderini, *Diz.* = Calderini, Aristide. 1935. *Dizionario dei nomi geografici e topografici dell'Egitto greco-romano*, vol. I/1. Cairo; Daris, Sergio. 1966. Vol. I/2. Madrid; *id.* 1973–77. Vol. II. Milan; *id.* 1978–83. Vol. III. Milan; *id.* 1983–86. Vol. IV. Milan; *id.* 1986. Vol. V. Milan; *id.* 1988. Supplemento 1. Milan; *id.* 1996. Supplemento 2. Bonn; *id.* 2003. Supplemento 3. Pise; *id.* 2006. Supplemento 4. Pisa-Rome; *id.* 2010. Supplemento 5. Pisa-Rome.

Crum, *CD* = Crum, Walter C. 1939. *A Coptic Dictionary*. Oxford.

*CSBE*² = Bagnall, Roger S., and Klaas A. Worp. 2004. *Chronological Systems of Byzantine Egypt*. 2nd ed. Leiden.

FHN III = Eide, Tormod, Tomas Hägg, Richard Holton Pierce, and László Török. 1998. *Fontes Historiae Nubiorum. Textual Sources for the History of the Middle Nile Region between the Eighth Century BC and the Sixth Century AD*. Vol. III, *From the First to the Sixth Century AD*. Bergen.

MP³ + number = Mertens-Pack³ database (http://cipl93.philo.ulg.ac.be/Cedopal/MP3/dbsearch_en.aspx).

PAES IV B = Littmann, Enno. 1934. *Publications of the Princeton University Archaeological Expeditions to Syria*. Vol. IV. B, *Syriac Inscriptions*. Leiden.

PAT = Hillers, Delbert R., and Eleonora Cussini. 1996. *Palmyrene Aramaic Texts*. Baltimore.

PG = *Patrologia Graeca*.

PLRE = Jones, Arnold H. M., John R. Martindale, and John Morris. 1971. *The Prosopography of the Later Roman Empire*, vol. I; Martindale, John R. 1992. Vols. II–III. Cambridge.

Timm = Timm, Stephan. 1984–92. *Das christlich-koptische Ägypten in arabischer Zeit. Eine Sammlung christlicher Stätten in Ägypten in arabischer Zeit* (Beihefte zum Tübinger Atlas des Vorderen Orients, Reihe B, Geisteswissenschaften 41/1–6), 6 vols. Wiesbaden.

TM + number = Trismegistos texts database (http://www.trismegistos.org/index2.php).

WB = Preisigke, Friedrich. 1925–31. *Wörterbuch der griechischen Papyrusurkunden mit Einschluss der griechischen Inschriften Ausschriften Ostraka Mumienschilder usw. aus Ägypten*. Vols. I–III. Kiessling, Emil. 1944, Vol. IV. Berlin.

References

Aggoula, Basile. 1992. "Studia Aramaica III." *Syria* 69: 391–422.

Alcock, Anthony, and Peter J. Sijpesteijn. 2000. "Early 7th Cent. Contract from Aphrodito (P.Mich. Inv. 6898)." *Enchoria* 26: 1–19.

Amélineau, Émile. 1887. *Études sur le christianisme en Égypte au septième siècle*. Paris.

———. 1893. *La géographie de l'Égypte à l'époque copte*. Paris.

———. 1907. *Oeuvres de Schenoudi*. Vol. I. Paris.

Anagnostou-Canas, Barbara. 1998. "La 'justice' oraculaire en Égypte." *Revue historique de droit français et étranger* 76: 1–16.

Atiya, Aziz S. (ed). 1991. *The Coptic Encyclopedia*. 8 vols. New York-Toronto.

Aufrère, Sydney H. 1999. "La dernière ronde des hiéroglyphes . . . La mort des écritures égyptiennes traditionnelles et l'émergence des premiers signes coptes." In *Égyptes . . . L'Égyptien et le copte*, edited by Nathalie Bosson and Sydney H. Aufrère, 27–68. Lattes.

Bagnall, Roger S. 1988. "Combat ou vide: Christianisme et paganisme dans l'Égypte romaine tardive." *Ktèma* 13: 285–96.

———. 1993. *Egypt in Late Antiquity*. Princeton.

———. 2005. "Linguistic Change and Religious Change: Thinking about the Temples of the Fayoum in the Roman Period." In *Christianity and Monasticism in the Fayoum Oasis. Essays from the 2004 International Symposium of the Saint Mark Foundation and the Saint Shenouda the Archimandrite Coptic Society in Honor of Martin Krause*, edited by Gawdat Gabra, 11–19. Cairo-New York.

———. 2009a. *Early Christian Books in Egypt*. Princeton-Oxford.

———. 2009b. *Les livres chrétiens antiques d'Égypte* (École Pratique des Hautes Études, Sciences historiques et philologiques III, Hautes études du monde gréco-romain 44). Paris.

———. 2011. *Everyday Writing in the Graeco-Roman East* (Sather Classical Lectures 69). Berkeley.

Bagnall, Roger S., and Klaas A. Worp. 2004. "Dating the Coptic Legal Documents from Aphrodite." *Zeitschrift für Papyrologie und Epigraphik* 148: 247–52.

Bagnall, Roger S., Malcolm Choat, and Iain Gardner. 2004. "O.Douch I 40." *Zeitschrift für Papyrologie und Epigraphik* 147: 205–7.

Barney, Stephen A., Wanda J. Lewis, Jennifer A. Beach, and Oliver Berghof. With the collaboration of Muriel Hall. 2006. *The Etymologies of Isidore of Seville*. Cambridge.

Bastianini, Guido, and Guglielmo Cavallo. 2011. "Un nuovo frammento di lettera festale (PSI inv. 3779)." In *I papiri letterari cristiani. Atti del convegno internazionale di studi in memoria di Mario Naldini, Firenze, 10–11 giugno 2010* (Studi e Testi di Papirologia. N.S. 13), edited by Guido Bastianini and Angelo Casanova, 31–45. Florence.

Bell, Harold I. 1924. "The episcopalis audientia in Byzantine Egypt." *Byzantion* 1: 139–44.

Bell, Harold I., and Herbert Thompson. 1925. "A Greek-Coptic Glossary to Hosea and Amos." *Journal of Egyptian Archaeology* 11: 241–46.

Benaissa, Amin. 2008. "Two Bishops Named Senuthes: Prosopography and New Texts." *Zeitschrift für Papyrologie und Epigraphik* 166: 179–94.

———. 2016. "The Provenance of the Greek-Coptic Glossary to Hosea and Amos." *Chronique d'Égypte* 91: 175–79.

Biedenkopf-Ziehner, Anneliese. 1983. *Untersuchungen zum koptischen Briefformular unter Berücksichtigung ägyptischer und griechischer Parallelen*. Würzburg.

Bolman, Elizabeth S. (ed.). 2016. *The Red Monastery Church: Beauty and Asceticism in Upper Egypt*. New Haven-London.

Bosson, Nathalie. 1999. "'Langue copte,' une réalité à visages multiples." In *Égyptes . . . L'Égyptien et le copte*, edited by Nathalie Bosson and Sydney H. Aufrère, 69–87. Lattes.

———. 2012. "Le *Papyrus Vatican Copte* 9 des Petits Prophètes." In *Coptic Treasures from the Vatican Library. A Selection of Coptic, Copto-Arabic and Ethiopic Manuscripts, Papers Collected on the Occasion of the Tenth International Congress of Coptic Studies (Rome, September 17th–22nd, 2012)* (Studi e Testi, 472.2), edited by Paola Buzi, and Delio V. Proverbio, 73–84. Vatican City.

Bosson, Nathalie, and Sydney H. Aufrère (eds.). 1999. *Égyptes . . . L'Égyptien et le copte*. Lattes.

Botte, Bernard. 1964. "L'euchologe de Sérapion est-il authentique?" *Oriens Christianus* 48: 50–56.

Boud'hors, Anne. 1998. "Un codex formé de tablettes (Musée du Louvre)." In *Études coptes V* (Cahiers de la Bibliothèque Copte 10), 3–5. Paris-Leuven.

———. 2008. "Du copte dans les archives d'Apollôs." In *Les archives de Dioscore d'Aphrodité cent ans après leur découverte. Histoire et culture dans l'Égypte byzantine* (Études d'archéologie et d'histoire ancienne), edited by Jean-Luc Fournet, 170–75. Paris.

———. 2018. "Dialectes et régionalismes: La langue des textes coptes documentaires." In *Written Sources about Africa and Their Study. Le fonti scritte sull'Africa e i loro studi* (Accademia Ambrosiana. Africana Ambrosiana 3), edited by Mena Lafkioui and Vermondo Brugnatelli, 19–33. Milan

Brashear, William M., and Helmut Satzinger. 1990. "Ein akrostichischer griechischer Hymnus mit koptischer Übersetzung (Wagner-Museum K 1003)." *Journal of Coptic Studies* 1: 37–58.

Brashear, William M., Wolf-Peter Funk, James M. Robinson, and Richard Smith. 1990. *The Chester Beatty Codex AC 1390* (Chester Beatty Monographs 13). Leuven-Paris.

Brock, Sebastian P. 1994. "Greek and Syriac in Late Antique Syria." In *Literacy and Power in the Ancient World*, edited by Alan K. Bowman and Greg Woolf, 149–60. Cambridge (= *id.* 1999. *From Ephrem to Romanos: Interactions between Syriac and Greek in Late Antiquity* [Variorum Collected Studies Series CS 664], Nr. I. Aldershot-Brookfield).

———. 2009. "Edessene Syriac Inscriptions in Late Antique Syria." In *From Hellenism to Islam: Cultural and Linguistic Change in the Roman Near East*, edited by Hannah M. Cotton, Robert G. Hoyland, Jonathan J. Price, and David J. Wasserstein, 289–302. Cambridge.

Browne, Gerald M. 1979. *Michigan Coptic Texts* (Papyrologica Castroctaviana 7). Barcelona.

Budge, Ernest A. W. 1914. *Coptic Martyrdoms etc. in the Dialect of Upper Egypt*. London.

Butts, Aaron M. 2016. *Language Change in the Wake of Empire, Syriac in Its Graeco-Roman Context* (Linguistic Studies in Ancient West Semitic 11). Winona Lake.

Cameron, Alan. 1965. "Wandering Poets: A Literary Movement in Byzantine Egypt." *Historia* 14: 470–509 (= *id.* 1985. *Literary and Society in the Early Byzantine World*, Nr. I. London; Cameron 2016, chap. 1).

———. 2016. *Wandering Poets and Other Essays on Late Greek Literature and Philosophy*. Oxford.

Camplani, Alberto. 2003. "Momenti di interazione religiosa ad Alessandria e la nascita dell'élite egiziana cristiana." In *Origeniana Octava. Origen and the Alexandrian Tradition*, edited by Lorenzo Perrone, vol. I, 31–42. Leuven.

———. 2004. "Coptic Fragments from a Festal Letter of the Late Sixth Century (John Rylands Library, Coptic Suppl. N. 47–48): Damian or Eulogius?" In *Coptic Studies on the Threshold of a New Millennium. Proceedings of the Seventh International Congress of Coptic Studies. Leiden, 27 August–2 September 2000* (Orientalia Lovaniensia Analecta 133), edited by Mattheus Immerzeel and Jacques van der Vliet, vol. I, 317–27. Leuven.

———. 2012. "A Pastoral Epistle of the Seventh Century Concerning the Eucharist (Pap. Berlin P. 11346)." In *Forschung in der Papyrussammlung. Eine Festgabe für das Neue Museum; für das Ägyptische Museum und Papyrussammlung-Staatliche Museen zu Berlin*, edited by Verena M. Lepper, 377–86. Berlin.

———. 2015. "Il copto e la chiesa copta. La lenta e inconclusa affermazione della lingua copta nello spazio pubblico della tarda antichità." In *L'Africa, l'Oriente mediterraneo e l'Europa tradizioni e culture a confronto*, edited by Paolo Nicelli, 129–53. Milan.

Cauderlier, Patrice. 1978. "Sciences pures et sciences appliquées dans l'Égypte romaine: Essai d'inventaire antinoïte." In *Recherches sur les "Artes" à Rome* (Publications de l'Université de Dijon 58), 47–76. Paris.

Cavallo, Guglielmo, Edoardo Crisci, Gabriella Messeri, and Rosario Pintaudi. 1998. *Scrivere libri e documenti nel mondo antico. Mostra di papiri della Biblioteca Medicea Laurenziana. Firenze, 25 agosto–25 settembre 1998* (Papyrologica Florentina 30). Florence.

Charles, Robert H. 1916. *The Chronicle of John, Bishop of Nikiu*. London-Oxford.

Chauveau, Michel. 2002. "Rive droite, rive gauche. Le nome Panopolite au IIe et IIIe siècles de notre ère." In *Perspectives on Panopolis: An Egyptian Town from Alexander the Great to the Arab Conquest* (Papyrologica Lugduno-Batava 31), edited by Arthur Egberts, Brian P. Muhs, and Jacques van der Vliet, 45–54. Leiden.

Choat, Malcom. 2006a. *Belief and Cult in Fourth-Century Papyri* (Studia Antiqua Australiensia 1). Turnhout.

———. 2006b. "The Unidentified Text in the Freer Minor Prophets Codex." In *The Freer Biblical Manuscripts. Fresh Studies of an American Treasure Trove* (Text-Critical Studies 6), edited by Larry W. Hurtado, 87–121. Atlanta.

———. 2007a. "The Archive of Apa Johannes: Notes on a Proposed New Edition." In *Proceedings of the 24th International Congress of Papyrology, Helsinki, 1–7 August, 2004* (Societas Scientiarum Fennica, Commentationes Humanarum Litterarum 122), edited by Jaakko Frösén, Tiina Purola, and Erja Salmenkivi, vol. I, 175–83. Helsinki.

———. 2007b. "Epistolary Formulae in Early Coptic Letters." In *Actes du huitième congrès international d'études coptes. Paris, 28 juin–3 juillet 2004* (Orientalia Lovaniensia Analecta 163), edited by Nathalie Bosson, and Anne Boud'hors, vol. II, 667–78. Leuven-Paris-Dudley (MA).

———. 2010. "Early Coptic Epistolography." In *The Multilingual Experience in Egypt, from the Ptolemies to the Abbasids*, edited by Arietta Papaconstantinou, 157–78. Farnham.

———. 2012. "Coptic." In *The Oxford Handbook of Roman Egypt*, edited by Christina Riggs, Oxford: 581–83.

Choat, Malcom, and Iain Gardner. 2003. "O.Douch I 49." *Zeitschrift für Papyrologie und Epigraphik* 143: 143–46.

———. 2006. "*P. Lond. Copt.* I 1123: Another Letter to Apa Johannes?" *Zeitschrift für Papyrologie und Epigraphik* 156: 157–64.

Choat, Malcolm, and Maria Chiara Giorda (eds.). 2017. *Writing and Communication in Early Egyptian Monasticism*. Leiden.

Clackson, Sarah J. 1995. "Four Coptic Papyri from the Patermouthis Archive." *Bulletin of the American Society of Papyrologists* 32: 97–116.

———. 2004. "Papyrology and the Utilization of Coptic Sources." In *Papyrology and the History of Early Islamic Egypt*, edited by Petra M. Sijpesteijn and Lennart Sundelin, 21–44. Leiden-Boston.

———. 2007. "Coptic Oxyrhynchus." In *Oxyrhynchus. A City and Its Texts* (Egypt Exploration Society. Graeco-Roman Memoirs 93), edited by Alan K. Bowman, Revel A. Coles, Nikolaos Gonis, Dirk Obbink, and Peter J. Parsons, 332–41. London.

———. 2010. "Coptic or Greek? Bilingualism in the Papyri." In *The Multilingual Experience in Egypt, from the Ptolemies to the Abbasids*, edited by Arietta Papaconstantinou, 74–104. Farnham.

Clarysse, Willy. 1987. "Greek Loan-Words in Demotic." In *Aspects of Demotic Lexicography. Acts of the Second International Conference for Demotic Studies* (Studia Demotica 1), edited by Sven P. Vleeming, 9–33. Leuven.

Coquin, René-Georges. 1991. "Constantine, Sixth-Seventh Century Bishop of Asyūṭ." In *The Coptic Encyclopedia*, edited by Aziz S., vol. II, 590–92. New York-Toronto.

Coquin, René-Georges, and Maurice Martin. 1991. "Dayr Anbā Shinūdah." In *The Coptic Encyclopedia*, edited by Aziz S. Atiya, vol. III, 761–66. New York-Toronto.

Cotton, Hannah M. 1995. "Subscriptions and Signatures in the Papyri from the Judaean Desert: The ΧΕΙΡΟΧΡΗΣΤΗΣ." *Journal of Juristic Papyrology* 25: 29–40.

———. 1999. "The Languages of the Legal and Administrative Documents from the Judaean Desert." *Zeitschrift für Papyrologie und Epigraphik* 125: 219–31.

———. 2003. "'Diplomatics' or External Aspects of the Legal Documents from the Judean Desert: Prolegomena." In *Rabbinic Law in Its Roman and Near Eastern Context* (Texte und Studien zum antiken Judentum 97), edited by Catherine Ezser, 49–61. Tübingen.

———. 2009. "Continuity of Nabataean Law in the Petra Papyri: A Methodological Exercise." In *From Hellenism to Islam: Cultural and Linguistic Change in the Roman Near East*, edited by Hannah M. Cotton, Robert G. Hoyland, Jonathan J. Price, and David J. Wasserstein, 154–74. Cambridge.

Cotton, Hannah M., Walter E. H. Cockle, and Fergus G. B. Millar. 1995. "The Papyrology of the Roman Near East: A Survey." *Journal of Roman Studies* 85: 214–35.

Cribiore, Raffaella. 1996. *Writing, Teachers, and Students in Graeco-Roman Egypt* (ASP, XXXVI). Atlanta.

Crisci, Edoardo. 2004. "I più antichi codici miscellanei greci. Materiali per una riflessione." *Segno e Testo* 2: 109–44.

Cromwell, Jennifer. 2010. "Aristophanes Son of Johannes: An Eighth-Century Bilingual Scribe? A Study of Graphic Bilingualism." In *The Multilingual Experience in Egypt, from the Ptolemies to the Abbasids*, edited by Arietta Papaconstantinou, 221–31. Farnham.

Crum, Walter E. 1934. "Un psaume en dialecte d'Akhmîm." In *Mélanges Maspero*, vol. II. *Orient grec, romain et byzantin*, 73–76. Cairo.

Dagron, Gilbert. 1969. "Aux origines de la civilisation byzantine: Langue de culture et langue d'État (IVe–VIe siècles)." *Revue historique* 489: 23–56 (= *id.* 2012. *Idées byzantines* [Bilans de recherche 8], vol. II, 204–31. Paris).

———. 2012. *Idées byzantines* (Bilans de recherche 8). 2 vols. Paris.

Dekker, Renate. 2011. "Reconstructing and Re-editing the Archive of Bishop Pesynthios of Koptos/Keft (7th Century)." In *Current Research in Egyptology 2010. Proceedings of the Eleventh Annual Symposium Which Took Place at Leiden University, the Netherlands, January 2010*, edited by Marteen Horn, Joost Kramer, Daniel Soliman, N. Staring, Carina van den Hoven, and Lara Weiss, 33–41. Oxford.

———. 2018. *Episcopal Networks and Authority in Late Antique Egypt: Bishops of the Theban Region at Work* (Orientalia Lovaniensia Analecta 264). Leuven-Paris-Bristol.

Delattre, Alain. 2004. "Un contrat de prêt copte du monastère de Baouît." *Chronique d'Égypte* 79: 385–89.

Delattre, Alain, and Jean-Luc Fournet. 2018. "La première pétition en copte: Révision de *SBKopt.* IV 1709." *Chronique d'Égypte* 93: 167–86.

Depauw, Mark. 2003. "Autograph Confirmation in Demotic Private Contracts." *Chronique d'Égypte* 78: 89–105.

———. 2009. "Bilingual Greek-Demotic Documentary Papyri and Hellenization in Ptolemaic Egypt." In *Faces of Hellenism. Studies in the History of the Eastern Mediterranean (4th Century B.C.–5th Century A.D.)* (Studia Hellenistica 48), edited by Peter van Nuffelen, 113–46. Leuven-Paris-Walpole (MA).

———. 2011. "Physical Descriptions, Registration and εἰκονίζειν. With New Interpretations for P. Par. 65 and P. Oxy. I 34." *Zeitschrift für Papyrologie und Epigraphik* 176: 189–99.

Diebner, Bernd J., and Rodolphe Kasser. 1989. *Hamburger Papyrus Bil. 1: Die alttestamentlichen Texte des Papyrus Bilinguis 1 der Staats- und Universitätsbibliothek Hamburg* (Cahiers d'Orientalisme 18). Geneva.

Diethart, Johannes M., Denis Feissel, and Jean Gascou. 1994. "Les *prôtokolla* des papyrus byzantins du Ve au VIIe siècle. Édition, prosopographie, diplomatique." *Tyche* 9: 9–40.

Drescher, James. 1947. *Three Coptic Legends: Hilaria, Archellites, The Seven Sleepers* (Supplements to ASAE 4). Cairo.

Drew-Bear, Marie. 1979. *Le nome Hermopolite. Toponymes et sites* (ASP 21). Ann Arbor.

———. 1992. "La culture grecque à Hermoupolis Magna." In *Proceedings of the XIXth International Congress of Papyrology*, vol. II, 195–204. Cairo.

Dummer, Jürgen. 1968. "Angaben der Kirchenväter über das Koptische." In *Probleme der koptischen Literatur* (Wissenschaftliche Beiträge der Martin-Luther-Universität Halle-Wittenberg 1968/1 [K 2]), edited by Peter Nagel, 17–55. Halle (= *id.* 2006. *Philologia sacra et profana. Ausgewählte Beiträge zur Antike und zu ihrer Wirkungsgeschichte*, edited by Meinolf Vielberg [Altertumswissenschaftliches Kolloquium 16], 140–71. Stuttgart).

Egberts, Arthur, Brian P. Muhs, and Jacques van der Vliet (eds.). 2002. *Perspectives on Panopolis: An Egyptian Town from Alexander the Great to the Arab Conquest* (Papyrologica Lugduno-Batava 31). Leiden.

Emmel, Stephen. 2002. "From the Other Side of the Nile: Shenute and Panopolis." In *Perspectives on Panopolis: An Egyptian Town from Alexander the Great to the Arab Conquest* (Papyrologica Lugduno-Batava 31), edited by Arthur Egberts, Brian P. Muhs, and Jacques van der Vliet, 95–113. Leiden.

———. 2007. "Coptic Literature in the Byzantine and Early Islamic World." In *Egypt in the Byzantine World 300–700*, edited by Roger S. Bagnall, 83–102. Cambridge.

———. 2016. "Editing Shenoute, Old Problems, New Prospects: The Date of Shenoute's Death." In *Coptic Society, Literature and Religion from Late Antiquity to Modern Times: Proceedings of the Tenth International Congress of Coptic Studies, Rome, September 17th–22th, 2012, and Plenary Reports of the Ninth International Congress of Coptic Studies, Cairo, September 15th–19th, 2008* (Orientalia Lovaniensia Analecta 247), edited by Paola Buzi, Alberto Camplani, and Federico Contardi, vol. II, 937–44. Leuven-Paris-Bristol.

Emmel, Stephen, and Bentley Layton. 2016. "Pshoi and the Early History of the Red Monastery." In *The Red Monastery Church: Beauty and Asceticism in Upper Egypt*, edited by Elizabeth S. Bolman, 11–15. New Haven-London.

Erman, Adolf. 1894. "Schenute und Aristophanes." *Zeitschrift für ägyptische Sprache und Altertumskunde* 32: 134–35.

Feissel, Denis. 1996. "La réforme chronologique de 537 et son application dans l'épigraphie grecque: Années de règne et dates consulaires de Justinien à Héraclius." *Ktèma* 18: 171–88 (= *id.* 2010. *Documents, droit, diplomatique de l'Empire romain tardif* [Bilans de recherche 7], Nr. XX: 503–24. Paris).

Feissel, Denis, and Jean Gascou. 1989. "Documents d'archives romains inédits du Moyen Euphrate (IIIe s. après J.-C.)." *Comptes rendus de l'Académie des Inscriptions & Belles-Lettres* juillet-décembre: 535–61.

———. 1995. "Documents d'archives romains inédits du Moyen Euphrate (IIIe s. après J.-C.). I. Les pétitions (*P. Euphr.* 1 à 5)." *Journal des Savants* janvier–juin: 65–119.

———. 1997. "Documents d'archives romains inédits du Moyen Euphrate (IIIe s. après J.-C.). II. Les actes de vente-achat (*P. Euphr.* 6 à 10)." *Journal des Savants* janvier–juin: 3–57.

———. 2000. "Documents d'archives romains inédits du Moyen Euphrate (IIIe s. après J.-C.). III. Actes divers et lettres (*P. Euphr.* 11 à 17)." *Journal des Savants* juillet–décembre: 157–208.

———(eds.). 2004. *La pétition à Byzance* (Centre de recherche d'histoire et civilisation de Byzance, Monographie 14). Paris.

Ferguson, Charles A. 1959. "Diglossia." *Word* 15: 325–40.

Festugière, André-Jean (ed.). 1961. *Historia monachorum in Aegypto* (Subsidia Hagiographica 34). Brussels.

———(trans.). 1964. *Les moines d'Orient.* Vol. IV/1. *Enquête sur les moines d'Égypte (Historia monachorum in Aegypto)*. Paris.

———.1965. *Les moines d'Orient.* Vol. IV/2, *La première vie grecque de saint Pachôme*. Paris.

Fishman, Joshua A. 1967. "Bilingualism with and without Diglossia; Diglossia with and without Bilingualism." *Journal of Social Issues* 23/2: 29–38.

Flinders Petrie, William M. 1908. *Athribis*. London.

Förster, Hans. 2002. *Wörterbuch der griechischen Wörter in den koptischen dokumentarischen Texten* (Texte und Untersuchungen zur Geschichte der altchristlichen Literatur 148). Berlin.

———. 2012. "Edition von P.Vat.Copt. Doresse 5. Verkauf von Grundbesitz durch Taham an Kolluthos und Markos." *Aegyptus* 92: 55–74.

Förster, Hans, and Fritz Mitthof. 2004. "Ein koptischer Kaufvertrag über Anteile an einem Wagen. Edition von P.Vat. Copt. Doresse 1." *Aegyptus* 84: 217–42.

Förster, Hans, Jean-Luc Fournet, and Tonio S. Richter. 2012. "Une *misthôsis* copte d'Aphrodité (P.Lond. inv. 2849): Le plus ancien acte notarié copte?" *Archiv für Papyrusforschung und verwandte Gebiete* 58/2: 344–59.

Fournet, Jean-Luc. 1993. "L'inscription grecque de l'église Al-Muʿallaqa." *Bulletin de l'Institut Français d'Archéologie Orientale* 93: 237–44.

———. 1999. *Hellénisme dans l'Égypte du VIe siècle. La bibliothèque et l'œuvre de Dioscore d'Aphrodité* (MIFAO 115). 2 vols. Cairo.

———. 2000a. "Coptos dans l'Antiquité tardive (fin IIIe-VIIe siècle)." In *Coptos, l'Égypte antique aux portes du désert*, Musée des Beaux-Arts de Lyon, RMN, 196–215. Paris.

———. 2000b. "Un nom rare du boulanger: ΑΡΤΟΚΟΛΛΗΤΗΣ." *Revue des Études Grecques* 113: 392–412.

———. 2003. "Between Literary Tradition and Cultural Change. The Poetic and Documentary Production of Dioscorus of Aphrodite." In *Learned Antiquity. Scholarship and Society in the Near East, the Greco-Roman World, and the Early Medieval West* (Groningen Studies in Cultural Change 5), edited by Alasdair A. MacDonald, Michael W. Twomey, and Gerrit J. Reinink, 101–14. Leuven.

——(ed.). 2008. *Les archives de Dioscore d'Aphrodité cent ans après leur découverte. Histoire et culture dans l'Égypte byzantine* (Études d'archéologie et d'histoire ancienne). Paris.

——. 2009a. *Alexandrie: Une communauté linguistique? Ou la question du grec alexandrin* (Alexandrie médiévale 3). Cairo.

——. 2009b. "I papiri di Antinooupolis. La collezione e gli scavi fiorentini." In *100 anni di istituzioni fiorentine per la papirologia: 1908. Società Italiana per la ricerca dei Papiri, 1928. Istituto Papirologico "G. Vitelli." Atti del Convegno internazionale di studi. Firenze, 12–13 giugno 2008* (Studi e Testi di Papirologia N.S. 11), edited by Guido Bastianini and Angelo Casanova, 115–32. Florence.

——. 2009c. "The Multilingual Environment of Late Antique Egypt: Greek, Latin, Coptic, and Persian Documentation." In *Oxford Handbook of Papyrology*, edited by Roger S. Bagnall, 418–51. Oxford.

——. 2010a. "Les pétitions des *Acta Conciliorum Œcumenicorum* comparées à celles de la documentation papyrologique (Ve–VIe s.): Libelle, *didaskalia* et *anaphora*." In *Quellen zur byzantinischen Rechtspraxis. Aspekte der Textüberlieferung, Paläographie und Diplomatik, Akten des internationalen Symposiums Wien, 5.–7. 11. 2007* (Veröffentlichungen zur Byzanzforschung 25), edited by Christian Gastgeber, 61–79. Vienna.

——. 2010b. "Sur les premiers documents juridiques coptes." In *Études coptes XI. Troisième journée d'étude (Marseille, 7–9 juin 2007)* (Cahiers de la Bibliothèque Copte 17), edited by Anne Boud'hors and Catherine Louis, 125–37. Paris.

——. 2014. "Rapport des conférences en papyrologie grecque." In *Annuaire de l'École Pratique des Hautes Études, Section des sciences historiques et philologiques, 145e année, 2012–2013*, 104–6. Paris.

——. 2016. "Sur les premiers documents juridiques coptes (2): Les archives de Phoibammôn et de Kollouthos." In *Études coptes XIV, Seizièmes journées d'études coptes (Genève, 19–21 juin 2013)* (Cahiers de la Bibliothèque Copte 21), edited by Anne Boud'hors and Catherine Louis, 115–41. Paris.

——. 2018a. "Les documents bilingues gréco-coptes: Essai de typologie." In *Written Sources about Africa and Their Study. Le fonti scritte sull'Africa e i loro studi* (Accademia Ambrosiana. Africana Ambrosiana 3), edited by Mena Lafkioui and Vermondo Brugnatelli, 59–83. Milan.

——. 2018b. "Sur les premiers documents juridiques coptes (3): Les 'archives' d'Apa Abraham." In *Études coptes XVI, Dix-septième journée d'études coptes (Lisbonne, 18–20 juin 2015)* (Cahiers de la Bibliothèque Copte 23), edited by Anne Boud'hors and Catherine Louis, 199–226. Paris.

——. Forthcoming. "Les signes diacritiques dans les papyrus documentaires grecs." In *Signes dans les textes. Recherches sur les continuités et les ruptures des pratiques scribales en Égypte pharaonique, gréco-romaine et byzantine*. Liège.

Fournet, Jean-Luc, and Jean Gascou. 2004. "Liste des pétitions sur papyrus des Ve–VIIe siècles." In *La pétition à Byzance* (Centre de recherche d'histoire et civilisation de Byzance, Monographie 14), edited by Denis Feissel and Jean Gascou, 141–96. Paris.

Frakes, Robert M. 2001. Contra Potentium Iniurias*: The Defensor Civitatis and Late Roman Justice* (Münchener Beiträge zur Papyrusforschung und antiken Rechtsgeschichte 90). Munich.

Funk, Wolf-Peter. 1991. "Dialects, Morphology of Coptic." In *The Coptic Encyclopedia*, edited by Aziz S. Atiya, vol. VIII, 101–8. New York-Toronto.

Gagos, Traianos, and Peter van Minnen. 1994. *Settling a Dispute. Toward a Legal Anthropology of Late Antique Egypt*. Ann Arbor.

Gardiner, Alan H. 1916. *Notes on the Story of Sinuhe*. Paris.

Gardner, Iain. 1999. "An Old Coptic Ostracon from Ismant El-Kharab?" *Zeitschrift für Papyrologie und Epigraphik* 125: 195–200.

Gardner, Iain, and Malcolm Choat. 2004. "Towards a Palaeography of Fourth Century Documentary Coptic." In *Coptic Studies on the Threshold of a New Millennium. Proceedings of the Seventh International Congress of Coptic Studies. Leiden, 27 August–2 September 2000* (Orientalia Lovaniensia Analecta 133), edited by Mat Immerzeel and Jacques van der Vliet, I, 495–503. Leuven.

Garel, Esther. 2015. "Les testaments des supérieurs du monastère de Saint-Phoibammôn à Thèbes (VIIe siècle). Édition, traduction, commentaire." PhD diss., EPHE, Paris.

Garel, Esther, and Maria Nowak. 2017. "Monastic Wills: The Continuation of Late Legal Roman Tradition." In *Writing and Communication in Early Egyptian Monasticism*, edited by Malcolm Choat and Maria Chiara Giorda, 108–28. Leiden.

Gascou, Jean. 1983. "Notes de papyrologie byzantine." *Chronique d'Égypte* 58: 226–34.

———. 1985. "Les grands domaines, la cité et l'État en Égypte byzantine (Recherches d'histoire agraire, fiscale et administrative)." *Travaux et Mémoires* 9: 1–90 (= Gascou 2008: 125–213, Nr. IX).

———. 1998. "Ducs, *praesides*, poètes et rhéteurs au Bas-Empire." *Antiquité Tardive* 6: 61–64.

———. 2004a. "L'Égypte byzantine (284–641)." In *Le Monde byzantin*. I. *L'Empire romain d'Orient (330–641)*, edited by Cécile Morrisson, 403–36. Paris.

———. 2004b. "Les pétitions privées." In *La pétition à Byzance* (Centre de recherche d'histoire et civilisation de Byzance, Monographie 14), edited by Denis Feissel and Jean Gascou, 93–103. Paris.

———. 2008. *Fiscalité et société en Égypte byzantine* (Bilans de recherche 4). Paris.

———. 2009a. "The Papyrology of the Near East." In *Oxford Handbook of Papyrology*, edited by Roger S. Bagnall, 473–94. Oxford.

———. 2009b. "Procès-verbal d'audience du juge Ammonius." *Zeitschrift für Papyrologie und Epigraphik* 170: 149–55.

———. 2011. "La montagne d'Antinoopolis, hagiographie et papyrus." In *I papiri letterari cristiani. Atti del convegno internazionale di studi in memoria di Mario Naldini, Firenze, 10–11 giugno 2010* (Studi e Testi di Papirologia N.S. 13), edited by Guido Bastianini and Angelo Casanova, 161–71. Florence.

Gascou, Jean, and Klaas A. Worp. 1982. "Problèmes de documentation apollinopolite." *Zeitschrift für Papyrologie und Epigraphik* 49: 83–95.

Gauthier, Henri. 1903. "La déesse Triphis." *Bulletin de l'Institut Français d'Archéologie Orientale* 3: 165–81.

Giorda, Maria Chiara. 2009. "Bishops-Monks in the Monasteries: Presence and Role." *Journal of Juristic Papyrology* 39: 49–82.

———. 2017. "Writing Monastic Testaments: A Communication from Generation to Generation." In *Writing and Communication in Early Egyptian Monasticism*, edited by Malcolm Choat and Maria Chiara Giorda, 129–50. Leiden.

Goehring, James E. 1986. *The Letter of Ammon and Pachomian Monasticism.* Berlin.

Goldstein, Jonathan A. 1966. "The Syriac Bill of Sale from Dura-Europos." *Journal of Near Eastern Studies* 25: 1–16.

Gonis, Nikolaos. 2008. "Further Letters from the Archive of Apa Ioannes." *Bulletin of the American Society of Papyrologists* 45: 69–85.

Grossman, Eitan, Peter Dils, Tonio S. Richter, and Wolfgang Schenkel. 2017. *Greek Influence on Egyptian-Coptic: Contact-Induced Change in an Ancient African Language* (DDGLC Working Papers 1, Lingua Aegyptia Studia Monographica). Hamburg.

Halkin, François (ed.). 1932. *Sancti Pachomii Vitae Graecae* (Subsidia Hagiographica 19). Brussels.

———. 1982. *Le corpus athénien de saint Pachôme* (Cahiers d'Orientalisme 2). Geneva.

Hammerstaedt, Jürgen. 1997. "Photios über einen verlorenen Codex mit Autoren des vierten Jahrhunderts n.Chr. aus Mittel- bzw. Oberägypten." *Zeitschrift für Papyrologie und Epigraphik* 115: 105–16.

Hardy, Edward R. 1931. *The Large Estates of Byzantine Egypt.* New York.

Harris, Jill. 1999. *Law and Empire in Late Antiquity.* Cambridge.

Hauben, Hans. 2002. "Aurêlios Pageus, alias Apa Paiêous, et le monastère mélitien d'Hathor." *Ancient Society* 32: 337–52.

Huck, Olivier. 2008. "Ad episcopale iudicium provocare. Fondements spirituels, cadre institutionnel et implications sociales des recours laïcs à la justice épiscopale (Ier–Ve siècle)." PhD diss., Marc Bloch University, Strasbourg.

Johannsen, Tanja. 2017. *Das Privatrecht der griechischen Urkunden vom Mittleren Euphrat P.Euphr. 6-P.Euphr. 15* (Münchener Beiträge 114). Munich.

Johnson, Maxwell E. (ed.). 1995. *The Prayers of Sarapion of Thmuis: A Literary, Liturgical, and Theological Analysis* (Orientalia Christiana Analecta 249). Rome.

Johnson, Scott F. (ed.). 2015. "The Social Presence of Greek in Eastern Christianity, 200–1200 CE." In *Languages and Cultures of Eastern Christianity: Greek* (The Worlds of Eastern Christianity, 300–1500), edited by Scott F. Johnson, 1–122. Farnham-Burlington.

Jones, Arnold H. M. 1937. *Cities in the Eastern Roman Provinces*. Oxford.

———. 1964. *The Later Roman Empire, 294–602*. Oxford.

Kaiser, Anna. Forthcoming. "Flavius Athanasius, *dux et Augustalis Thebaidis*—A Case Study on Landholding and Power in Late Antique Egypt." In *Land and Power in the Ancient and Post-Ancient World, Proceedings of the 3rd International Conference of the Research Network Imperium & Officium*, edited by Stephan Procházka and Sven Tost. Vienna.

Kasser, Rodolphe. 1958. *Papyrus Bodmer III. Évangile de Jean et Genèse I–IV, 2 en bohairique* (CSCO 177–78, SC 25–26). Leuven.

———. 1960. *Papyrus Bodmer VI. Livres des proverbes* (CSCO 194–95, SC 27–28). Leuven.

———. 1966. "Dialectes, sous-dialectes et 'dialecticules.'" *Zeitschrift für Ägyptische Sprache und Altertumskunde* 92: 106–15.

———. 1990. "A Standard System of Sigla for Referring to the Dialects of Coptic." *Journal of Coptic Studies* 1: 141–51.

———. 1991a. "Alphabets, Coptic." In *The Coptic Encyclopedia*, edited by Aziz S. Atiya, vol. VIII, 32–41. New York-Toronto.

———. 1991b. "Vocabulary, Copto-Greek, Autochthonous Coptic." In *The Coptic Encyclopedia*, edited by Aziz S. Atiya, vol. VIII, 215–22. New York-Toronto.

———. 2001. "Le Papyrus Bodmer III réexaminé: Amélioration de sa transcription." *Journal of Coptic Studies* 3: 81–112.

———. 2004. "Protodialectes coptes à systèmes alphabétiques de type vieux-copte." In *Coptic Studies on the Threshold of a New Millennium. Proceedings of the Seventh International Congress of Coptic Studies. Leiden, 27 August–2 September 2000*, vol. I, 77–123. Leuven.

Kelly, Benjamin. 2011. *Petitions, Litigation, and Social Control in Roman Egypt*. Oxford.

Kenyon, Frederic G. 1937. *The Chester Beatty Biblical Papyri. Descriptions and Texts of Twelve Manuscripts on Papyrus of the Greek Bible. Fasc. VI, Isaiah, Jeremiah, Ecclesiasticus*. London.

Kovaric, Sophie. 2014. "Das spätantike Notariat. Kanzleipraxis des 4.–8. Jh. n. u. Z. am Beispiel Arsinoites (Mittelägypten)." PhD diss., University of Vienna.

Krause, Martin. 1956. "Apa Abraham von Hermonthis. Ein oberägyptischer Bischof um 600." 2 vols. PhD diss., Humboldt-Universität Berlin.

———. 1985. "Die Beziehungen zwischen den beiden Phoibammon-Klöstern auf dem thebanischen Westufer." *Bulletin de la Société d'Archéologie Copte* 27: 31–44.

———. 1991. "Abraham of Hermonthis." In *The Coptic Encyclopedia*, edited by Aziz S. Atiya, vol. I, 13. New York-Toronto.

Kreuzsaler, Claudia. 2010. "Die Beurkundung aussergerichtlicher Streitbelegung in den ägyptischen Papyri." In *Quellen zur byzantinischen Rechtspraxis. Aspekte der Textüberlieferung, Paläographie und Diplomatik*, edited by Christian Gastgeber, 17–26. Vienna.

Külzer, Andreas. 1998. "Die 'Festbriefe' (Ἐπιστολαὶ Ἑορταστικαί)—Eine wenig beachtete Untergattung der byzantinischen Briefliteratur." *Byzantinische Zeitschrift* 91: 379–90.

Lammeyer, Joseph. 1933. "Die 'audientia episcopalis' in Zivilsachen der Laien in römischen Kaiserrecht und in den Papyri." *Aegyptus* 13: 193–202.

Layton, Bentley. 2011. *A Coptic Grammar. With Chrestomathy and Glossary. Sahidic Dialect* (Porta Linguarum Orientalium, Neue Serie 20). 3rd ed. Wiesbaden.

———. 2014. *The Canons of Our Fathers. Monastic Rules of Shenoute*. Oxford.

Lefort, Louis-Théophile. 1933. "Athanase écrivain copte." *Le Muséon* 46: 1–33.

———. 1948. "ⲉⲓⲙⲏⲧⲓ dans le Nouveau Testament sahidique." *Le Muséon* 61: 153–70.

Lewis, Naphtali. 1993. "The Demise of the Demotic Documents: When and Why." *Journal of Egyptian Archaeology* 79: 276–81.

———. 2001. "The Demise of the Aramaic Documents in the Dead Sea Region." *Scripta Classica Israelica* 20: 179–81.

Loprieno, Antonio. 1982. "Methodologische Anmerkungen zur Rolle der Dialekte in der ägyptischen Sprachentwicklung." *Göttinger Miszellen* 53: 75–95.

MacCoull, Leslie S. B. 1984. "Redating the Inscription of El-Moallaqa." *Zeitschrift für Papyrologie und Epigraphik* 64: 230–34

———. 1995. "Further Notes on Interrelated Greek and Coptic Documents of the Sixth and Seventh Centuries." *Chronique d'Égypte* 70: 341–53 (= *ead.* 2011. *Documenting Christianity in Early Egypt, Sixth to Fourteenth Century* [Variorum Collected Studies CS 981], Nr. II. Farnham-Burlington [VT]).

———. 1997. "Dated and Datable Coptic Documentary Hands before A.D. 700." *Le Muséon* 10: 349–66 (= *ead.* 2011. *Documenting Christianity in Early Egypt, Sixth to Fourteenth Century* [Variorum Collected Studies CS 981], Nr. III. Farnham-Burlington [VT]).

———. 2002–3. "*CPR* IV 34 = *P. Rain. Unterricht* 112 = *MPER* XVIII 223 descr.: Aspects of the Training of a Bilingual Scribe." *Analecta Papyrologica* 14–15: 187–95.

———. 2007a. "Philosophy in Its Social Context." In *Egypt in the Byzantine World 300–700*, edited by Roger S. Bagnall, 67–82. Cambridge.

———. 2007b. "Why Do We Have Coptic Documentary Papyri before A.D. 641?" In *Actes du Huitième Congrès international d'Études coptes. Paris, 28 juin–3 juillet 2004* (Orientalia Lovaniensia Analecta 163), edited by Nathalie Bosson and Anne Boud'hors, II, 751–58. Leuven-Paris-Dudley (MA) (= *ead.* 2011. *Documenting Christianity in Egypt, Sixth to Fourteenth Centuries* [Variorum Collected Studies Series CS 981], Nr. IV. Farnham-Burlington [VT]).

MacDonald, Alasdair A., Michael W. Twomey, and Gerrit J. Reinink (eds.). 2003. *Learned Antiquity. Scholarship and Society in the Near East, the Greco-Roman World, and the Early Medieval West* (Groningen Studies in Cultural Change 5). Leuven.

MacMullen, Ramsay. 1966. "Provincial Languages in the Roman Empire." *American Journal of Philology* 87: 1–18 (= *id.* 1990. *Changes in the Roman Empire. Essays in the Ordinary*. Nr. 4, 32–40. Princeton).

Mannino, Vincenzo. 1984. *Ricerche sul "defensor civitatis"* (Pubblicazioni dell'Istituto di Diritto Romano e dei Diritti dell'Oriente Mediterraneo 62). Milan.

Mansi, Gian Domenico. 1743. *Sacrorum conciliorum nova et amplissima collectio*, vol. IX. Florence.

Maraval, Pierre (ed.). 1982. *Égérie. Journal de voyage (Itinéraire)* (Sources chrétiennes 296). Paris.

Mason, Hugh J. 1974. *Greek Terms for Roman Institutions: A Lexicon and Analysis* (ASP 13). Toronto.

Matthews, John F. 1984. "The Tax Law of Palmyra: Evidence for Economic History in a City of the Roman East." *Journal of Roman Studies* 74: 157–80.

McClure, M. L., and Charles L. Feltoe. 1919. *The Pilgrimage of Etheria*. London.

Meyer, Béatrice. 1997. "'Gymnase' et 'Thermes' dans l'Égypte romaine et byzantine." In *Akten des 21. Internationalen Papyrologenkongresses* (APF Beiheft 3), vol. II, 691–95. Stuttgart-Leipzig.

Miguélez Cavero, Laura. 2008. *Poems in Context. Greek Poetry in the Egyptian Thebaid 200–600 AD* (Sozomena. Studies in the Recovery of Ancient Texts 2). Berlin-New York.

Mihálykó, Ágnes. 2019. "The Persistance of Greek and the Rise of Coptic in the Early Christian Liturgy in Egypt." In *Proceedings of the 28th International Congress of Papyrology* (Scripta Orientalia 3), edited by Alberto Nodar and Sofía Torallas Tovar, 698–705. Barcelona.

Milik, Józef T. 1968. "Parchemin judéo-araméen de Doura-Europos, an 200 ap. J.-C." *Syria* 45: 97–104.

Milizia, Paolo. 2016. "Problemi di grafia e fonologia nel lessico copto-greco." *Linguarum varietas* 5: 177–90.

Millar, Fergus. 2009. "The Syriac Acts of the Second Council of Ephesus, 449." In *Chalcedon in Context: Church Councils 400–700* (Translated Texts for Historians, Contexts 1), edited by Richard Price and Mary Whitby, 45–69. Liverpool (= Millar 2015, Nr. XXII, 529–52).

———. 2011. "Greek and Syriac in Edessa and Osrhoene, 213–363." *Scripta Classica Israelica* 30: 93–111 (= Millar 2015, Nr. XXIII, 553–76).

———. 2015. *Empire, Church and Society in the Late Roman Near East: Greeks, Jews, Syrians and Saracens. Collected Studies, 2004–2014* (Late Antique History and Religion 10). Leuven.

Mirecki, Paul Allan, Iain Gardner, and Anthony Alcock. 1997. "Magical Spell, Manichaean Letter." In *Emerging from Darkness to Light*, edited by Paul A. Mirecki and Jason D. BeDuhn, 1–32. Leiden.

Morelli, Federico. 2007. "*Grammatêphoroi* e vie della giustizia nell'Egitto tardo antico." In *Symposion 2005*, edited by Eva Cantarella, 351–71. Vienna.

Morgan, Teresa. 2003. "Literary Culture in Sixth-Century Egypt." In *Learned Antiquity. Scholarship and Society in the Near East, the Greco-Roman World, and the Early Medieval West* (Groningen Studies in Cultural Change 5), edited by Alasdair A. MacDonald, Michael W. Twomey, and Gerrit J. Reinink, 147–61. Leuven.

Moyle, John B. 1913. *The Institutes of Justinian*. 5th ed. Oxford.

Müller, C. Detleff G. 1991. "John of Parallos, Saint." In *The Coptic Encyclopedia*, edited by Aziz S. Atiya, vol. V, 1367–68. New York-Toronto.

Ochała, Grzegorz 2011. "The Date of the Dendur Foundation Inscription Reconsidered." *Bulletin of the American Society of Papyrologists* 48: 217–24.

Oréal, Elsa. 1999. "Contact linguistique: Le cas du rapport entre le grec et le copte." *Lalies* 19: 289–306.

Orlandi, Tito. 1986. "Coptic Literature." In *The Roots of Egyptian Christianity* (Studies in Antiquity and Christianity), edited by Birger A. Pearson and James E. Goehring, 51–81. Philadelphia.

———. 1991. "John of Shmūn." In *The Coptic Encyclopedia*, edited by Aziz S. Atiya, vol. V, 1369. New York-Toronto.

Papaconstantinou, Arietta. 2008. "Dioscore et la question du bilinguisme dans l'Égypte du VIe siècle." In *Les archives de Dioscore d'Aphrodité cent ans après leur découverte. Histoire et culture dans l'Égypte byzantine* (Études d'archéologie et d'histoire ancienne), edited by Jean-Luc Fournet, 77–88. Paris (= *ead*. 2015. "Dioscorus and the Question of Bilingualism in Sixth-Century Egypt." In *Languages and Cultures of Eastern Christianity: Greek* (The Worlds of Eastern Christianity, 300–1500), edited by Scott F. Johnson, 249–60. Farnham-Burlington).

———(ed.). 2010. *The Multilingual Experience in Egypt, from the Ptolemies to the Abbasids*. Farnham.

———. 2014. "Egyptians and 'Hellenists': Linguistic Diversity in the Early Pachomian Monasteries." In *Le myrte et la rose. Mélanges offerts à Françoise Dunand par ses élèves, collègues et amis*, edited by Gaëlle Tallet and Christiane Zivie-Coche, 15–21. Montpellier.

Parkinson, Richard B. 1997. *The Tale of Sinuhe and Other Ancient Egyptian Poems (1940–1640 BC)*. Oxford.

Parsons, Peter J. 1970. "A School-Book from the Sayce Collection." *Zeitschrift für Papyrologie und Epigraphik* 6: 133–49.

Peust, Carsten. 1999. *Egyptian Phonology: An Introduction to the Phonology of a Dead Language* (Monographien zur ägyptischen Sprache 2). Göttingen.

Porten, Bezalel. 1996. *The Elephantine Papyri in English. Three Millenia of Cross-Cultural Continuity and Change*. Leiden-New York-Cologne.

Price, Richard, and Michael Gaddis. 2005. *The Acts of the Council of Chalcedon Translated with Introduction and Notes* (Translated Texts for Historians 45). Liverpool.

Quack, Joachim F. 2017. "How the Coptic Script Came About." In *Greek Influence on Egyptian-Coptic: Contact-Induced Change in an Ancient African Language* (DDGLC Working Papers 1, Lingua Aegyptia Studia Monographica), edited by Eitan Grossman, Peter Dils, Tonio S. Richter, and Wolfgang Schenkel, 27–96. Hamburg.

Quaegebeur, Jan. 1975. *Le dieu égyptien Shaï dans la religion et l'onomastique* (Orientalia Lovaniensia Analecta 2). Leuven.

———. 1982. "De la préhistoire de l'écriture copte." *Orientalia Lovanensia Periodica* 13: 125–36.

———. 1991a. "Pre-Coptic." In *The Coptic Encyclopedia*, edited by Aziz S. Atiya, vol. VIII, 188–90. New York-Toronto.

———. 1991b. "Pre-Old Coptic." In *The Coptic Encyclopedia*, edited by Aziz S. Atiya, vol. VIII, 190–91. New York-Toronto.

Rees, Brinley R. 1952. "The Defensor Civitatis in Egypt." *Journal of Juristic Papyrology* 6: 73–102.

Reintges, Chris. 2001. "Code-Mixing Strategies in Coptic Egyptian." *Lingua Aegyptia* 9: 193–237.

Richter, Tonio S. 2000. "Spätkoptische Rechtsurkunden neu bearbeitet (II): Die Rechtsurkunden des Teschlot-Archivs." *Journal of Juristic Papyrology* 30: 95–148.

———. 2006. "'Spoken' Sahidic. Gleanings from Non-Literary Texts." *Lingua Aegyptia* 14: 311–23.

———. 2008a. "Greek, Coptic, and the 'Language of the Hijra.' Rise and Decline of the Coptic Language in Late Antique and Medieval Egypt." In *From Hellenism to Islam: Cultural and Linguistic Change in the Roman Near East*, edited by Hannah M. Cotton, Robert G. Hoyland, Jonathan J. Price, and David J. Wasserstein, 398–443. Cambridge.

———. 2008b. *Rechtssemantik und forensische Rhetorik. Untersuchungen zu Wortschatz, Stil und Grammatik der Sprache koptischer Rechtsurkunden* (Philippika. Marburger altertumskundliche Abhandlungen 20). 2nd ed. Wiesbaden.

———. 2010. "Koptische Rechtsurkunden als Quellen der Rechtspraxis im byzantinischen und frühislamischen Ägypten." In *Quellen zur byzantinischen Rechtspraxis. Aspekte der Textüberlieferung, Paläographie und Diplomatik. Akten des internationalen Symposiums, Wien, 5.–7.11.2007* (Veröffentlichungen zur Byzanzforschung 25 = Österreichische Akademie der Wissenschaften. Philosophisch-historische Klasse. Denkschriften 413), edited by Christian Gastgeber, 39–60. Vienna.

Russo, Simona. 1998. "Il corredo dotale di una giovane antinoita." In *Antinoe cent'anni dopo*, edited by Loretta Del Francia Barocas, 149–53. Florence.

Salomons, Robert P., and Peter J. Sijpesteijn. 1987. "Varia Coptica no. 5 Made Complete." *Enchoria* 15: 55–59.

Sanders, Henry A., and Carl Schmidt. 1927. *The Minor Prophets in the Freer Collection and the Berlin Fragment of Genesis* (University of Michigan Studies, Humanistic Series 21). New York.

Sauneron, Serge, Dominique Valbelle, Pascal Vernus, Jean-Pierre Corteggiani, Michel Vallogia, Jean Gascou, Guy Wagner, and Gérard Roquet. 1978. "Douch—Rapport préliminaire de la campagne de fouille 1976." *Bulletin de l'Institut Français d'Archéologie Orientale* 78: 1–33.

Schenke, Gesa. 2007. "Anweisung zur Übergabe von Textilien und Weizen in O. Douch. I 40 und 49." *Zeitschrift für Papyrologie und Epigraphik* 162: 220–22.

Schiffman, Lawrence H. 2003. "Witnesses and Signatures in the Hebrew and Aramaic Documents from the Bar Kokhba Caves." In *Semitic Papyrology in Context: A Climate of Creativity. Papers from a New York University Conference Marking the Retirement of Baruch A. Levine*, edited by Lawrence H. Schiffman, 165–86. Boston.

Schiller, A. Arthur. 1957. "Coptic Documents: A Monograph on the Law of the Coptic Documents and a Survey of Coptic Legal Studies 1938–1956." *Zeitschrift für Vergleichende Rechtswissenschaft* 60: 190–211.

———. 1971. "The Courts Are No More." In *Studi in onore di Edoardo Volterra*, vol. I, 469–502. Milan.

Selb, Walter, and Hubert Kaufhold. 2002. *Das syrisch-römische Rechtsbuch.* Vienna.

Sheridan, J. Mark. 1998. *Rufus of Shotep: Homilies on the Gospels of Matthew and Luke. Introduction, Text, Translation, Commentary.* Rome.

Shifman, Ilia S. 2014. *The Palmyrene Tax Tariff* (Journal of Semitic Studies Supplement 33), translated by Svetlana Khobnya and John F. Healey. Oxford.

Signes Codoñer, Juan. 2014. "New Alphabets for the Christian Nations: Frontier Strategies in the Byzantine Commonwealth between the 4th and 10th Centuries." In *New Perspectives on Late Antiquity in the Eastern Roman Empire*, edited by Ana de Francisco Heredero, David Hernández de la Fuente, and Susana Torres Prieto, 116–65. Cambridge.

Simon, Dieter. 1971. "Zur Zivilgerichtsbarkeit im spätbyzantinischen Ägypten." *Revue Internationale des Droits de l'Antiquité*, 3rd ser., 18: 623–57.

Simonin, Jacky, and Sylvie Wharton. 2013. *Sociolinguistique du contact. Dictionnaire des termes et des concepts.* Paris.

Smith, Mark. 1998. "Coptic Literature, 311–425." In *The Cambridge Ancient History*, edited by Averil Cameron, Bryan Ward-Perkins, and Michael Whitby, vol. XIII, 720–35. Cambridge.

Stadler, Martin A. 2008. "On the Demise of Egyptian Writing: Working with a Problematic Source Basis." In *The Disappearance of Writing Systems. Perspective on Literacy and Communication*, edited by John Baines, John Bennet, and Stephen D. Houston, 157–81. London-Oakville.

Steinwenter, Artur. 1929. "Zur Lehre der episcopalis audientia." *Byzantinische Zeitschrift* 30: 660–68.

———. 1931. "Die Ordinationsbitten koptischer Kleriker." *Aegyptus* 11: 29–34.

———. 1955. *Das Recht der koptischen Urkunden* (Rechtsgeschichte des Altertums im Rahmen des Handbuch der Altertumswissenschaft 4/2). Munich.

Taylor, David G. K. 2002. "Bilingualism and Diglossia in Late Antique Syria and Mesopotamia." In *Bilingualism in Ancient Society. Language Contact and the Written Word*, edited by James N. Adams, Mark Janse, and S. Swain, 298–331. Oxford (= *id.* 2015. *Languages and Cultures of Eastern Christianity: Greek* (The Worlds of Eastern Christianity, 300–1500), edited by Scott F. Johnson, 183–220. Farnham).

Teixidor, Javier. 1990. "Deux documents syriaques du IIIe siècle après J.-C., provenant du Moyen Euphrate." *Comptes rendus des séances de l'Académie des Inscriptions et Belles-Lettres*: 147–54.

———. 1993 (1991/1992). "Un document syriaque de fermage de 242 après J.-C." *Semitica* 41/42: 195–208.

Thomas, John D. 1998. "P.Ryl. IV 654: The Latin Heading." *Chronique d'Égypte* 73: 125–34.

Thür, Gerhard. 2013. "Syro-Roman Law Book." In *The Encyclopedia of Ancient History*, edited by Roger S. Bagnall, Kai Brodersen, Craige B. Champion, Andrew Erskine, and Sabine R. Huebner, 6495–96. Oxford.

Till, Walter C. 1947. "Die koptischen Steuerquittungsostraka der Wiener Papyrussammlung." *Orientalia*, n.s., 16: 525–43.

———. 1954. *Erbrechtliche Untersuchungen auf Grund der koptischen Urkunden*. Vienna.

———. 1962. *Datierung und Prosopographie der koptischen Urkunden aus Theben*. Vienna.

———. 1964. *Die koptischen Rechtsurkunden aus Theben* (Sitzungsberichte—Österreichische Akademie der Wissenschaften. Philosophisch-Historische Klasse, 244/3). Vienna.

Torallas Tovar, Sofía. 2001. "Los *riparii* en los papiros del Egipto tardoantiguo." *Aquila legionis* 1: 123–51.

———. 2003. "La situación lingüística en los monasterios egipcios en los siglos IV–V." *Collectanea Christiana Orientalia* 1: 233–45.

———. 2010. "Linguistic Identity in Graeco-Roman Egypt." In *The Multilingual Experience in Egypt, from the Ptolemies to the Abbasids*, edited by Arietta Papaconstantinou, 17–43. Farnham.

Turner, Eric G. 1977. *The Typology of the Early Codex* (Haney Foundation Series 18). Philadelphia.

Vanderheyden, Loreleï. 2015. "Les lettres coptes des archives de Dioscore d'Aphroditê (VIe siècle; Égypte)." 3 vols. PhD diss., EPHE, Paris.

Van der Vliet, Jacques. 2002. "Pisenthios de Coptos (569–632), moine, évêque et saint: Autour d'une nouvelle édition de ses archives." In *Autour de Coptos: actes du colloque organisé au Musée de Beaux-Arts de Lyon (17–18 mars 2000)* (*TOPOI. Orient-Occident Supplément* 3), edited by Marie-Françoise Boussac, 61–72. Lyon-Paris.

———. 2006. "L'épigraphie chrétienne d'Égypte et de Nubie: Bilan et perspectives." In *Huitième congrès international d'études coptes (Paris 2004)*, vol. I, *Bilans et perspectives 2000–2004* (Collections de l'Université Marc-Bloch-Strasbourg.

Études d'Archéologie et d'Histoire ancienne = Cahiers de la Bibliothèque copte 15), edited by Anne Boud'hors and Denyse Vaillancourt, 303–20. Paris.

——. 2013. "Coptic Documentary Papyri after the Arab Conquest." In *Papyrology AD 2013. 27th International Congress of Papyrology* [Keynote Papers] = *Journal of Juristic Papyrology* 43: 187–208.

——. 2017. "The Earliest Dated Epitaph in Coptic: A Second Look." *Chronique d'Égypte* 92: 412–18.

Van Minnen, Peter. 1994. "The Roots of Egyptian Christianity." *Archiv für Papyrusforschung und verwandte Gebiete* 40: 71–85.

Van Minnen, Peter, and Klaas A. Worp. 1993. "The Greek and Latin Literary Texts from Hermopolis." *Greek, Roman and Byzantine Studies* 34: 151–86.

Vecoli, Fabrizio. 2017. "Writing and Monastic Doctrine." In *Writing and Communication in Early Egyptian Monasticism*, edited by Malcolm Choat and Maria Chiara Giorda, 165–86. Leiden.

Wacke, Andreas. 1993. "Gallisch, Punisch, Syrisch, oder Griechisch statt Latein?" *Zeitschrift der Savigny-Stiftung für Rechtsgeschichte (Romanistische Abteilung)* 110: 14–59.

Ward, Benedicta (trans.). 1975 *The Sayings of the Desert Fathers* (Cistercian Studies Series 59). Kalamazoo-Oxford.

Watson, Alan. 1998. *The Digest of Justinian*. Revised English-language edition. 4 vols. Philadelphia.

Wipszycka, Ewa. 1984. "Le degré d'alphabétisation en Égypte byzantine." *Revue d'Études Augustiniennes et Patristiques* 30: 279–96 (= Wipszycka 1996, I.3).

——. 1992a. "Il vescovo e il suo clero. A proposito di *CPR* V 11." *Journal of Juristic Papyrology* 22: 67–81 (= Wipszycka 1996, II.3).

——. 1992b. "Le nationalisme a-t-il existé dans l'Égypte byzantine?" *Journal of Juristic Papyrology* 22: 83–128 (= Wipszycka 1996, I.1).

——. 1994. "Le monachisme égyptien et les villes." *Travaux et Mémoires* 12: 1–44 (= Wipszycka 1996, III.1).

——. 1996. *Études sur le christianisme dans l'Égypte de l'Antiquité tardive* (Studia Ephemeridis Augustinianum 52). Rome.

——. 2000. "The Nag Hammadi Library and the Monks." *Journal of Juristic Papyrology* 30: 179–91.

——. 2009. *Moines et communautés monastiques en Égypte (IVe-VIIIe siècles)* (*Journal of Juristic Papyrology*. Supplements 11). Warsaw.

Wise, Michael O. 2015. *Language and Literacy in Roman Judaea: A Study of the Bar Kokhba Documents*. New Haven-London.

Worp, Klaas A. 1990. "A Forgotten Coptic Inscription from the Monastery of Epiphanius: Some Remarks on Dated Coptic Documents from the Pre-Conquest Period." *Analecta Papyrologica* 2: 139–43.

Worrell, William H. 1935. "An Early Bohairic Letter." *American Journal of Philology* 56: 103–12.

Zakrzewska, Ewa. 2015. "L* as a Secret Language: Social Functions of Early Coptic." In *Christianity and Monasticism in Middle Egypt: Al Minya and Assyut*, edited by Gawdat Gabra and Hany N. Takla, 185–98. Cairo.

———. 2016. "Why Did Egyptians Write Coptic? The Rise of Coptic as a Literary Language." In *Copts and Society: Documentary-Historical Studies. Proceedings of the First International Coptic Studies Conference "Life in Egypt during the Coptic Period: Towns and Villages, Laymen and Clergy, Bishops and Dioceses." Alexandria 21–23 September 2010*, edited by Ahmed Mansour, 227–36. Alexandria.

———. 2017. "'A Bilingual Language Variety' or 'The Language of the Pharaohs'? Coptic from the Perspective of Contact Linguistics." In *Greek Influence on Egyptian-Coptic: Contact-Induced Change in an Ancient African Language* (DDGLC Working Papers 1, Lingua Aegyptia Studia Monographica), edited by Eitan Grossman, Peter Dils, Tonio S. Richter, and Wolfgang Schenkel, 115–61. Hamburg.

Zuckerman, Constantin. 1995. "The Hapless Recruit Psois and the Mighty Anchorite, Apa John." *Bulletin of the American Society of Papyrologists* 32: 183–94.

GENERAL INDEX

When a term pertains to the caption of a figure, the page number is given followed by the figure number in parentheses. When a term pertains to the text of the page plus the caption, the page number and figure number are both given without parentheses.

INDEX OF ANCIENT SOURCES

1. *Documentary Papyri*

2. *Literary Papyri*

CPSIA information can be obtained
at www.ICGtesting.com
Printed in the USA
LVHW092318261121
704522LV00004B/4

9 780691 230238